THE IDENTIFICATION OF AUTISTIC ADULTS' PERCEPTION OF THEIR OWN DIAGNOSTIC PATHWAY

A Research Dissertation submitted for the Degree of
Master of Autism
at Sheffield Hallam University

Rod Morris

BAhons (University of Leeds) PGCE (University of Huddersfield)
PGC Asperger Syndrome (Sheffield Hallam University)

School of Development and Society
Sheffield Hallam University

Order this book online at www.trafford.com
or email orders@trafford.com

Most Trafford titles are also available at major online book retailers.

Print information available on the last page.

ISBN: 978-1-4907-6608-9 (sc)
ISBN: 978-1-4907-6609-6 (e)

Library of Congress Control Number: 2015917497

Trafford rev. 10/26/2015

Trafford
PUBLISHING® www.trafford.com
North America & international
toll-free: 1 888 232 4444 (USA & Canada)
fax: 812 355 4082

CONTENTS

ABSTRACT

The Identification of Autistic Adults' Perception of Their Own Diagnostic Pathway

This research focuses on the perceptions of autistic adults regarding the identification/diagnosis process(es) of being autistic, with a strong element of ethical practices involved throughout the research process(es) including participatory and emancipatory components. Participants ages range from thirty nine to seventy years of age, with age of when diagnosis being conducted ranging from thirty two to sixty five years of age, and they all live in various parts of England. Eight participants were interviewed and consent to use their data was provided. Grounded Theory principles were used to carry out Thematic Analyses of the data; the findings are matrices that were formed with regards to pre-diagnosis, diagnosis and post-diagnosis. The themes tend to inter-twine, e.g. perception and identity, and discussions regarding each matrix has been carried out. The findings suggest that more ethical research that utilizes a social model ought to be carried out. Furthermore, recommendations for autistic people, researchers or/and diagnosticians have been outlined.

ACKNOWLEDGEMENTS

I would like to thank the following people:

The participants who contributed to this research for trusting me with their life narratives and experiences.

My supervisor Luke Beardon for his invaluable insights and experience on autism and sharing these perspectives with me.

Hayrunisa Pelge for her unwavering expert support and ongoing friendship.

My mother Elizabeth Marlow for making this truly possible.

And all of those who have inadvertently over the years contributed positively to this research.

You are all truly inspirational human beings.

LIST OF FIGURES

FOREWORD

As an academic, researcher and professional in the area of the autism spectrum and an autistic I was engaged with Rod Morris's writing from the first paragraph. Suitable for a wide audience, this book provides lived experience insights in a clear and well-researched manner, which would seem to prove that autistics do indeed have a theory of mind, in contrast to early research in this area. The clear descriptions of the research process and underlying methodology are interesting and give an insight into collaborative and respectful research that is based in an ideology of nothing about us without us.

Insights into the very human and powerful diagnostic journey are provided through a range of quotes and summaries of shared information. These insights will be of use to anyone thinking about seeking an autism spectrum diagnosis for themselves or a friend or family member. For adults who are in the midst of the diagnostic process, this book will provide a support and assurance that the range of feelings and reactions that can accompany this process are experienced by others and that they are not alone in their journey. The recommendations for going forward shine a light on ideas that would drive positive and supportive policy for the large autistic population going forward into the future. This section is a must read for policy makers and researchers in the areas of aging, housing, and health. Researchers seeking guidance on true co-production of research in the area of the autism spectrum would also benefit from this great example of inclusive and respectful research.

Rod Morris captures the experiences and views of autistic adults and presents them in a respectful way that both contributes to academic and theoretical research around the autism spectrum but is also accessible to the a wider audience. This unusual book captures the attention and invites multiple readings to gain a variety of perspectives, challenge current thinking and increase understanding of the richness of autistic lives.

Dr. Emma Goodall

FOREWORD

It is striking that the mechanics of diagnosing autism are often distanced from the needs of the patients receiving the diagnosis. Specialists usually base their diagnosis on behavioral evaluations. These specialists may be developmental behavioral pediatricians, psychiatrists or psychologists using different screening algorithms under varying environmental settings. In essence the approach to diagnosis is just as variable as the clinical presentations of autistic individuals. The author summarizes his views succinctly: "Is autism in and of itself, a spectrum (people on a spectrum), or is this more a reflection of a spectrum of opinion and perspective of differing professionals and schools of thought?"

Obtaining a medical diagnosis is an individual experience that is often relegated to a distant afterthought by the diagnostician. It would be an advantage, instead of classifying patients into prescribed labels, mental health professionals should take this opportunity in order to alleviate suffering. To do anything else is to dehumanize an individual by stereotyping him/her into a collective group.

Rod Morris has written an extremely useful book, based on originally sourced reference material, focusing on the diagnostic process of autism. It is a sensitive overview of a person's belief's and emotional state before, during, and after the diagnostic process along with a helpful discussion on how to improve the same. In doing so the book provides a source of guidance and inspiration based on personal testimonies as to a journey marked by the angst caused by self-imposed doubts (pre-diagnosis) all the way to what, under proper circumstances would be, an enlightened future (post-diagnosis). As the author states this book, "… in itself is geared towards being a piece of work that an autistic person, or someone who suspects they may be autistic, can read and feel more empowered and informed by, in terms of seeking or/and attaining a diagnosis of autism as well as hopefully what to avoid."

Manuel F. Casanova, MD

CHAPTER I

Introduction

1.1 Options for How to Read this Document

As this thesis involves perception, and as this will include the perception of the reader, there are two methods which can be taken when approaching this text:

1. Read in the traditional style (from the beginning through to the end)
2. Read first from Appendix F onwards (interview data), form conclusions and opinions based on the data, then read this document from the beginning.

These two different approaches are designed to facilitate how different perceptions may differ from the author and also how the readers' perceptions may differ. Fuller explanations for this approach will become clear within this document.

1.2 Information Regarding the Direct Quotes of Dr. Hans Asperger

The author of this thesis has secured by commission fresh translations of Dr. Hans Asperger's writings. The original German papers were obtained from various worldwide locations and were translated in full by Dr. Herbert Murbach into English. Herbert had no knowledge of autism or Asperger's prior to translation:

> *I am a retired teacher of a secondary school in Germany and I have lived in England for a few years. I studied at a University in Germany, which included maths, biology, theology, philosophy, psychology, pedagogy, physics and chemistry. Besides my professional work as a*

teacher I studied (home study) in the field of "carer for older people" - especially the medical aspects. I wrote many tests and examined test papers for students. My partner was a teacher in an institute for the education of carers. Of course all important literature must be analysed - so for example I have the ability to translate English scientific text into German language and vice versa.

(Dr. Herbert Murbach, 2013. Pers. Comm.)

1.3 Language, Terms and Accessibility

Inline with Article 1 of The Universal Declaration of Human Rights that *"All human beings are born free and equal in dignity and rights"* (United Nations, 1948, online), the basis of this thesis and indeed the principles set herein, will be presented in the framework of universal language and dignity for all persons. In an attempt to be as sensitive as possible, this researcher will also be using reflective perspectives and language, which is inline with this.

Therefore, overt medical and academic language will be avoided, except in quotes where this will be unavoidable. Throughout the document, terms such as *"Predominant Neurotype"* (PNT) (Cornwell and Beardon, 2007/2008, p.181), *"neurodiversity"* (Singer, 1999, p.64), diagnosis and identification will also be used. The use of images will also be incorporated so as to communicate complex concepts in an accessible form.

In terms of using this research for further study and reference, the author asserts that referencing the direct quotes of participants either from the Appendices or the main body of this thesis is strictly prohibited. These are largely due to ethical issues, which will be outlined within the ethics section of this document.

On a technical note and in the interest of research ethics, the author has obtained as many originally sourced reference materials as is possible, including the works of Hans Asperger, thereby limiting the use of multiple impressions and interpretations upon the core sources for this thesis, thus limiting bias. Furthermore, regarding

Asperger's papers, it was felt that having a suitably qualified professional without much prior knowledge about autism translating such texts might bring to light fresh translations and interpretations of his works, and the use of fully translated papers (rather than partial translations that are present in the academic field) one may gain a deeper perspective of Asperger's knowledge regarding autism.

1.4 Rationale and Objectives

With the Autism Act (2009) Section 15(5) as legal legislation on the Statue Book and the first ever disability-specific law to be passed in England, calling for:

(a) the provision of relevant services for the purpose of diagnosing autistic spectrum conditions in adults;
(b) the identification of adults with such conditions;
(c) the assessment of the needs of adults with such conditions for relevant services;
(d) planning in relation to the provision of relevant services to persons with autistic spectrum conditions as they move from being children to adults;
(e) other planning in relation to the provision of relevant services to adults with autistic spectrum conditions;
(f) the training of staff who provide relevant services to adults with such conditions;
(g) local arrangements for leadership in relation to the provision of relevant services to adults with such conditions.

(Great Britain, *Autism Act 2009, online*)

And for

there to be a clear pathway to diagnosis in every area and local areas should appoint a lead professional to develop diagnostic and assessment services. The pathway should be from initial referral through to assessment of needs. Diagnosis should lead to a person-centred assessment of need and should be recognised as a catalyst for a carer's assessment. Assessment of eligibility for care services cannot be denied on the grounds of the person's IQ. Any assessment of needs should be carried out by a professional who has a good understanding of autism and reasonable adjustments made to the process to enable the adult with autism to take part fully. All NHS practitioners should be able to identify signs of autism and refer for assessment and diagnosis if necessary. They should also then be able to understand how to adapt their behaviour and communication for a patient with autism.

(Department of Health, 2014, p.47)

Combined with

The clear vision is that: All adults with autism are able to live fulfilling and rewarding lives within a society that accepts and understands them. They can get a diagnosis and access support if they need it, and they can depend on mainstream public services to treat them fairly as individuals, helping them make the most of their talents.

(Department of Health, 2014, P.4)

Although *"Each area should put in place a clear pathway for diagnosis of autism, from initial referral through to assessment of needs"* (Department of Health, 2010, p.16), even though

the diagnoses of an autistic spectrum disorder are broadly applied to children who have widely divergent life histories, although different labels are applied to differentiate children based on age of onset and severity of impairments (Nadesan, 2005, p.10),

the only officially recognized guide for adults is that of the NICE (2012) guideline. Additionally, research on the lived process of adult diagnosis and its impact appears very limited at present especially with older adults (Piven and Rabins, 2011, p.2151-2155; Happe and Charlton, 2011, p.70-78; NICE, 2012, p.108), women, transgender people and black and minority groups (NICE, 2012, p.107-109). Because *"autism is a lifelong condition"* (NICE, 2012, p.18); and that *"it is important that autism is seen not only as a medical diagnosis for which the NHS has responsibilities, but also as a social care responsibility"* (NICE, 2012, p.21) and in consideration that

The rights of people with autism has become an important social issue and professionals need to be sensitive to the view that many individuals on the autism spectrum regard themselves as an excluded minority whose rights have been overlooked by a 'neurotypical' majority (see Chapter 4). Alongside using medical diagnostic terminology to define themselves, they also use the key concept of 'neurodiversity' to remind society that there are many different routes along which the brain can develop, that one is not necessarily better or worse than another, and that society has to adapt to make space for this diversity (NICE, 2012, p.21),

for the individual, the process could be seen by some as an identification process rather than just a diagnostic one as *"this is the generation that missed the opportunity to be identified and understood"* (Attwood, 2008, p.10). Another consideration is that *"however autism is perceived, it is unarguable that all autistic people are "human beings born free and equal in dignity and rights""* (Beardon and Chown, 2013, p.6). However, as autism is currently diagnosed by the identification of certain traits the scope for observational bias is vast and as *"autism involves both difference and disability, in that the diagnosis of autism is only made when the person is experiencing difficulties arising from their difference"* (NICE, 2012, p.22), the consequences of framing already vulnerable people around purely deficit based medical models as listed in the DSM-5 (2013) as used in the United States of America and ICD-10 (2010) as used in the United Kingdom, how this is communicated to the individual and possibly those around them may have very real consequences. An additional aspect is that of the implications for research, especially as common sense would suggest, that at the heart of how autism is understood is that of the diagnostic process/criteria and whom is deemed to reach the criteria, especially as

> the process of identification and assessment is well understood but is
> limited by the availability of well-validated tools for case identification
> and the lack of specialist services to undertake the necessary
> assessments (NICE, 2012, p.24).

However, as all of the different identification tools used in clinical assessment, *"demonstrate that despite guidelines there is still no single clear manner of identification"* (Beardon, 2014. Pers. Comm.); as the following from the NICE guideline illustrates:

> To aid more complex diagnosis and assessment for adults, consider using a formal assessment tool, such as:
>
> • the following tools for people who do not have a learning Disability:
>
> - The Adult Asperger Assessment (AAA; includes the Autism Spectrum Quotient [AQ] and the Empathy Quotient [EQ])25
>
> - the Autism Diagnostic Interview – Revised (ADI-R)26
>
> - the Autism Diagnostic Observation Schedule – Generic (ADOS-G)27
>
> - the Asperger Syndrome (and high-functioning autism) Diagnostic Interview (ASDI)28
>
> - The Ritvo Autism Asperger Diagnostic Scale – Revised (RAADS-R)29
>
> • The following tools in particular for people with a learning Disability:
>
> - The ADOS-G
>
> - The ADI-R.
>
> 5.4.7.5 To organise and structure the process of a more complex assessment, consider using a formal assessment tool, such as the Diagnostic Interview for Social and Communication Disorders (DISCO)30, the ADOS-G or the ADI-R.
>
> (NICE, 2012, p.137).

In summary:

> Having reviewed the formal assessment instruments, the GDG [Guideline Development Group] did not judge that any single instrument had sufficient properties to recommend its routine use in the assessment of adults with autism over any other instrument (NICE, 2012, p.131).

Additionally, aspects relating to how the individual's perceptions of their adult diagnosis as well as how others in turn will perceive that individual could have additional consequences. This is likely to ultimately affect how autism is understood and researched. It would seem apparent that with autism being constructed from an observational basis, any post diagnostic support may or may not be currently based on the individual's experiences of this world but by the interpretation and perception of the observer of that person, which in return may affect the support provided or not provided to that person. In essence, this research aims to examine the perception of autistic adults' and their own diagnostic journey. The main research aims is to examine the perceptual experiences of autistic adults regarding;

(a) Why they sought a diagnosis;
(b) How they felt about the diagnostic procedure;
(c) What impact the diagnosis has had on the understanding of who they are.

An additional objective of this research is to provide a document which can help guide and better inform those who are seeking, or are considering seeking a diagnosis and for those who have already been through the process, a benchmark with which to measure their own pathway through diagnosis. The authors' view is that it is pivotal that any assessment of this nature is accurate as to the persons' experiences and that there are standards of practice which do not impede an individuals' life, but to have meaning and purpose for a positive way forward. In this sense this could also be a guide for clinicians and diagnosticians on which to measure how they practice in this area.

CHAPTER 2

Literature Review

2.1 Introduction

This Literature Review will focus on the history and different schools of thought and perception up until the present in the 'Autism Constructs' sub-section. Ethical issues in autism research will follow this and how the tools and approaches the clinician uses affects the outcomes of identification/diagnosis. With the wide myriad of research available do any of us truly understand autism? Does the process of identification lead to further disability in itself? A pertinent question is that is autism a modern-day pseudonym for witchcraft? Does the awareness of being recognized as being different lead to further disablement? Is it something so unstructured that it is not possible to research it? Has the way autism been defined breaking the Equality Act (2010) and human rights law to live as a person is? Is the construct of autism just as problematic of society's views of difference? These questions, in part will be highlighted. However, the reader will ultimately be required to apply critical thinking in order to provide the answers and solutions on the understanding that:

> People diagnosed with autism and AS do experience difference and are experienced as different. These differences are both produced and rendered visible by complex institutional matrices including built environments, social institutions and professional role identities, and cultural practices and values. Yet, individuals who are singled out and whose behaviors are rendered meaningful by the diagnosis of autism are not passive agents
>
> (Nadesan, 2005, p.210)

2.2 Autism Constructs

"If the doors of perception were cleansed everything would appear to man as it is: Infinite. For man has closed himself up, till he sees all things through narrow chinks of his cavern" (Blake, 1790, p.14).

What follows is an analysis of a selection of original research papers from different professionals, which have largely formed the basis for how autism is recognized and seen today in the United Kingdom. The timeline of the papers selected begin from the early twentieth century through to more recent studies and hypotheses by examining the perceptions of autism by these different authors.

> Over the course of time, there have been major changes in ideas on the nature of autistic conditions. Before there was any understanding of the relationship of brain and behavior, causes were suggested – 'a changeling child' or 'demonic possession' (Wing, 2002, p.21). In 1487 a manual called *Malleus Maleficarum,* known as the 'handbook of the witch-hunters' and written by two German Catholic friars, Jakob Sprenger and Heinrich Kramer, stated that children with impairments were born to mothers who were involved with witchcraft and sorcery. Disabled people provided living proof of Satan's existence and of his power over humans. Thus, visibly impaired children were seen as 'changelings', the Devil's substitutes for human children. The book explained how to identify witches by their impairments, by 'evidence' of them creating impairments in others, or by their giving birth to a disabled child. It stated that 'creatures can be made by witches, although they necessarily must be very imperfect creatures and probably in some way deformed'
>
> (Quarmby, 2011, p.32).

One could observe this early diagnostic manual to formally label people as being 'different' was produced by Jakob Sprenger and Heinrich Kramer in 1487. One wonders how much has changed and how much has remained the same, especially when considering Blake's (1790, p.14) quote and that man "*sees all things through narrow chinks of his cavern",* one is led to the different perspectives and theories regarding each others' differences - this may explain why

> In the history of autism studies, expertise has been claimed by many differing academic schools of thought, practitioners, parents, quacks and so on. Yet, the one voice that has been traditionally silenced within the field is that of autistic people themselves (Milton, 2014, p.7).

"We now know that it was probably a Russian neurology scientific assistant, Dr Ewa Ssucharewa, who first published a description of children that we would describe today as having Asperger's Syndrome" (Attwood, 2008, p.36). In her 1926 paper that appeared in the 'Monatsschrift für Psychiatrie und Neurologie 60:235-261' entitled 'Die schizoiden Psychopathien im Kindesalter' (Wolff, 1996), the female assistant examined six boys aged between 2 and 14 years of age over a two-year period. She provided for each case detailed generational family history, using a multi-dimensional approach including details regarding their physiology, neurology and psychology. Although she used the accepted subsumed term 'autistic thinking', she did not use the over-arching term 'autism', as this was later extrapolated as a separate entity by Leo Kanner (1943) and Hans Asperger (1944), and not formally entered into the diagnostic classification system until 1980 with DSM III (APA, 1980, p.86-92).

Leo Kanner described autism as a disturbance of affective contact and extreme autistic aloneness in his 1943 paper where he studied in narrative form, 11 children (8 boys and 3 girls) aged between 3 and 11 years old between the years 1938 to 1943, although these ages and dates were staggered with intermittent visits.

Hans Asperger described autism as 'autistic psychopathy', although *"this has led to misunderstanding because of the popular tendency to equate psychopathy with sociopathic behaviour"* (Wing, 1981 p.115); first in a training lecture he gave on 9th October 1938 where he described two children (one aged ten and the one aged seven and a half), then in his 1944 thesis where he described the autistic personality in 4 boys aged between 6 and 11 years old over a period of between 5 and 6 years continually within a special educational setting. He examined areas such as autistic intelligence, behavior in the community, appearance and symptomology. Asperger, while noting similarities with autism, regarded what he observed as a distinct and stable personality type.

The common aspects to these three descriptions by Ssucharewa, Kanner and Asperger, apart from the same use of the same term 'autism', is that all of the children originated from parents who had the funds and the resources to ascribe such service and observation and all the parents were described as very intelligent. Additionally, the authors recognized various differences/conditions in the parents of these children as well as the wider family lineage; a Swedish study with approximately 3,000 participants, the largest study to date (Gaugler et al. 2014), confirms that most genetic aspects of autism are common in the population, rather than being rare, and passes down the family lineage via the interplay of variants of such genes.

The rationale for highlighting the processes these three pioneers undertook was to examine the very different approaches and perspectives to assessment, which again highlight issues of consistency in approaches and how, while there may be similarities, there appear to be many differences. It would have been interesting if these professionals had examined each other's subjects in a blind study where the results could be examined to determine the variables within their descriptions. An additional aspect in relation to diagnosis and assessment is that these subjects were observed over a period of time.

In their Camberwell study, Lorna Wing and Judith Gould examined 132 children in their epidemiological and classification study of severe impairments of social interaction and associated abnormalities in children. There are however, discrepancies regarding the ages of participants, in-depth particulars on the methods used and the timeframe used for the research process. For example, on the first page of the method section, it states *"the subjects were selected from children aged under 15 years on the census day, December 31, 1970"* (Wing and Gould, 1979, p.13) and at the end of this section it is stated *"At the time of the detailed interviews with parents and teachers, the ages of the children ranged from 2 years 2 months to 18 years"* (Wing and Gould, 1979, p.14).

In this this study the researchers sought much information, including medical history, local authority records and the environment they resided in. Even after the study they remained in contact with the families with support and information provided on an ongoing basis; *"More work on the children studied, including follow-up, is being undertaken"* (Wing and Gould, 1979, p.27) and *"The investigators have remained in touch with the children since the interviews and tests were completed"* (Wing and Gould, 1979, p.14). Therefore, they took the time to understand the participants and families. It is interesting to note, that unlike the previous studies mentioned, this study was conducted in a *"...mainly working-class area..."* (Wing and Gould, 1979, p.13) which highlights autism being evident throughout the social classes.

Wing and Gould (1979) referred to a number of authors who had developed their own syndromes, including Hans Asperger, Leo Kanner as well as Eugene Bleuler. Key themes were identified and elements that ran through these different diagnoses:

> Children with severe impairments of social interaction, abnormalities of language development involving both speech and gesture, and a behavioral repertoire consisting of mainly repetitive, stereotyped activities and beginning from birth or within the first few years of life have been described by a number of writers (Wing and Gould, 1979, p.11 – 12).

And that:

> These "syndromes," although thought by their proponents to be specific, have many features in common. Individual children may show more than one syndrome, making diagnosis difficult. When discussing this subject, Anthony (1958a) wrote, "The cult of names added chaos to an already confused situation, since there did not seem to be a

sufficiency of symptoms to share out among the various prospectors, without a good deal of overlap" (Wing and Gould,1979, p.12).

Although not mentioned by name, a triad-of-impairments were identified as running throughout certain conditions and in order to bring some consensus, by having these as the fundamental diagnostic elements and placing them under a 'spectrum umbrella' would achieve this. It does appear though that by speaking of a spectrum of professionals in disagreement with each other; one of the aims it seems was to try and develop a consensus.

With this, it would seem probable that any professional can seemingly and erroneously provide one diagnosis over another for the simple reason that there may be services and resources for particular diagnoses, therefore the availability of service provision may be the determining factor of what type of diagnosis is being provided, or replaced - *"The patterns of impairments and behavioral abnormalities described could be classified in a variety of ways, the value of each depending on the purpose for which it was undertaken"* (Wing and Gould, 1979, p.27). A spectrum of professionals is illustrated here again in terms of identification, which leads to the question: Is autism in and of itself, a spectrum (people on a spectrum), or is this more a reflection of a spectrum of opinion and perspective of differing professionals and schools of thought? It is also interesting that *"the authors also express the hope that some name more suitable than "autism" or "psychosis" will eventually be coined for the behavioral patterns discussed here"* (Wing and Gould, 1979, p.27).

In her 1981 paper 'Asperger's syndrome: a clinical account', Lorna Wing presented it with the following synopsis:

> The clinical features, course, aetiology, epidemiology, differential diagnosis and management of Asperger's syndrome are described. Classification is discussed and reasons are given for including the syndrome, together with early childhood autism, in a wider group of

conditions which have, in common, impairment of development of social interaction, communication and imagination (Wing, 1981, p.115).

Wing attempts to make a case for what Asperger described to be subsumed within her autistic spectrum concept. Asperger's papers were read and themes drawn out including speech, non-verbal communication, social interaction, repetitive activities and resistance to change, skills and interest and experiences at school. These components were then applied to the spectrum concept that had already been developed.

> In 1981, Lorna wing coined the term "Asperger's Syndrome." She did not believe it was a separate condition from autism, unlike Hans Asperger himself, but rather that it lay on the autistic continuum. They discussed the matter together when Asperger visited London in the late 1970s, and agreed to differ (Feinstein, 2010, p.179).

Modifications were also made to Asperger's account where *"the present author has noted a number of additional items in the developmental history, not recorded by Asperger"* (Wing, 1981, p.117) and *"there are two points on which the present author would disagree with Asperger's observations"* (Wing, 1981, p.117). Wing then produced and selected six male case histories, which form the appendices, utilizing her amendments. Asperger and Wing did appear to disagree on many aspects including the following:

> Techniques of behaviour modification as used with autistic children can possibly be helpful if applied with sensitivity. However, Asperger (1979) expressed considerable reservations about using these methods with children with his syndrome who are bright enough to be aware of and, as Asperger put it, 'to value their freedom' (Wing, 1981, p.124-125).

It would appear from this, that Hans Asperger's perspective was with knowledge and appreciation of human rights law, as well as a respect for the individuality of the individual, where, in contrast Lorna Wing's concept of her spectrum seemingly must enter behavioral modification programs with the end goal to have those who are identified to be made indistinguishable from their peers as the preferred intervention and/or 'medical treatment'.

In addition to the Wing/Gould school of thought regarding autism, an additional cohort has consisted of Uta Frith, with her former students Simon Baron-Cohen and Francesca Happe. A summary of a selection of Simon Baron-Cohen's theories follows with views questioning them. In his paper 'Does the Autistic child have a theory of mind?' (1985) Simon Baron-Cohen sites Premack and Woodruff (1978) who define this theory as *"the ability to impute mental states to oneself and to others. The ability to make inferences about what other people believe to be the case in a given situation allows one to predict what they do"* (Baron-Cohen, 1985, p.39). This theory is formally explored here through the Sally-Anne test, which did appear to confirm the validity of this theory in the assessment of 61 children (20 autistic children against 41 controls - 14 with Downs Syndrome and 27 PNT).

In a later paper 'Is autism an extreme form of the "male brain"?' (1997) Simon Baron-Cohen and Jessica Hammer explored an idea which stated thus: *"The core aim of this article is to propose a model to explain the connection between autism and being male"* (Baron-Cohen and Hammer, 1997, p.8). In this paper the authors highlight recent experimental evidence to address this model in the form of eight experiments; ranging from an experiment asking *"Are males superior on the embedded figures test?"* (Baron-Cohen and Hammer, 1997, p.12), to an experiment asking *"Are children with autism/Asperger Syndrome impaired on the faux pas test?"* (Baron-Cohen and Hammer, 1997, p.17). The empathizing and systemizing theory (Baron-Cohen, 2002/2009) is explained thus:

> This new theory explains the social and communication difficulties in autism and Asperger syndrome by reference to delays and deficits in empathy, while explaining the areas of strength by reference to in tact or even superior skill in systemizing (Baron-Cohen, 2009, p.71).

In this paper Baron-Cohen (2009) refers to deficits in cognitive and affective empathy. The NICE (2012) guidelines state that autistic people apparently lack cognitive empathy:

> … in people with autism it is the cognitive component of empathy that is impaired ('theory of mind' or recognising what others may be thinking or feeling) while affective empathy (having an appropriate emotional reaction to/caring about other's feelings) may be intact. In contrast, whereas in psychopathy the cognitive component of empathy is intact (enabling them to deceive and manipulate others) affective empathy is impaired (they do not care about others' suffering, for example) (NICE, 2012, p.23).

However, the counter-argument to this theory was highlighted by Beardon (2008) where he outlines his 'cross-neurological ToM' concept:

> … are we really sure that all individuals with autism lack a Theory of Mind when assessed in context of their own cognitive styles? For example, I would argue that in some cases individuals with autism demonstrate excellent Theory of Mind with other people with autism. In many cases, the level of understanding can be of a very high level, and appear to be totally intuitive. In fact, I have met some individuals who appear to communicate empathically non verbally, which could be seen as a very well developed Theory of Mind. … It is surely time to recognize that assessing individuals simply in a PNT context is not going to give a full picture of an individual's skills level and areas of competency. Perhaps it is time to recognize that as a PNT population we lack a Theory of Mind in relation to those with autism to a high degree. Perhaps we should relook at PNT led concepts and rethink how we think. (Beardon, 2008, p.20)

The argument above is also in line with ideas put forward by Milton (2012) who outlines that:

> The 'double empathy problem': a disjuncture in reciprocity between two differently disposed social actors which becomes more marked the wider the disjuncture in disprositional perceptions of the lifeworld – perceived as a breach in the 'natural attitude' of what constitutes 'social reality' for 'non- autistic spectrum' people and yet an everyday and often traumatic experience for 'autistic people'. (Author's concept and definition) (Milton, 2012, p.2)

In addition to his 'Is autism an extreme form of the "male brain"?' (1997) theory, Simon Baron-Cohen produced a paper entitled 'The hyper-systemizing, assortative mating theory of autism' (2006) which

> proposes that the systemizing mechanism is set too high in people with autism. As a result, they can only cope with highly lawful systems, and cannot cope with systems of high variance or change (such as the social world of other minds). They appear 'change-resistant'. This proposal extends the extreme male brain theory of autism. Finally, evidence is reviewed for autism being the genetic result of assortative mating of two high systemizers (Baron-Cohen, 2006, p.865)

The consequences of these research perspectives can be observed in the 2012 paper by *Krahn and Fenton, who state that:*

> ... the EMB [Extreme Male Brain] theory of autism by linking empathy with femininity and systemizing with masculinity, not only plays upon but also, in turn, reifies sex stereotypes in its treatment of ASDs as inherently masculine. Our concern is that this theory of autism and its research mandate have been too quick to gender ASDs and that more care and investigation is needed to better understand sex-related profiles amongst those diagnosed with an ASD. Indeed, more care and investigation are needed to discern what is being built *into* the research of what are "male" versus "female" brains and behaviours. (Fine, 2010a; Jordan-Jung, 2010). Unfortunately, the very language used to describe ASDs is now laden with certain gender expectations as a result, this may be informing how ASDs are recognized in children and youth, perhaps explaining the under-diagnosis of girls on the autism spectrum. If this is correct, seeing ASDs through a gendered lens may be adversely inhibiting early diagnosis and treatment in girls... .....a corresponding lack of such boys on the spectrum may prove disadvantaging for them as well. In certain practical ways then, Baron-Cohen's EMB theory of autism may inadvertently be contributing to systematic constraints that are unjustly locking in the life prospects of some girls and boys with ASDs. (Krahn and Fenton, 2012. p.99-100)

The argument above is also in line with Rivett and Matson's (2010) paper in their 'review of gender differences', whereby they call for more research into females. This all in itself illustrates that *"autism, or more specifically, the idea of autism is fundamentally socially constructed"* (Nadesan, 2005, p.2). In addition, Manual Casanova states the following in his blog post – 'Ludwig Wittingenstein debunks theory of mind in autism':

> I will end by repeating my own opinion about Theory of Mind and other psychological theories of autism: "Without hard evidence in terms of neuropathology psychological theories are too malleable, confluent, and easy to paint themselves into a corner. Most psychological theories offer nothing more than common sense. It has been the failure of psychologists not to pursue their theories with neurobiological techniques. Thus far they all remain unidimensional and only offer the perspective of the people that developed them". (Casanova, 2014, online)

However, *"To make the claim that the idea of autism is socially constructed is not necessarily to reject a biological basis for the conditions or symptoms that come to be labeled as 'autistic'"* (Nadesan, 2005, p.2).

In light of these views and with the evidence presented thus far, there is a question mark as to whether the professions of Psychiatry and Psychology can claim medical expertise in relation to how other medical professions operate when measured in terms of progress that has been made. This is reinforced by the following:

> The goal of this new manual, as with all previous editions, is to provide a common language for describing psychopathology. While DSM has been described as a "Bible" for the field, it is, at best, a dictionary, creating a set of labels and defining each. The strength of each of the editions of DSM has been "reliability" – each edition has ensured that clinicians use the same terms in the same ways. The weakness is its lack of validity. Unlike our definitions of ischemic heart disease, lymphoma, or AIDS, the DSM diagnoses are based on a consensus about clusters of clinical symptoms, not any objective laboratory measure. In the rest of medicine, this would be equivalent to creating diagnostic systems based on the nature of chest pain or the quality of fever. Indeed, symptom-based diagnosis, once common in other areas of medicine, has been largely replaced in the past half century as we have understood that symptoms alone rarely indicate the best choice of treatment. Patients with mental disorders deserve better (Insel. T, 2013, online).

This would confirm that the mind is still not understood, therefore it would follow that autism is still not understood. Additionally, with autism there is no single behavior or set of behaviours:

> One of the most fundamental issues related to diagnosis that is flawed is the concept of diagnostic criteria. One of the very few aspects related to autism that pretty much everyone can agree on is that there is no single behaviours - that is specific to autism. While there may be all sorts of behaviours that are common amongst the population, it is entirely incorrect to suppose that any behaviour or groupings of behaviours can define autism; certain behavioural profiles can be indicative of autism, certainly, but define it? No. However, a simple glance at sets of diagnostic criteria will leave you in no doubt that we are led to believe that a diagnosis can be made based on sets of behaviours. Not only is this misleading, it is in fact, in direct contrast to the fundamental notion that autism can *not*, in fact be diagnosed thus. (Beardon, 2013, p.1)

The word autism has been adopted in a literal sense through a behavioral model, preventing both the safety and the right to proper diagnosis. This will be further discussed in sub-section *2.3 Ethical Issues in Autism Research*. In conclusion to this section, it is highlighted here that there are many different views, which will inform the identification of autism. From a diagnostic pathway perspective, this would confirm that the issues of clear and consistent pathways run deep and it is based on luck as to who conducts the assessment. It is entirely possible that the concept of a spectrum of autism is a consequence and a reflection of professional disagreement rather than diagnostic fact.

This would not only confirm different perspectives but also the realization that no one can make an absolute statement about autism or the individuals these statements refer. The same conclusions could be reached regarding more positive constructs when considering the more complex the individual i.e. multiple diagnoses, and complex environments/opportunities, the less likely there is to be a true representation of that individuals' profile or potential given the constraints and contradictions within theory and practice presented thus far.

2.3 Ethical Issues in Autism Research

It is of course very easy to find quotes and to refer to selected text from authors who both agree or disagree with the researcher's perspective and then to divert a reader's attention through discourse analysis, whereas it is much harder to conduct wide-ranging research with a very heterogeneous population made up of complex people with identities which cannot be encapsulated by a medical model (Waltz, 2014). It is unfortunate therefore, as the following figure illustrates, that funded research is very much uneven and not directed into developing research methodologies, frameworks and practices that lend themselves to be truly participatory and emancipatory.

Figure 1: Autism Research Funding by Research Category (Pellicano, Charman and Dinsmore., 2013, p.22) Image design by Daniel Sinclair; courtesy of CRAE: @CRAE_IOE

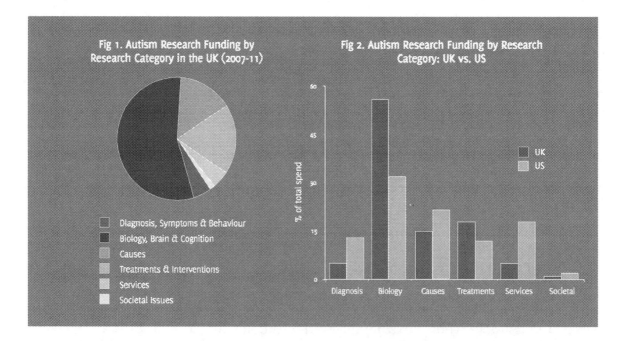

Although participatory and emancipatory research exists, for example the 'ASPECT report' (Beardon and Edmonds, 2007) and 'Very late diagnosis of

Asperger's Syndrome 2013 UK survey report' (Wylie and Heath, 2013), funded research is disproportionately directed towards biology, brain and cognition, yet so little funding is directed toward researching diagnosis, creating an unethical paradigm whereby participants who form the biological group would have been identified through an underfunded process of diagnosis. The irony is that autism has always been about social communication difficulties, yet very little funding is provided for researching societal issues, highlighting the lack of qualitative research being undertaken across this range of discourses.

For example, in a survey of 2000 people with autism and a carer or parent of someone with a diagnosis completed a UK diagnostic survey with the following conclusion under the heading 'Autism diagnostic tool: Which one do we use?'

> At this time the action of diagnosing 'Autism' is lacking any direction. For too many years now people have been trying to make a big issue fit a box that it never will. There is a want to classify and make the Autistic Spectrum something smaller and more defined than it actually is, in doing that we now have too many cases of people not receiving a diagnosis or having to wait for years of medical in-fighting around them to gain one. Even down to the very basics of which diagnostic tool is used is not clear. On the one hand the NHS sets out that ICD-10 IS the diagnostic tool recognised and used. On the other hand professionals WITHIN the NHS state they diagnosing to what the DSM-V states and often misunderstanding what is within it. Instead of giving an ASD diagnosis, as was meant to happen, we now have evidence of families being told 'ah we would have given you a diagnosis before but under DSM-V 'Aspergers' no longer exists and as your child's symptoms meet with what we view as Aspergers we can no longer diagnose'. Unless all health professionals FULLY understand the 'Big Picture' that Autism is and the full scope of the Spectrum and are given a ONE go to point to diagnose from this system is always going to fail (Kennedy, 2013, p.7).

This would confirm the essential role of a code of ethics for multi-disciplinary teams who diagnose autism, similar to that outlined by Cox (2012). However, this may affect the individual who is being assessed, therefore, for an individual who struggles with social communication it may be inappropriate and it may not be what families require. In terms of adult identification, the following quote entitled 'ASAN statement on Frein study on autism and "recovery"' in which is a rebuttle to a study which claims that autistic children recover from autism:

> Adults who clearly met criteria for autism as young children may not show up as Autistic on current behavioral tests, but may by self-report so or appear to by social cognitive testing[ii] or brain scans[iii],[iv]. Moreover, the Workgroup that recently revised the ASD diagnosis stated that current criteria work best for 5-to-8-year-olds[v] (Autistic self advocacy network, 2013).

This would appear to confirm that identification and diagnosis of autism cannot be made using sets of diagnostic criteria as highlighted by Beardon (2013) and that criteria based on childhood presentation should certainly not be used for an adulthood assessment. Moreover, this would suggest that adults are being provided with an 'Aspergers' diagnosis, even if they may be 'autistic'.

The following study utilized EEG (electroencephalogram), which is the process of picking up and recording the impulses and recording brain activity. Brain cells continually send messages to each other that can be picked up as small electrical impulses on the scalp.

Figure 2: Asperger's Syndrome and autism spectrum disorders population distributions (Duffy et al., 2013, p.9) Courtesy of BioMed

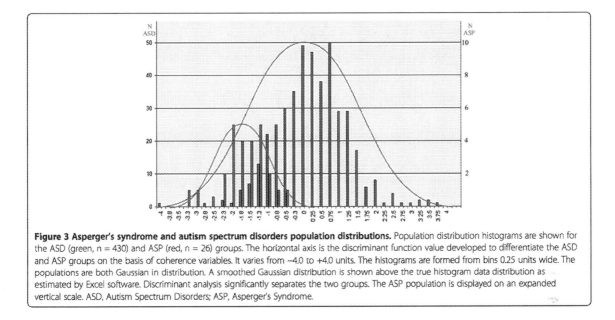

Figure 3 Asperger's syndrome and autism spectrum disorders population distributions. Population distribution histograms are shown for the ASD (green, n = 430) and ASP (red, n = 26) groups. The horizontal axis is the discriminant function value developed to differentiate the ASD and ASP groups on the basis of coherence variables. It varies from –4.0 to +4.0 units. The histograms are formed from bins 0.25 units wide. The populations are both Gaussian in distribution. A smoothed Gaussian distribution is shown above the true histogram data distribution as estimated by Excel software. Discriminant analysis significantly separates the two groups. The ASP population is displayed on an expanded vertical scale. ASD, Autism Spectrum Disorders; ASP, Asperger's Syndrome.

A diagnostic classifier based upon EEG spectral coherence data, previously reported to accurately classify controls and ASD subjects [36], has identified ASP subjects as within the ASD population. Thus, there is justification to consider Asperger's Syndrome as broadly belonging within the Autism Spectrum Disorders. However, there is also evidence demonstrating that ASP subjects can be physiologically distinguished from ASD subjects. Just as dyslexia is now recognized as the low-end tail of the reading ability distribution curve [63], so Asperger's Syndrome may be similarly and usefully defined as a distinct entity within the higher functioning tail of the autism distribution curve. Larger samples are required to determine whether ASP subjects should be considered as an entity physiologically distinct from the ASD population or whether they form an identifiable population within the higher-functioning tail of ASD. EEG spectral coherence data, as presented, provide easily obtained, unbiased, quantitative, and replicable measures of brain connectivity differences relevant to these issues (Duffy et al., 2013, p.10).

This is also reinforced by an earlier study by Yu et al (2010) where they used MRI (Magnetic Resonance Imaging), which is a type of scan that uses strong magnetic fields and radio waves to produce detailed images of the inside of the body and the brain. Yu and colleagues concluded that

> This summery of a rich VBM MRI data set has important implications for how we categorize people on the autism spectrum and cautions that mixing individuals with autism and Asperger syndrome may at times obscure important characteristics manifested in one or the other condition alone (Yu et al., 2010,p.419).

It should be highlighted, though that the NICE guidelines recommend the following - *"Do not use biological tests, genetic tests or neuroimaging for diagnostic purposes routinely as part of a comprehensive assessment"* (NICE, 2012, p.138) because *"In the review of the literature of diagnostic instruments no good-quality evidence for the use of these tests in routine care was found and therefore no recommendations for their routine use were developed"* (NICE, 2012, p.132).

It would seem that despite resources directed towards biological research, there are still barriers to using these techniques alongside traditional methods of identification. Furthermore, it would seem that a person seeking a diagnosis is likely to encounter resistance from the very professionals who carry out such a diagnosis.

> The controversial point was the discussion with Simon Baron Cohen about whether all people with autistic traits need a diagnosis. He believes that it is up to clinicians to judge whether a diagnosis ought to be given or withheld, based on their assessment of how autistic traits affect the "everyday functioning" of the individual. This seems to be a contradictory argument: if a person is having sufficient difficulties that they are seeking a clinical diagnosis, it clearly is affecting their life. Unless the clinician is dismissive of the patient's perspective, there is no case to consider. (Michael, 2014, p.11)

It seems that the individual has to prove that they are autistic, whereas maybe the clinician should be using say the aforementioned technological techniques to provide evidence for the support of their opinion of a diagnosis thus alleviating burden of proof encountered by both sides while adhering to the Hippocratic Oath of 'do no harm'.

When considering research that indicates family lineage and naturally occurring genetic variations (Gaugler et al., 2014), when researchers discuss 'treating autistic children' or 'curing autism' they are actually discussing and advocating wiping out generations of families. Technically, by researchers focusing on individual children and a lack of research with adults, it could lead to professionals providing vulnerable undiagnosed parents with advice or 'treatment' that solely focuses on the child, which in itself is highly unethical. It would be wise for anybody examining the area of autism to research widely and wisely in a manner that would provide a positive future. Here William Blake's assertion comes to mind: *"I must Create a System or be enslav'd by another Man's. I will not Reason and Compare: my business is to Create"* (Blake, 1700s/1994, p.IX).

To be ethical, new research paradigms have to be created where the solutions involve being an autistic researcher. As with any construct, it is illusory and designed to trap you within a paradigm, giving you limited power, so the creation of a new paradigm is required.

This section justifies that Asperger's is also an aspect of autism, therefore, reinforcing the notion that the participants who took part in the study are autistic. This section also reinforces certain elements of participants' reports and validity about experiences at the hands of the NHS regarding a diagnosis and having similar experiences regarding the way they were treated.

2.4 The Identification/Diagnostic Process and Autistic Perception

"Adults with autism will have had very different experiences, depending on factors such as their position on the autistic spectrum, the professionals they have come into contact with and even how and when they got their diagnosis" (Department of Health, 2014, p.46) Therefore, the diagnostic process itself affects perceptions regarding

ones' own identity; an assessment and conclusion based on the perceived expression of themselves (Bagatell, 2007, Bains, 2012; Molloy and Vasil, 2002; Jaci et al., 2008).

2.4.1 Introduction

This section will focus on the existing literature of the experienced view of identification and diagnosis of autism, which will later be cross-referenced within the discussion elements in chapter 4. This section is comprised of three components (pre-diagnosis, diagnosis and post-diagnosis) in order to manage the data more efficiently and to provide clarity for the reader.

Two reports, which will be referred to within this section, are the 'APECT Consultancy Report' (Beardon and Edmonds, 2007) and the 'Very Late Diagnosis of Asperger's Syndrome 2013 UK Survey Report' (Wylie and Heath, 2013). The two main reasons for referring to these particular reports is that (i) they are both UK based and (ii) the two reports were led by both autistic and non-autistic individuals, so fall in line with the perception aspect of this study. Quotes from these sources, unless otherwise stated pertain to the participants of these studies and not the researchers themselves.

The ASPECT report is a national research document where *"a total of 237 questionnaires were received and recorded. As far as we know this is the largest consultation with adults with AS to date"* (Beardon and Edmonds, 2007, p.4). The research methodology design, although not explicitly stated, does appear to be of mixed methods. It does state the use of questionnaires combined with an open day for the adult participants. Although this report covers many different areas, only elements of the diagnostic process will be utilized here.

The research by Wylie and Heath (2013) is a market survey report with a sample of twenty adult participants. The research methodology design, although not explicitly stated, states that it is with a focus on statistical analysis using the method of questionnaires, which were completed through telephone conversations or emailed/posted by participants. Both reports include statistical analysis of data and include the edited highlights of the lived experiences and views of participants. Both documents can be read as companions to this research.

2.4.2 Pre-Diagnosis

Wylie and Heath's research in the section on 'Initial source of diagnosis' outlines that *"...there were no cases of medical doctors initiating the AS diagnostic process"* and that *"...65% of the people surveyed discovered their condition on their own, or via comments by their spouses, relationship partners of friends"* (Wylie and Heath, 2013). Also highlighted was that *"37.5% of respondents who self-diagnosed their condition via personal research did so after discovering that a close relative is on the autism spectrum"* (Wylie and Heath, 2013). Highlights from participants cited within the ASPECT report relating to Pre-diagnosis follow:

> I did see a psychologist who was seeing me for depression but she did not diagnose anything further. I thought on looking back that the times we spent together over a period of six months or so might have given her some pointers. I would never have gone for diagnosis except that my younger sister was diagnosed Asperger's syndrome a year before me and we are very similar (Beardon and Edmonds, 2007, p.62).

"There was no route of any sort available. Diagnosis was made after many frustrating years and numerous stand-up rows" (Beardon and Edmonds, 2007, p.43).

"I had to take my own route to a diagnosis, I felt it totally pointless to go to the doctors, feeling I'd be dismissed. I probably would have been." (Beardon and Edmonds, 2007, p.23).

"My then GP said the diagnosis would not provide any benefit, as there is no cure for Aspergers Syndrome. Thus the PCT would not fund it" (Beardon and Edmonds, 2007, p.27).

"I was left to find a diagnostic centre by myself, and was actively discouraged from seeking a diagnosis by health professionals" (Beardon and Edmonds, 2007, p.45).

While examining the elements within the literature as to how and why participants sought a diagnosis, and with much disagreement between professionals as previously highlighted, when an individual is being assessed, does the individual actually know which school of thought has influenced the clinician's approach to assessment and how this will effect the final decision?

2.4.3 Diagnosis

Although in both reports, there is no mention of the overall process of the lived experience of the diagnostic interview, Wylie and Heath do highlight that *"45 percent of respondents had their AS condition misdiagnosed previously"* and that *"many GPs and Psychiatrists are poorly equipped with knowledge about autism"* (Wylie and Heath, 2013).

> During diagnosis, I was questioned for over two and a half hours using a method that was aimed at parents of young children. I had no family members or friends for support and could answer very few of the questions asked of me. The doctor only stopped when I became very distressed. Is there not a method for diagnosing adults without demeaning, distressing and bullying the person? (Beardon and Edmonds, 2007, P.341 and 342)

An additional element regarding the diagnostic procedure is the ethical nature and the relevance of how this is conducted, and how the information clinicians write in reports feeds into further research, which informs other clinicians. The following is a visual representation of a clinical diagnostic procedure, which highlights not only the different perspectives but also how this leads to very different outcomes and referral routes post-diagnosis.

Figure 3: Bad-Science + Observational Bias (Fisher, 2012, online) Courtesy of Karla Fisher at Karla's ASD page on Facebook

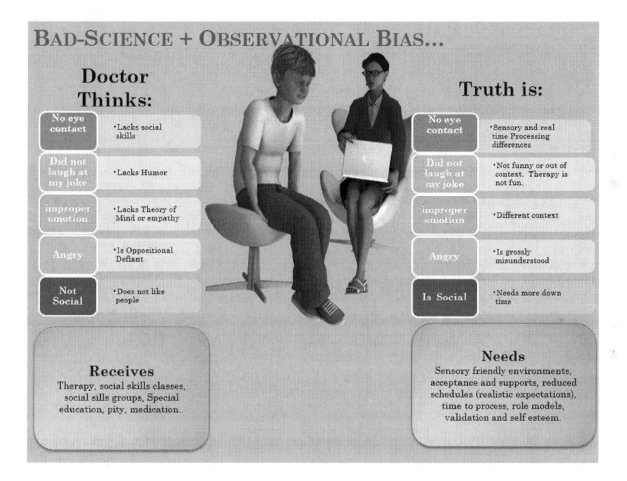

As previously highlighted in the 'autism constructs' section of this thesis, pertaining to the psychological behavioral model of assessment, including empathy and Theory of Mind, these theories remain unproven and therefore unsafe, especially in light of recent research by (Owen, et al., 2013) who suggest *"abnormal white matter as a biological basis for SPD* [Sensory Processing Disorder] *and may also distinguish SPD from overlapping clinical conditions such as autism and*

attention deficit hyperactivity disorder" and (Chang, et al., 2014) who state that *"Over 90% of children with Autism spectrum Disorders (ASD) demonstrate atypical sensory behaviors".* Subsequently, Tavassoli, Hoekstra and Baron-Cohen (2014) have devised *'The sensory perception quotient (SPQ)'* which *"assesses basic sensory hyper and hyposensitivity across all five modalities".* Their conclusion states that:

> The SPQ shows good internal consistency and concurrent validity and differentiates between adults with and without ASC. Adults with ASC report more sensitivity to sensory stimuli on the SPQ. Finally, greater sensory sensitivity is associated with more autistic traits. The SPQ provides a new tool to measure individual differences on this dimension. (Tavassoli, Hoekstra and Baron-Cohen, 2014, P.1)

However, it seems logical that there may be an issue regarding such instruments, as the individual would require a reference point for which to measure their own level of sensory differences against someone who is not affected in this way. This would require the assessor to engage with the individual on a more intimate level in order to ascertain this information. Although there are many good books on sensory differences; particularly by Olga Bogdashina, sensory aspects, although referenced by the early investigators of autism, such as Ssucharewa (1926) and Asperger (1944) it is only recently with the publication of DSM-5 (2013) that sensory aspects have been formally included within the classification system for autism. There needs to be a greater dialogue between individuals and professionals in order to reach a proper conclusion in these matters, which is highlighted in the following by participants who contributed to the ASPECT report:

"A formal study is urgently required to inform health professionals about the severe personal identity issues/damage arising from diagnosis in adults, especially high performing adults due to enormous pendulum swing in confidence" (Beardon and Edmonds, 2007, p.324).

"Better method of diagnosis" (Beardon and Edmonds, 2007, p.322)

"My official diagnosis is "(high functioning) atypical autism" but I believe (and my GP agrees) that AS is more appropriate in practice. (Official diagnosis possibly influenced by misunderstandings in assessment/ narrow interpretation of AS criteria.)" (Beardon and Edmonds, 2007, p.33)

"The sheer mind boggling, overwhelming inaccessibility of it all the inability of 'experts' to agree the diagnosis (AS and comorbids)" (Beardon and Edmonds, 2007, p.113).

> Stop saying that AS was only just recognised and that's why people get late diagnosis. rubbish! - if GP's were better prepared and taught they wouldn't miss the signs and treat us like we are mentally ill. the law needs to recognise this and make sure that GP's who misdiagnose or don't recognise people with AS who are adults or misdiagnose with other mental illnesses are reprimanded and fined/banned from practicing (Beardon and Edmonds, 2007, p.266 and 267)

"There are positive traits in Asperger Syndrome as well as weaknesses. These need to be concentrated on as well" (Beardon and Edmonds, 2007, p.334)

"I do not feel that the current diagnostic criteria accurately define the autistic and specific learning difficulty spectra, so although I am technically defined in a particular way it does not mean that I accept this diagnosis" (Beardon and Edmonds, 2007, p.19)

For a final comment for this section and one it is hoped will filter down into professional practice and become common practice: *"I suggest that people with autism make sense of the world differently, and that, in the social realm, they are differently able to participate in sense-making with others"* (De Jaegher, 2013).

2.4.4 Post-Diagnosis

Wylie and Heath's research in the section on 'Reactions to diagnosis' outlines that *"20 percent of the survey respondents reported no surprise when they received their AS diagnosis because they already suspected it"* and *"Fred Smith said that he felt relief initially, 'although lately I have felt quite confused and bewildered by my situation'"*, *"Jennifer Marks experienced shock initially, although she already suspected she had AS"*, *"John Carlisle said that he experienced relief, confusion and anger simultaneously after his AS diagnosis because he suspected that he would not now be able to receive adequate support from the NHS"* and *"Chris Stevens, who experienced relief and confusion afterwards, said he needed some time to get used to his new self-identity, but the diagnosis made sense and he can live with it"* (Wylie and Heath, 2013). In addition to this, highlights from participants cited within the ASPECT report relating to Post-diagnosis follow:

"In the event my diagnosis hasn't made any difference whatsoever to the total absence of service I receive from the NHS; I suppose it was useful in that it gave my efforts at self-treatment a clearer direction" (Beardon and Edmonds, 2007, p.36)

"I felt entirely on my own after getting my diagnosis, especially living in the rural Highlands, where there is little or no support" and that *"no other psychological syndromes, such as downs or Williams are merely given a diagnosis and left"* (Beardon and Edmonds, 2007, P.335).

"Post-diagnostic support and explain diagnosis" (Beardon and Edmonds, 2007, p.77), *"by not being as vague about the fact that they are giving you an official diagnosis"* and *"stop their ignorance and not doing what they are professionally required to when making a diagnosis"* (Beardon and Edmonds, 2007, p.76).

"Since diagnosis I actually feel more protected in some areas e.g. dealing with police, emergency services etc" (Beardon and Edmonds, 2007, p.271).

"A key advantage of diagnosis, arising from the survey, is that it helps to explain past issues" (Wylie and Heath, 2013).

"I could have been diagnosis from the age of 3 if our GP had taken my mum's concerns seriously and agreed to have me assessed" (Beardon and Edmonds, 2007, p.50).

2.4.5 Conclusion

While these two reports demonstrate the effective collaboration of diversity of researchers and with the aims of each study researched very professionally, in relation to the aims of this particular thesis there are methodological limitations in the sense that (i) mixed methods were used in the form of questionnaires, which enable ascertaining limited narrative information; (ii) these studies do not focus exclusively on the diagnostic process itself in a narrative form and (iii) the holistic nature of the lived experience regarding the process of identification are not fully addressed, but are presented as a series of statements of experiences. Therefore, this study herein addresses these issues by carrying out face-to-face interviews with autistic people in a manner that enables a lengthened amount of their narratives to be attained.

This study expands upon existing literature and is aimed at further exploring autistic people's diagnostic journey. Furthermore, this thesis in itself is geared towards being a piece of work that an autistic person, or someone who suspects they may be autistic, can read and feel more empowered and informed by, in terms of seeking or/and attaining a diagnosis of autism as well as hopefully what to avoid. This is especially relevant in light of the following:

The Division of Clinical Psychology (DCP) is a part of the British Psychological Society and is a professional body representing Psychologists across the United Kingdom. They work with bodies such as the NHS, Government, services users and carers. They were co-authors of the NICE guideline for autistic adults. Their position in the document 'Behaviour and experience in relation to functional psychiatric diagnoses: Time for a paradigm shift, DCP Position Statement' is summarized thus:

> The DCP [Division of Clinical Psychology] is of the view that it is timely and appropriate to affirm publicly that the current classification system as outlined in DSM and ICD, in respect of the functional psychiatric diagnoses, has significant conceptual and empirical limitations. Consequently, there is a need for a paradigm shift in relation to the experiences that these diagnoses refer to, towards a conceptual system which is no longer based on a 'disease' model
>
> (British Psychological Society, 2013, p.1).

Although this statement is not autism specific, it does highlight a shift in thinking towards focusing on the experiences of those who have been identified in order to improve the process including outcomes and a re-invention of how these issues are viewed. This is especially relevant with autistic adults wanting to be seen as experts in the field as well as consultants on these issues (Hurlbutt and Chalmers, 2002) and that

> Ethically, the approach put forward here is not one of laissez faire. On the contrary, it is one that starts from also taking seriously the perspective and subjectivity of people with autism themselves, in a principled, coherent, and comprehensive way. It is then that we can expect to be able to build bridges that are well-informed by both autistic and non-autistic experiences (De Jaegher, 2013).

However, *"Real participation and co-production of research takes extra time, can be challenging, and runs counter to the career goals that academics are incentivized to pursue"* (Waltz, 2014, p.2).

For this research, the main aims are to examine the perceptual experiences of autistic adults regarding;

    (i) Why they sought a diagnosis;

    (ii) How they felt about the diagnostic procedure;

    (iii) What impact the diagnosis has had on the understanding of who they are.

CHAPTER 3

Methodology and Methods

Rod Morris

3.1 Introduction

In order for research to be participatory and emancipatory participants ought to be assisted in the process of exercising their voice in the research process(es) and assisted in changing their perceptions regarding themselves in to more positive perceptions (Moore, Beazley and Maelzer, 1998). This often involves challenging the language people use when referring to themselves (Waltz, 2010). Better research methodologies and methods need to be thought out and created when carrying out research with 'autistic' persons (Waltz, 2010; Milton, 2014). The methodology of this research is based on qualitative assumptions, i.e. that one's lived experience is socially constructed (Nadesan, 2005), and qualitative methods of interviews were used to assist the participants to develop their voice and language in a more positive manner. Which in turn has hopefully led to (i) a more positive perception of themselves and (ii) provide the foundation for a way in which research, as well as the diagnosis procedure, can be made more inclusive. This is especially relevant, as diagnostic pathways have to be transparent and diagnostic protocol has to be clearly laid out (Autism Act, 2009), this research could assist clinicians and local authorities in their statutory duty of providing a smoother process. However, with the rush to provide better opportunities for individuals to seek and obtain a diagnosis, where autism currently sits (within a deficit medical model) and how it has been constructed may have unintended consequences concerning adults who are not under mental health services and who are residing within the community (Waltz, 2008).

Additional aims and objectives will be to assess the following:

- Is a diagnosis as it is currently carried out at the moment beneficial to the individual and to others around them?

- Does the effect of a diagnosis of autism on adults within the community adhere to medical ethics of 'do no harm'?

- This research also aims to explore which profession and level of professional believe they are qualified and knowledgeable to diagnose.

3.2 Grounded Theory Principles and Thematic Analysis

3.2.1 Definition

Grounded Theory aims to be explicit about the process of data collection and analyses so as to bring forth how theory is constructed; it provides relevant applications and methods of investigation for social scientists (Glaser and Strauss, 1967/1999). The principles of Grounded Theory were used to carry out Thematic Analyses of the data collected via semi-structured interviews. Thematic Analysis is the point at which the researcher produces themes from the data whilst using the principles of Grounded Theory (Guest, MacQueen & Namey, 2012). The diagram by Bernard & Ryan (1998) (in Guest, MacQueen & Namey 2012, p.9) illustrate the range of qualitative research processes.

Figure 4 – The Range of Qualitative Research (Guest et al., 2012; p.9).

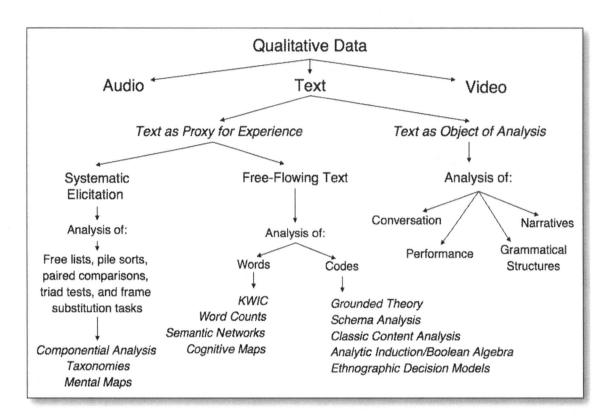

3.2.2 Discussion of Advantages and Disadvantages

The following illustrates the advantages of using Grounded Theory principles to carry out thematic analyses:

> Thematic Analyses, as in Grounded Theory and development of cultural models, require more involvement and interpretation from the researcher. Thematic Analyses move beyond counting explicit words or phrases and focus on identifying and describing both implicit and explicit ideas within the data that is themes. Codes are then typically developed to represent the identified themes and applied or linked to raw data as summary markers for later analysis.
>
> (Guest et al., 2013, p.10).

This method of analyzing enables the researcher to work with the reported experiences of participants in an open and ethical manner, whereby the research process(es) and how interpretations are formed are explicitly outlined. Furthermore, this method enables a researcher to be more culturally sensitive to participants' perceptions and therefore enhances the relevance of the study for autistic people. During the analysis process(es) the researcher was very mindful of participants' narratives and lived experiences, therefore, one attempted to focus more so on the practical and interpersonal aspects of participants' stories. Hence, at the heart of the 'autistic' perception in this study are the matrices, whereby the findings have not been 'diluted' by the process(es) of having other researchers or/and editors reading through it and providing feedback to change it. This is equally applicable to the raw data presented in the appendices.

A disadvantage is that the researcher can impose one's own views upon the data, however, in order to address this factor this researcher has attempted to be as open as possible and has also sought confirmation from participants with regards to their transcripts – which all did confirm. The figure "Comparative Summary of Three Theme-Based Approaches to Analysis" (Guest, MacQueen & Namey 2012, p.17) highlights more in-depth the different approaches, as well as strengths and limitations:

Figure 5 – Comparative Summary of Three Theme-Based Approaches to Analysis (Guest et al., 2012; p.17).

	Phenomenology	*Grounded Theory*	*Applied Thematic Analysis*
Defining Features	• Focuses on subjective human experience • Analysis is typically thematic in nature • Often used in humanist psychology, but approach has been adopted in humanities and social sciences	• Uses a systematic comparative technique to find themes and create codes • Properly done, requires an exhaustive comparison of all text segments Theoretical models built on themes/ codes that are "grounded" in the data	• Identifies key themes in text. Themes are transformed into codes and aggregated in a codebook. • Uses techniques in addition to theme identification, including word searches and data reduction techniques. • Can be used to build theoretical models or to find solutions to real-world problems.
Epistemological Leaning	• *Interpretive* • Subjective meaning is interpreted and extrapolated from discourse	• *Interpretive/Positivist* • Interpretive in that quantification is not included • Positivist in that it is systematic and assertions are required to be supported with evidence (text)	• *Positivist/Interpretive* • Positivist in that assertions are required to be supported with evidence (text). • Processes are also systematic and quantification can be employed. • Methods and processes in ATA (except those of a quantitative nature) can also be used in an interpretive analysis.
Strengths	• Good for smaller data sets • Has latitude to explore data more deeply and extrapolate beyond the text • Good for cognitively oriented studies	• Good for smaller data sets • Exhaustive coverage of data • Interpretation supported by data • Can be used to study topics other than individual experience (e.g., social process, cultural norms, etc.)	• Well suited to large data sets • Good for team research. • Inclusion of non-theme-based and quantitative techniques adds analytic breadth. • Interpretation supported by data • Can be used to study topics other than individual experience.
Limitations	• Focuses only on human experience • May interpret too far beyond what's in the data • Not necessarily systematic	• Does not include quantification • Time consuming ; logistically prohibitive for large data sets	• May miss some of the more nuanced data.
Key Sources	• Giorgi (1970, 2009), Moustakas (1994), Smith, Flowers, and Larkin (2009)	• Glaser and Strauss (1967), Corbin and Strauss (2008), Charmaz (2006)	• No one text. • Elements of inductive thematic analysis can be found in numerous books on qualitative data analysis.

3.3 Ethical Considerations & Methods Used to Address Ethical Issues

The very nature of autism being communication based, with the formal identification process(es) being hugely personal, particular attention was paid not just to research practices in general but also wider recognition and accommodation of differences within participants. As such, the process(es) was quite rigid but also flexible.

With the process of recruitment and retention, participants were informed of the processes and that they could withdraw at any point. The time between sending out the questions and conducting the interview was lengthy due to awareness of processing differences, the researcher ensured that participants had time and space to recall and consider what they wanted to communicate and chose the day and time of the interview – therefore, they led the process. The semi-structured interview questions were presented in a narrative form so as to ease recollection of one's experiences.

The medium by which the researcher and each participant communicated was dictated to by the participant, whereby it could take place via video conferencing or in person, but needed to be recorded. Due to processing differences, for example, which some participants are likely to have had, the researcher made sure not to disturb them whilst they were talking and this ensured that they were able to delve into the topics as much as they wanted without losing their train of thought or be influenced by the researcher.

After the researcher typed up the transcripts word-for-word for each interview, each participant was emailed a copy of the transcript to read and confirm. When one has processing difficulties and is interviewed in a real time situation, whereby one feels pressure, one is likely to have said things that one may not have otherwise said. Also, something, which is presented in an audio format, can be interpreted very differently in print. Therefore, participants were sent their transcripts and given time to read through them and respond in their own time. Additionally, during the period between the interview and the reading of the transcript, participants may have contemplated their experiences more thoroughly; therefore participants were advised that they could edit their interview transcripts any way they saw fit. This also acted as a second filtering mechanism (with the first being the measures taken with the interview process itself) to ensure that differences in communication and thinking styles were accommodated.

An additional ethical issue arises through the very nature of the subject being researched and the very personal nature of each individual's journey and experiences, which may illicit emotional issues, therefore, the researcher informed each participant that if they required additional support or dialogue at any point then they are welcome to make further contact. Ultimately it is hoped that by partaking in this process and by revisiting this period in their lives, participants may have identified areas of their pathway which were previously hidden, and/or provided a different perspective on the process. This may also have highlighted an awareness of just how far they have come since the diagnosis.

An additional aspect to the ethical design of this research and the processes is when participants read the complete thesis they will then be able to compare how their process faired in relation to others' pathways. One of the problems any individual being assessed is that individuals have nothing to compare it with. Therefore, participants may not have been made fully aware of whether their process was good or bad or what the standard is or should be. Hence, reading the thesis may better clarify the process(es) participants lived through.

3.4 Processes Used for this Research

After developing the proposal for this research, including the protocols developed by the researcher and approved by the supervisor and referenced in appendices B to E, approval from the ethics committee was sought and granted (Appendix A) with some issues including language which were addressed before commencing.

Invitations to participate (Appendix B) were emailed to a number of different organizations and groups. Those who responded were sent further information (Appendix C), which provided an outline of the principle questions. This also highlighted their rights as a participant. Along with this was sent a consent form (Appendix D). Once this consent form was signed and returned participants were sent the protocol (Appendix E), which included all the interview questions. Given the potential differences in communication styles across participants choices were provided as to how they wanted to conduct the interview; either by e-mail, Skype or in person. Additionally, participants were provided with sufficient time to read the questions and to process the information before commencing.

During the interviews, each question was read out line-by-line, so the researcher did not deviate into other matters. Though after the formal questions some participants wanted to discuss things further and this took place. With their permission this additional information was also transcribed and used for analyses. The audio records were then transcribed word-for-word and transcripts were produced. These transcripts were then e-mailed to the relevant participant, in order for them to make any changes that they saw fit. These transcripts make up Appendix F, which is the raw interview data.

Figure 6 – The Range of Qualitative Research (Guest et al., 2012; p.96).

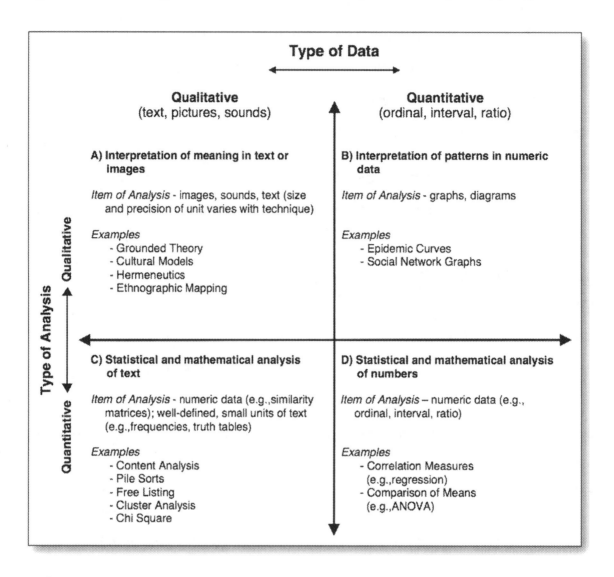

3.4.1 Analysis of Data

Once these transcripts were approved by the participants, the researcher then read through the transcripts many times and made analytical notes/memos; this is coding level 1 and 2, which are outlined in Appendix G.

The figure "Qualitative and Quantitative data analysis" (adapted by Bernard, 1996) cited in (Guest, MacQueen & Namey 2012, p.6), illustrates the different types of research and analyses. The processes used by this researcher involved transcribing data in the form of sounds in to a textual format, and this in itself involved a form of analyses, whereby the researcher was paying attention to the participant's tone of voice, silences, the way in which words were used and not used etc. This aspect was another dimension of the transcribing process(es) whereby the researcher had to step out of one's own standpoint at times and try and imagine the reported experiences of participants and what it would be like to live such experiences, yet simultaneously then step away from this and analyze the material with a rounded perspective, providing rich data and analyses. Therefore, this research is of a qualitative nature.

The transcripts and memos were then analyzed via comparison, focusing on similarities and differences across participants' experiences (Appendix G), to make up the themes that make up the main body matrix; focusing on the explicit (e.g. practical) and implicit (e.g. emotional) subjective meanings of the participant(s).

CHAPTER 4

Findings and Discussion

4.1 Introduction

Presented in this chapter are the results with discussion. This includes preliminary data pertaining to each participant followed by three matrices, which outline the perception of participants' diagnostic pathway. Each matrix is followed by a discussion identifying common themes outlined in the literature review, what can be discerned from the findings and possible ways forward.

4.1.1. Participant Particulars

The following information provides data to the background of each participant. This, in addition to the matrices and the discussions enhance and provides depth to the conclusion and summary of recommendations, which follow afterwards. In summary, eight participants represent an equal male to female ratio with age at time of interview ranging from thirty nine to seventy years of age, with age of when diagnosis being conducted ranging from thirty two to sixty five years of age.

Natalie

Current age: 39

Age when diagnosis was conducted: 38

Current social and economic situation: Married with 5 children. Currently a qualified Science teacher and stay at home mum. Runs an autistic group.

Official diagnoses by name: Asperger's syndrome (no additional diagnoses)

Christine

Current age: 40

Age when diagnosis was conducted: 32

Current social and economic situation: *"I'm out of work I am applying to go back to university but I need funding to do that. I am in quite a vulnerable economic situation: having had a very disheartening experience in trying to find disability support in the workplace, and having left that workplace where I was unhappy, and now wanting to go back to university in middle life. I have years of experience and good qualifications but don't see myself being able to cope in a mainstream workplace, I need to do other things with my life, but economically I feel, no I am very vulnerable."*

Official diagnoses by name: Asperger Syndrome (Diagnosed as dyslexic as a child, aged 6)

Isaac

Current age: 65

Age when diagnosis was conducted: 55 (2003)

Current social and economic situation: *"I'm retired now. I had to give up work for medical reasons, not because of Asperger's. I was a postman."*

Official diagnoses by name: Asperger's

"I had tremendous difficulty in obtaining a diagnosis because some of the places wanted my parents input, but my parents were deceased. I had it done at a hospital in Birmingham."

Jack

Note: Ethically, the author of this thesis declares he has known this participant for many years, but this does not interfere with the content as the experiences presented here occurred long before first contact.

Current age: 70

Age when diagnosis was conducted: 65 (2008)

Current social and economic situation: *"Both good; It's something that I've always known was important to me and I have worked on both of them all my life; I have a strange habit of wanting to stay in touch with people that go back years. I play a lot of sport, which helps me to meet people. The social aspects of my life have always been important to me because when I was young I couldn't relate well to people; I wanted to but I didn't quite know how to engage, so throughout my life I was observant as to how people conducted themselves, and it is a learning process I am still doing."*

Official diagnoses by name: Asperger Syndrome

Leanne

Current age: 51

Age when diagnosis was conducted: 44 (2006)

Current social and economic situation: Has two jobs but are both part-time, both term-time, doesn't have a salary. *"I'm in a scary financial position, because my youngest son is 19 he is still in full time education for the next few weeks. In September the child benefit will stop and so will the child tax credits and family tax credits so I will be about £200 a week worse off, which is scary."* *"The last few weeks since my dad died, my boy has been brilliant and helped loads, he's answered the phone when I can't talk to anybody and he just tells everybody to go away; he has coped fantastically; I don't know what I'd have done without him and he doesn't get any recognition for that and he shouldn't have to have that responsibility but it's just the way it is."* Leanne has two sons and a daughter; *"both of my son's have been diagnosed but my daughter hasn't although this doesn't mean she is not on the spectrum."*

Official diagnoses by name: Asperger Syndrome

James

Current age: 59

Age when diagnosis was conducted: 57 (2011)

Current social and economic situation: *"I'm trained and work as a Social Worker. I'm comfortable being in the community and believe myself to be middle class, but not sure. I own my own house, am married with no children but I have two relationships with wife's children and am financially not too bad."*

Official diagnoses by name: *"Asperger Syndrome (at the top of the scale, she said)"*

Rachel

Current age: 39

Gender: Transgender (male to female, currently in transition)

Age when diagnosis was conducted: *"When I went to see the Doctor for depression I think he initially figured out I had Asperger's, I was 28 (2002) at the time but it wasn't until I was 30 (2004) that I saw him again specifically for getting an Asperger's diagnosis from him."*

Current social and economic situation: *"I'm married and we have a mortgage and I'm an IT consultant and run a limited company and I do freelance web design work as well"*

Official diagnoses by name: *"I think its Mild Asperger Syndrome. I've not got depression at the moment but did have in 2002. I think the main reasons for that were a mixture of relationship problems with a previous relationship and it was around the first anniversary that my father had died and things were getting stressful at work as well, so with all that going on together it caused depression at that time."*

Russell

Current age: 58

Age when diagnosis was conducted: *"I was told unofficially by a psychiatrist with specialism in autism about 10 years ago (48 years old), then 3 years later I had an official diagnosis. (51 years old) I went back as I needed an official diagnosis."*

Current social and economic situation: *"I work full time for BT and I have worked since I was 16, I do work too hard for some of my peers and they don't like how much work I do; at home I am very lazy and I can't be bothered to do anything; I employ a cleaner to do everything; I'm divorced; I was married for 18 years; got divorced, again at age 48; I currently have a girlfriend whom I have been seeing for 8 years, but we don't live together; financially I am ok with no worries; I don't have any friends and I don't go out; If you took away all the professional people I know and my girlfriend, I wouldn't have anybody. I see a councilor and have regular massages. I find it hard to socialize in the normal way; there has to be something keeping us together, like work or school, in the school days. I have no children as I couldn't have any with my wife; I never found out why; we did have IVF for a few years."*

Official diagnoses by name: *"Asperger's Syndrome, Dyslexia, Dyscalculia, potential long-term memory problems which I am trying to get assessed but its like banging my head against a brick wall, Depression, Stress and Anxiety, very poor sleep."* (These were all diagnosed separately but around about the same time – between the ages of 48 and 50)

The following three matrices consist of the following. The first matrix is about participants' drivers and expectations, i.e. the reasons why they sought an assessment. The second matrix concerns their diagnostic perception and how this affected the understanding of themselves, spanning from the pre-assessment stage through to the post-diagnostic perception, covering aspects pertaining to the environment and the type of professional. The third matrix is more so with regards to post-diagnostic perception, dealing with participants' perception directly after the interview, the participants' reading of the report, to reflection and the long-term practical impact.

4.2 Findings/Results Matrices and Discussion

The following are matrices of the arising themes of participants' data. Leanne, Isaac and Natalie were diagnosed via NHS procedures whereas private clinicians diagnosed Russell, Rachel, James and Jack. There will be two quotes from Christine (e.g. Christine 1, Christine 2) as she was first diagnosed privately and then by the NHS, hence the use of "(P)" at the end of the quotes regarding the private diagnosis and "(N)" regarding her NHS diagnosis; this is also the case with Russell, however he was first diagnosed by the NHS and then privately. The sub-themes are often inter-related. The reasons are complex and multi-faceted. The quotes on the left side of the matrix are to do with the practical aspects of participants' experiences and perception (i.e. 'this is what happened') and the quotes on the right side are to do with how they interpreted the event(s) and how they felt.

4.2.1 Matrix of Themes 1: Pre-Diagnosis; Drivers

Primary Reasons for Diagnosis	Participant Quotes	Secondary Factors: Implications Regarding Identity	Participant Quotes
Employment and education	Christine 1: *"After the friend said that she thought I was on the spectrum I said to my disability adviser at my workplace that this friend of mine said that I may be on the spectrum…it was she who arranged my diagnosis, which my workplace paid for."* (P) James: *"I was having problems with concentration at University and ended up teaching most of the stuff to myself. I couldn't cope with University, getting around and getting there."* (P) Russell 2: *"I lost my post at work and had to find a new one, and they were trying to force people into call centers, and I knew that there was no way I could work in a call center, so I went to get an official diagnosis to help me with this, so that they would have to treat me as disabled and make reasonable adjustments for me."* (P)	Personal Identity	Christine 1: *"I have been aware all my life that there was something different about me that I couldn't explain. I felt like a complete failure as a human being and I hadn't put two and two together at all."* (P) James: *"I'd lost who I was; that was one of the reasons I wanted the assessment was to find out who I was, so I can put it quite clearly, maybe this is just behavioral or it's just the way I think, I don't know."* (P) Russell 2: [After losing his job, Russell's wife left him, please refer to the next section.]

Marriage/ Relationships	Isaac: *"We were having problems with the marriage and we went to Relate and one of the Relate councilors, who wrote books on Asperger's and she could see Asperger's in me."* (N) Rachel: *"When I was in the early stages of the relationship with a lady who I went on to marry, she suspected that I might have Asperger's… and then she suggested that I should get a diagnosis of it just so there is a record of it."* (P) Russell: *"I became initially aware that this was a problem through a TV program, which covered a family where the husband had Asperger's; not long after that my wife left me, so all the old problems reared their head such in socializing and trying to find another partner."* (P+N)
Personal and family identity	Russell: *"After the divorce I felt that I was back to square one, back to when I was in my teens and no better off, so I wanted to know what it was, and if it wasn't Asperger's then I'll carry on looking."* (P+N)

Theme	Quotes	Theme	Quotes
Their Children	Jack: "My daughter, who was a speech and language therapist, worked with some people with Autism and said to me one day 'I think you and I, dad, may have it'. So, that was important for me to find out and at the time I was retired which gave me time to think about it and to negotiate a diagnosis and how to get one." (P) Natalie: "One of my children (6 at the time) was having some problems at school... fitted on to the autistic spectrum, specifically Asperger' Syndrome." (N) Leanne: "A couple of people independent of each other said that he had traits of Asperger Syndrome/Autism... I was researching on behalf of my son, then I recognized the symptoms/traits in myself, then I went to my GP and she referred me." (N)	Personal and Family Identity	Jack: The thought process I went through at the time, was reflecting on the aspects of my quality of life...as it turned out it became an important question to me, so I decided to go after it." (P) Natalie: "So, I knew that I was the same, and I procrastinated for about a year... I decided yes because I didn't want him to feel alone." (N) Leanne: "This is where very personal, family history comes in... I also have memories going back to my childhood of my mum saying... very negative things.... I was arguing with myself... I wasn't looking for something to be wrong with me...it wasn't about me it was about my son. (N)
Health Concerns	Christine 2: "I then went to my GP and said I needed mental health services, which were relevant to autistic people, and the local hospital where such services are delivered kicked up a fuss and said oh no, we only treat people we have diagnosed ourselves...I went along with this because they were the only service provider in my area, so I went for an NHS diagnosis at this local hospital." (N)	System Identity	Christine 2: "My particular case is a rather messy one...I thought was totally ridiculous because people could of course move into the neighborhood, and why is one diagnosis different from another?" (N)

Prior Knowledge	Rachel: *"I had quite a decent understanding of Autism before then as well; mainly through books and the internet."* (P) Jack: *"None at all, apart from what I knew about myself. It was obvious that I did understand a lot because of all the self-analysis".* (P) Isaac: *"I had never heard about Asperger's up until that time. Even my GP had not heard of Asperger's and had to use the computer to look it up."* (N) Christine 1: *"Not much really; I had heard of it...* "*I had family members who were part of that generation who were never diagnosed.... In terms of autism itself, I didn't know very much about it; I started to read about it and so re-defined myself. I knew that there was something about me that I couldn't explain. I hadn't joined all the dots, but when I read books on autism I began to piece things together."* (P)
Expectations	Rachel: *"I expected that I would most likely have a diagnosis of Asperger's before actually attending."* (P) Jack: *"What I was hoping for was a positive diagnosis one way or the other; I wanted confirmation, one way or the other and that is what I was looking for, and I was somewhat apprehensive. I didn't know what it would unveil but it was like waiting to attend your own court case, but I wanted an answer."* (P) Isaac: *"I just wanted an answer; had I got it or hadn't I got it. I was nervous, as I didn't know what they were going to come up with"* (N) Christine 1: *"That I would simply be diagnosed as Autistic, that the diagnostic process would make sense, that I would be able to get some form of support as a result of diagnosis; I was quite naive regarding the types of support that were available. I thought I would be helped to gain a better understanding of myself and helped to cope better in the world."* (P)

	Christine 2: *"I think that I was fairly ignorant prior to my assessment and if I had understood autism's messy history with the mental health profession and how diagnosis worked before I asked my GP for diagnosis I would not have allowed my GP to refer me to a mental health team or even used an NHS service at all, but because I didn't have this knowledge diagnosis was mishandled and I was blocked from accessing services."* (N)
	Natalie: *"An awful lot of knowledge I've developed from research from various sources. I read all and anything I could about AS, including information specific to women… I found that the whole clinical side of it was very negative and I don't feel it needs to be negative."* (N)
	Leanne: *"I did some research and I went on to a number of websites and I recognized the symptoms, so I self-diagnosed… I went to the doctor with all the research I got and he asked 'why do you think you have Asperger Syndrome?'… I was actually convinced that I did actually have Asperger's Syndrome, but I also have memories going back to my childhood."* (N)
Christine 2: *"I was on a waiting list for some months, but that's how the NHS works."* (N)	
Natalie: *"I expected it to be quite clinical and quite formal… It was pretty much what I expected."* (N)	
Leanne: *"I can't remember having any expectations prior to diagnosis."* (N)	

James: "I had a basic knowledge.... I didn't have an in-depth knowledge of exactly what goes on. I had an interest; I had suspicions but I wasn't self-diagnosing. I knew Autism existed and Asperger's Syndrome but I wasn't clear what the difference was. It was an interest but I was reading anything too in-depth about it." (N)

Russell: "Not a lot. I always thought of Autism as that of little kids in a world of their own, who don't communicate with people. This was my view of Autism before I knew about Asperger's. It was only after the divorce that I was having real problems again that I started looking into it." (P+N)

James: "I thought it might have given me a reason of who I am, also I was apprehensive about where do I go if it isn't. I wanted an answer and for somebody to explain but I also wanted someone who could professionally do that... My expectations were to have a resolution as to whether I was right or whether I was wrong, or another reason as to why I was having such difficulties in such simple areas." (N)

Russell 1: "With the first one, when I just wanted to know what was wrong, my expectations were that it was Asperger's and that I was hoping that I was right. With the second one, I was still unsure because I believed that I didn't have the symptoms that badly, some of the people I have told since don't believe I have Asperger's as they can't see that I have a problem." (N)

Russell 2: "So, I was nervous the second time round but this surrounded the question as to whether I was bad enough to have a diagnosis, and I didn't know how this diagnosis thing worked, how bad you have to be to have a diagnosis. I was also worried about my job situation; without a diagnosis they would force me into an unsuitable post, which would make my mental health worse and leave me having to leave the job, and we don't like change." (P)

4.2.2 Discussion of Matrix 1

<u>Employment and Education</u>

In relation to existing literature highlighted in the literature review, Hans Asperger was an educator and was evaluating his students in an educational setting, Lorna Wing was evaluating within community settings in a mainly working class area; participants here, have been informed of the idea of autism via a friend and/or literature; in this sample medical professionals are not leading the way in identifying potential autistic persons. One could state that this is due to a lack of GP training, however these individuals would have been in contact with various other professionals, e.g. dentists, educators etc. throughout their lives. Regardless of whether someone has the acknowledgement of a formal assessment of autism, others would have identified him or her as being different.

Hans Asperger and Leo Kanner both included information about parents and their employment(s) but with a focus on the children. Here, James was having problems at university and could not cope, and now works as a Social Worker, and sought a diagnosis to find out who he was. He was seeking to make sense of his life and seeking to understand his identity. If one does not have a clear sense of identity this affects every aspect of one's life. Christine's first diagnosis was private and her work place paid for it. It was a Disability Adviser who arranged for the diagnosis to take place. An aspect of Russell's experiences is that he lost his post at work because the work place were forcing people in to call centers; he recognized his difficulties with this situation and this came about due to changes in the work place.

When such changes occur in people's lives as well as within society, this then brings differences to the fore in the form of disability. However, most research focuses on the biological aspects of autism rather than social research (Pellicano et al., 2014); therefore, research ought to be spread equally across these different domains in a coherent manor so as to gain a clearer picture of the issues. Due to a lack of societal research there is little all-encompassing data as to why individuals seek a diagnosis, and the data as above in Matrix 1 addresses these aspects.

Personal Identity

This aspect of personal identity is one of the core features of perception itself and participants' perceptions regarding the autism diagnosis process. Christine was aware that there was something different about her, and she identified herself as being a complete failure, however, because this was something she could not explain or put two and two together she seems to be describing in some aspects what James describes, i.e. feeling lost as she who she was. If a professional encounters something like this then it will not be obvious and a hidden facet which the person is likely to be covering up by other means. The danger occurs when different people tell someone with such an issue different things about themselves.

Regarding this aspect of personal identity, Karla's figure on page 32 is useful; it is about fluid interaction with other people including professionals. In situations where it may be inferred that the individual lacks empathy, the truth is quite different, yet one does not know what that something else is; this affects all aspects of functioning. This describes how being neurologically different and being informed by socially constructed views blend and differ (e.g. Casanova, 2014 versus Nadesan, 2005). If one has a hidden element of one's being it pervades through everything and it takes knowledge of such a thing to be able to communicate it to others and also receive some understanding from others.

Marriage and Relationships (Two People)

As highlighted in the previous section, many professionals are not fully aware of autism, though when Isaac accessed the service RELATE due to having problems with his marriage, the professional had written about autism and managed to provide them with information. By what Isaac reports it is evident that the RELATE therapist was using a social constructivist approach. However, Rachel's situation when compared with Isaac's is that her partner suggested going for a diagnosis; with Rachel there may have been more emotional depth with her partner, partly maybe because the partner is disabled, and recommended she see someone.

Russell initially became aware also because his wife left him. This appears to have had a major impact on his personal identity, whereby he felt like a teenager again and trying to fathom who he was, as his identity had been primarily through his partner. Russell's experiences do lead to an ethically pertinent question: when you have a family and they are viewing a TV program about autism which is presented as such that there is one person in a family who is presented as 'the problem' with sympathy with other family members, what effect would this have on a family if multiple viewers are in the same family are effected? If one notes the earlier studies where similar aspects were identified in the family lineage (Gaugler et al., 2014), ethically TV programs could be informing families of an inaccurate paradigm which could effect the identity and wellbeing of these families. Likewise, if a professional who has stereotypical views about autism and such power dynamics informs couples.

Marriage and Family; Children (Personal and Family Identity)

In relation to existing literature highlighted in the literature review, Leo Kanner's paper describes the children and their parents. Within this research, Jack's daughter was working as a Speech and Language Therapist and she recognized autism in herself and Jack; highlighting this to her father. This aspect brings about two factors; (i) a Speech and Language therapist who recognizes herself as being autistic and (ii) a genetic lineage whereby autism is seen as so rather than a disease.

Natalie and Jack both had time to procrastinate about deciding whether to formally obtain a diagnosis, as Jack was retired and Natalie was a stay-at-home mum; there was no immediate pressure for them to seek a diagnosis. Leanne, Natalie and Jack all have other family members who have been formally diagnosed which highlight situations of the genetic variability across the generations. Christine made inferences to family members being autistic but "were part of that generation who were never formally diagnosed". In Jack's case it was daughter that mentioned autism, in Natalie's case it was a self-identification via her child's difficulties and recognized the similarities, and Leanne sought a diagnosis after two people recognized the traits in her son and whilst she was carrying out research she recognized the traits in her self, thereby going to her GP to request a diagnosis.

The participants and their family members felt comfortable enough to share knowledge with each other. These adults had spent most their lives not formally knowing they were autistic, however, it took their children to more so recognize this aspect of themselves. This is ironic in that the child is pointing the way for the parent. Clearly, even when an autistic person is older, they are still as vulnerable as a child. Maybe as people become older they become more aware of their vulnerability, despite not having a name for this. Again, the aspects of participants experiences raised so far highlight the result of how little paid research goes in to societal aspect as highlighted by Pellicano's diagram and research.

A most beautiful quote by a participant: Natalie: "I decided yes because I did not want him to feel alone". This parent is identifying with her child rather than this construct called 'autism'.

Health Concerns

Christine required mental health services that were relevant to autistic people, and yet the local hospital stipulated that they would only see those who had been recognized via the NHS – discounting her private diagnosis. This links in with Kennedy's (2013) research, in that people are stuck between the medical in-fighting that is taking place and do not receive diagnoses or/and wait for years for a diagnosis, therefore, families and individuals are not receiving support. Politics is clearly affecting people's lives and further supports the need for a code of ethics as outlined by Cox (2012).

The System and Identity

Christine's experience also brings about the issue of if someone has been formally assessed in one area of the country, and a local hospital or/and Local Authority has a particular pathway in place whilst another has a different pathway, and say if a person moves from one place to another, this can be used by the NHS as an excuse to not provide relevant services. When there is brain scanning technology that may be able to assist with the process of identification, as is outlined in the Literature Review, for the NHS to not use such technology, standard approaches to diagnosis leads to a lottery of different diagnosis(es). This further highlights how the NHS's political agenda is affecting people's lives.

Expectations and Prior Knowledge

The previous themes have outlined the circumstances surrounding the driving factors of participants' reasons for seeking a diagnosis. The themes presented here combine prior knowledge and expectations, which are closer to the time of the diagnosis. Rachel suspected that she most likely had autism through having read books and the Internet; therefore, she had a certain expectation. From what this researcher has researched so far, there is no actual document that outlines how it feels to go through the process of diagnosis, but it is reasonable to infer that the knowledge a person has beforehand will affect the diagnosis.

Jack was hoping for a positive diagnosis either way, despite his anxieties, and wanted the diagnosis to be over and done with. He did not want his knowledge to affect the process and he avoided doing much research in to autism. It would seem that nobody knows what to expect and people have not been given much information by the actual practitioner beforehand. Both Jack and Isaac stated that they wanted an answer either way. Isaac had never heard of Asperger's, and neither had his GP - who had to look it up on the Internet! These two participants were not sure what to expect due to a lack of prior knowledge, however, the other participants had some prior knowledge and were more certain with their expectations. Christine admits that she was fairly ignorant prior to diagnosis, which highlights how much knowledge does the professional and the individual have of each other for such a potentially life-defining event? With Christine stating "I was blocked from accessing services", the NHS may have a case to answer in that the diagnosis of Autism may be used in order to block people from accessing services, but also that diagnostic labels could be applied or changed in order that the NHS staff can manipulate figures and provide inappropriate services – a labeling system that is based on service availability and not on services to meet the needs of an accurate diagnosis. This addresses the importance of the aspect of the Autism Act (2009) whereby the diagnosis process itself is required to be made more transparent. For example, if Christine had not gone for the initial private diagnosis, which felt positive, would she have been able to compare this experience with the NHS process and feel negative about it?

Natalie expected the process to be quite clinical and it was pretty much what she expected. This was likely partly due to her conducting extensive research, not just on behalf of her son or witnessing her son's diagnosis, but also in the intervening year before her own assessment. This may have been similar to Leanne, although she did not remember having any expectations. James had basic knowledge and expectations pertaining to his identity and a clear-cut resolution. Russell's knowledge was sparse and with a stereotypical view of autism. With his first assessment he was looking to know what was wrong; with the second one he was nervous as to the outcome as it surrounded where he would meet the criteria and how this surrounded his work situation.

Prior to assessment, each participant had very different levels of knowledge; most did not know about how the process worked and therefore did not know what to expect. It would seem that assessment under such circumstances might deter individuals from seeking assessment. This highlights that participants were not properly informed, unlike with other medical procedures, which highlights potential legal and ethical issues surrounding informed consent.

The following matrix further expands on self-identification (practical and interpersonal) and further explores expectations (with reflections). The narrative then proceeds to the process itself from the day of the assessment and through the diagnostic interview, which includes environmental factors and suitability of the type of professional who carried out the interview.

4.2.3 Matrix of Themes 2: Diagnostic Perception

Practical Perception	Participant Quotes	Personal perception and identity	Participant Quotes
Diagnosis of self (Practical reasons)	Christine 1: *"This reading began mainly after diagnosis"* (P) Christine 2: *"I needed mental health services, which were relevant to autistic people…The local hospital said that their test was better because it asked more questions and involved more people."* (N) James: *"The first person to mention anything of the sort was my mother when I was 7 years old…whilst working with service users I started noticing traits in myself."* (N) Leanne: *"When I realized I brought three books. I couldn't have picked three better books because they did what they said on the tin; yea, that's what it's like."* (N)	(Interpersonal)	Christine 1: *"I think that I was fairly ignorant prior to my assessment"* (P) Christine 2: *"I went along with this because they were the only service provider in my area."* (N) James: *"I was a person who didn't fit in; strange; on the wrong end of everything… but it became more apparent the more research I did, so I had arguments in my head, am I inducing this or is it me…is prior knowledge a good thing or a bad thing; maybe you shouldn't seek a diagnosis if you have already got suspicions! That is what brought the anxiety up."* (N) Leanne: *"I think the overriding thing was how do I be autistic?…So now I've got to learn how to be autistic; I spent so many years pretending to be normal, which didn't fucking work, but I don't know how to be autistic at all, so I was thinking crazy mad things."* (N)

Natalie: *"That was a strange experience...I thought there's something wrong with me, I'm defective and I felt quite depressed... then I realized that I am just different, and I was just quite cross about the clinical things I have read and the negative things I have read, and then discovered this whole other ethos, and then I just felt extremely positive...ultimately I feel very positive and very empowered, but also very frustrated...I felt that I was somehow useless and really blamed myself whereas I was just dealing the negative social behavior of other people who should have been well enough behaved not to have manifested it...I'm smart, not defective and I just find the whole thing really interesting.* (N)

Russell 1: *"It has come to me realizing that something is wrong with me; something is stopping me from socializing in the normal way, particularly with women, finding partners and girlfriends."* (N)

Natalie: *"I took the AQ test online and got 37...I did some more reading and research...I wanted to bring my children up to be positive and also to reach out to other people and really dispel the whole myths of us having something the matter with us... This positivity comes from me realizing that all my life I have been in these situations where people were really negative and I just didn't know how to deal with it...I suddenly realized that none of this is my fault. I have a different kind of brain...I quite like learning for real that I am different rather than this horrible suspicion that I've had all my life, and wondering why the hell I don't fit in. So I approached it from that kind of angle."* (N)

Russell 1: *"I wasn't bothered about an official diagnosis or having a bit of paper; I just wanted to know what is happening."* (N)

Reflections	Expectations
Christine 1: *"I was quite naive regarding the types of support that were available. I thought I would be helped to gain a better understanding of myself and helped to cope better in the world."* (P)	Christine 1: *"That I would simply be diagnosed as Autistic, that the diagnostic process would make sense, that I would be able to get some form of support as a result of diagnosis"* (P)
Isaac: *"I was nervous, as I didn't know what they were going to come up with."* (N)	Isaac: *"I just wanted an answer; had I got it or hadn't I got it."* (N)
Jack: *"I was somewhat apprehensive. I didn't know what it would unveil but it was like waiting to attend your own court case, but I wanted an answer."* (P)	Jack: *I had this overall mission on getting a positive answer, yea or nea."* (P)
James: *"My expectations were to have a resolution as to whether I was right or whether I was wrong, or another reason as to why I was having such difficulties in such simple areas."* (N)	James: *"I wanted an answer and for somebody to explain but I also wanted someone who could professionally do that, not just patting me on the head and saying you're on, because that's what happens to a lot of people I've seen since."* (N)
Natalie: *"I was quite frightened...I was quite worried that because I was being diagnosed that someone would tell social services and they would come snooping around my family with all these awful suspicions, so I was quite paranoid and a little bit worried."* (N)	Natalie: *"I had read some quite damning things about people with Asperger's as parents."* (N)

Rachel: "*I was not aware of his inclination of Asperger's when I went to see him for depression. When I went to see him for the Asperger's diagnosis he said at the time the main focus was getting the depression treated and sorted, so he didn't want to cloud the issue with mentioning Asperger's.*" (P)

Russell 1: "*I just wanted to know what was wrong…. I was very unsure of myself back then and I didn't know that I was intelligent; I knew that I was different; I felt different; I felt that I couldn't get on with people like other people do. I was searching for answers, and that with an answer I could do something about it and improve my life.*" (N)

Russell 2: "*I was still unsure because I believed that I didn't have the symptoms that badly, some of the people I have told since don't believe I have Asperger's as they can't see that I have a problem. So, I was nervous the second time round.*" (P)

Rachel: "*I had figured out about my Asperger two years ago; it was just to rubber-stamp the fact that I had Asperger's.*" (P)

Russell 1: "*My expectations were that it was Asperger's and that I was hoping that I was right. I wasn't looking forward to putting in all the work, time and energy trying to find out what it was if it wasn't Asperger's…I was nervous going to it.*" (N)

Russell 2: "*This surrounded the question as to whether I was bad enough to have a diagnosis, and I didn't know how this diagnosis thing worked, how bad you have to be to have a diagnosis. I was also worried about my job situation; without a diagnosis they would force me into an unsuitable post, which would make my mental health worse and leave me having to leave the job, and we don't like change.*" (P)

	Reflections	
Pre-assessment	Jack: *"it was down in London and we had driven down there; we arrived early so therefore I had time to kill and my wife suggested that I have something to eat, but I didn't fancy anything, so we just walked."* (P)	Jack: *"I was considerably nervous…I was apprehensive, just straightforward apprehensive; I didn't know what to expect, I was nervous of what might come about"* (P)
	James: *"I was numb. I was apprehensive prior to going. I was quite worried and scared and questioning whether I have done the right thing; is this a good idea? Maybe we'd better forget it."* (N)	James: *"I was trying to find a solution and it might not be there, so where do I go, what do I do after that. I was trying to put that out of my head…*
	James: *"When I got there, she was very specific in what was going to happen. I was told that 'no matter what happens in here, you are going to be the same person when you get out; you're not going to be a different person.'"* (N)	James: *"These alleviated my anxieties and worries that I had prior."* (N)
	Natalie: *"Before the diagnosis I cleared that up and asked if this diagnosis could be used against me, am I going to be judged? Actually I'm not, they don't do that…and that no, because I have never done anything wrong, that wouldn't happen… I wrote them a letter of documentation before I went and mentioned that I clearly had some sensory issues"* (N)	Natalie: *"once she had reassured me…I went through the process and it was almost, well, I didn't really feel anything at all, other than lets get to the end of it and you can just tell me and I'll have my piece of paper and that's that and I can move on."* (N)

(Interpersonal perception)	Rachel: "I wasn't particularly apprehensive, so I think it was just going on to see the Doctor and expecting him to say I have Asperger's, but not worrying too much about it." (P) Russell 2: "I thought the NHS wouldn't be too happy if I went back wanting to go through it all again with the NHS paying." (P) Christine 1: "I was nervous about the actual process… the overwhelming feeling I have about this experience was I wish that someone had told me that I was autisitc as a teenager" (P)
Diagnostic interview (Practical)	Rachel: "By knowing the Doctor before this prevented a lot of anxiety…If it had been a stranger I think I would have been more apprehensive, but because it was somebody I've met before, I didn't have that much fear." (P) Russell 1: "I initially went to my GP. He wouldn't refer me to anyone who specializes in Autism to start with; he just wanted me to go to my local mental health unit and be interviewed there. Fortunately, they then agreed to send me to a Psychiatrist who specialized in Autism." (N) Russell 2: "The second time I went, I paid for it privately." (P) Christine 1: "the interview did look at some of my childhood behavior, but it also talked about who I was as an adult…which was handled by someone who knew what she was looking at (thinking difference disability); able to ask the right questions; the interview went on for 45 minutes, then the psychologist had the information she needed and she could draw a conclusion." (P)

Christine 2: "*I didn't realize that this was a mental health team who were only looking at autism as a possibility if they couldn't consider me to have some type of mental health condition…they said it was a full process…My parents were in the same room for part of the NHS diagnosis and part of the time they were interviewed separately…they asked questions which were prejudicial to the process…they couldn't see that their evidence was faulty.*" (N)

Isaac: "*It was in-depth, it lasted over 3 hours…There were 2 people involved in the process at the same time; a main consultant who asked me most of the questions and the other only asked me a few. It went right back through my childhood, school and work. My wife was with me so some of the questions they asked us both together, others were with me on my own. At the end, the doctor and me and my wife were told that with the information we have you have Asperger Syndrome.*" (N)

Jack: "*She explained the process and I think she came across as very caring and understanding and she actually told me about her work with her colleague.*" (P)

Christine 2: "*I found the diagnosis process quite overwhelming, quite humiliating, stressful; my parents had to be involved, they found it to be very confusing; I felt mocked by the person doing the interview as if he thought my religious beliefs were very silly…they weren't looking at autism from the point of view of an adult woman; they didn't look at sensory issues…Goodness knows what went on in that room when I wasn't there.*" (N)

Isaac: "*The questions weren't probing and were quite easy to answer. I kept thinking what are they going to find; have I got more than this. To me, the questions he asked were the right questions. They wanted to know about my childhood more than anything, how I got on/treated at school, the family background. I had a good childhood, it was hard because my father hadn't a well-paid job but I was treated alright*" (N)

Jack: "*Made me feel as though she was qualified. She made me get to the point where I felt that whatever she said was true, so I had faith in her.*" (P)

James: "She put the questions in a way that I could only give a direct answer to. There wasn't any loaded questions…she gave me plenty of time to answer the questions so it took a long time. It got easer as the process went on. She was very straight with the questions; there was none of this 'what do you think'…She was a very frank person, which I view as good. I got less anxious as it went along." (N)

Leanne: (On receiving a full profile assessment) "Yes, at the time. Since then I have realized they didn't have a fucking clue how to do it." (N)

James: "The Clinician asked about certain social situations and what the outcome was, did I have difficulties, were there any specific social issues that arose…There were time-limited tests, which were all very structured…She also interviewed my wife, both separately and together… When it ended, she went to make her assessment and I was notified later on through the post." (N)

Leanne: "I was thinking there was an interesting line in the skirting board; it was plastic skirting board and somebody made a really bad join and I was just looking at it all the time and she was wearing stripy trousers and ankle boots; I can't remember anything about what she looked like; I can just remember this wrong join in the skirting board in this little windowless office." (N)

Natalie: "I felt like I was being a nuisance in some sort of way...it felt slightly patronizing... made me feel a bit of a wally... I must be a screaming aspie! I just hanged loose and didn't behave myself or anything. She went and asked me about Star Trek, silly woman." (N)

Rachel: "Last time I saw him I was in a lot worse state by a long way. I was in a very bad state of depression, so seeing him again when my mental health was ok; it really wasn't much of a problem." (P)

Russell 2: "I was nervous going through the interview; I was quite upset, nye on crying... It was difficult and I was very worried about the outcome, and if I didn't get a diagnosis, what else could I do. (P)

Natalie: "it was just straight into it as the psychologist wanted to get me out of the way as she had a lot of other work to do...I had to read this children's book...I had to mimic brushing my teeth and things...They did no sensory test. I gave them the information on the day and they didn't bring it up at all...She decided that I fitted the diagnosis. She said at the beginning of the meeting that she would have to go away and discuss it, and at the end of the meeting she just told me straight out and said that their was no ambiguity she was quite sure that I fitted the criteria," (N)

Rachel: "It was a quick process and that he had already done the work about two years previously to the diagnosis." (P)

Russell 2: "Some of the questions I felt were (even for someone with Asperger's) too blunt and out of the blue, very personal questions that were just dropped on me out of the blue which I found very difficult to answer honestly to a stranger about. They were questions to do with my sexual life.... Psychiatrists do look back into childhood; unfortunately my parents are both dead. (P)

Environment	Suitability	Christine 1: *"They had clearly set out the building so it was a low-arousal environment, and they knew exactly what they were doing in terms of serving autistic people."* (P) Christine 2: *"The local hospital didn't have a clue…It was ghastly; the whole set-up made me feel really, really tense. It may have affected the assessment, but I think in their mind they didn't even recognize sensory overload as relevant when diagnosing autism. I think that the team assessing me didn't realize the building was going to produce some of the behaviour they were observing."* (N) Isaac: *"No adjustments made to environment, I was made to feel comfortable."* (N)
		Christine 1: *"The center where I was diagnosed had clearly been designed to be a low-arousal environment. The environment was suitable".* (P) Christine 2: *"It wasn't set up to be a supportive environment for autistic people… To get from the place where you could have a cup of tea to the room where I was actually seen was just a complete maze of corridors that badly needed a lick of paint; the whole place was a depressing, rabbit warren of a place; it clearly hadn't been designed with autistic people in mind at all."* (N) Jack: *"We found it ok, but I had a Satnav and we could park outside her offices, so that was good. The secretary met us and we had to wait for the clinician to arrive. She then appeared and then we walked up this huge set of stairs and along a long corridor with high ceilings, then eventually into a large boardroom. My wife and me sat to one side, and she sat on the other side.* Isaac: *"It was just an ordinary consulting room. It was alright"* (N)

James: "It was quite a small environment, it was comfortable, there wasn't anything getting in the way. There wasn't anything influencing me from the outside and didn't cause any bother; it was a nice small room; the lighting was ok as it wasn't bright; it wasn't a clinical environment and it was quite a small place. It wasn't a huge building which was good. Parking was easy also." (N)	James: "She did ask, 'is the environment ok?' and if there was anything that needed adjustment, to which I said there wasn't." (N)
Leanne: "It was like they made a little office out of a bigger place, and they had not done the skirting board right and I was staring at it all the time thinking that was just wrong, and I can't answer any better than that." (N)	Leanne: "No, I don't think they did. From what I have read since, I think the environment was very low arousal." (N)
Natalie: "I don't think they take on board that some people have sensory issues because they had buzzing strip lights…There were no questions such as "is the lighting ok?" "How did you feel about the level of sound?" (N)	Natalie: "I can deal with it, it annoys me but there may be others with worse sensory issues than me and I felt that was a strange thing to have in a place where you were conducting these types of tests. I thought that would be a really obvious one not to have." (N)

	Theme	
Rachel: *"They didn't ask or make any adjustments."* (P) Russell: *"They didn't ask me if any adjustments were needed to the environment. I have some sensory issues, but there was nothing that bothered me at the time of the interview."* (N+P)	Suitability	Christine 1: *"I thought that I was treated with respect...She knew about autism and from a background of seeing it as a thinking difference."* (P) Christine 2: *"They had the wrong view of autism, the wrong training and experience. They did the assessment as tick box exercise without understanding how autism presents in adults and in females...I have had an IQ test every time I have had my needs as a dyslexic person assessed at work and I spent the whole test explaining that I'd done all the tasks before and asking whether that would affect the outcome. The team member was clearly too junior to know."* (N)
Rachel: *"It was basically a room at the clinic which is a private hospital in Somerset, so I think it was the same place I had been to before to see him previously. It was a private hospital; the parking was ok; it was in a suburban part and not in the center."* (P) Russell 1: *"The NHS one was very clinical, hospital type environment* (N) Russell 2: *The second one where the official diagnosis happened was at a private clinic so it was quite homely.* (P)	Type of professional	Christine 1: *"A very well-known clinical psychologist."* (P) Christine 2: *"A mental health team conducting a general mental health assessment in which they would only diagnose autism if my behaviour and difficulties could not be explained as a form of mental health condition...The subtleties of my social expression were assessed by a junior team member who did not have English as her first language. The team leader was a psychiatrist I am not even sure what training the other team members had. I was also given an IQ tes t by a junior team member and do not know why this was relevant or what her qualifications were to deliver this test or assess the results."* (N)

Isaac: *"Yes…I get thrown when people say Asperger Syndrome isn't a psychiatric problem, and then someone else says it is a psychiatric problem, so if it isn't a psychiatric problem why do they get a psychiatrist to do the diagnosis. It throws you a bit. I, myself don't see it as a psychiatric problem, if it was a psychiatric problem, you wouldn't have done what you'd have done would you, you'd have been having happy pills in a Psychiatric hospital. Some people say, you're not normal, and I say what is normal. I view Asperger's as a difference. To some people it is an advantage, to others it is a disadvantage."* (N)

Jack: *"I don't think I could have got anyone better, as she was someone who had dealt with a lot of people on the spectrum over a considerable period of time, along with someone who I was assured was one of the guru's of the subject"* (P)

Isaac: *"I believe it was a psychiatrist."* (N)

Jack: *"Psychiatrist…The lady who assessed me turned out to be a very well respected and well-known clinician in the field of Autism."* (P)

James: *"The person who diagnosed me was an MSC Health Psychologist, councilor for a charity, diploma in casework and supervision. That is her title. She does counseling in the subject as well specializing in Asperger Syndrome over a 10-year period, 1st class honors degree etc."* (N)	James: *"I do believe that with the knowledge I have, that she was suitable. I don't know if a professional has to have a particular title before you can diagnose but she has many years of experience; she was well known and thought of by my occupational health doctor who thought highly of her. I assumed if she wasn't of a high standard or sufficiently positioned, she wouldn't have been able to give a diagnosis, or wouldn't have been allowed to. She seemed very detailed; I don't know if any of the other processes are any different. I didn't think at any time that it could have been any more in-depth, because I was an older adult and there were fewer resources to go on, but she seemed thorough."* (N)
Leanne: *"It was a person working in elderly mental health care"* (N)	Leanne: *"she must have downloaded this questionnaire off the Internet. She did the GADS (Gilliam Asperger's Disorder Scale) test, which is aimed at children. So I have a Pervasive Developmental Disorder, but I was 44. You know what, they didn't have a fucking clue; they just pulled somebody off elderly mental health care; I was only 44, you know; it's a joke."* (N)

Natalie: *"I had a clinical psychologist…she was far more formal, but she believed in the whole neurodiversity angle because she was very positive, which surprised me as I wasn't expecting that."* (N)	Natalie: *"I don't know if she was suitable or not…I think these people have an air of importance about them and you're just another one who has turned up who is going through the same process."* (N)
Rachel: *"It was a consultant Psychiatrist."* (P)	Rachel: *"Very much the right professional with the right qualifications."* (P)
Russell: *"I think they were quite high up specialists in the field. On both occasions, one person was assessing me…one was a professor, so they weren't any old local authority Psychiatrist's. They were not local professionals, but they were both psychiatrists, one of which was in Leicester."* (N+P)	Russell: *"I think they were appropriately qualified."* (N+P)

4.2.4 Discussion of Matrix 2

Diagnosis of self – practical and interpersonal

As highlighted by Bagatell (2007), Bains, (2012), Molloy and Vasil (2002), and Jaci et al. (2008), the diagnostic process effects ones' own perception of identity, this section examines participants' experiences within the timeframe of the initial awareness of the possibility of being autistic and formal recognition through the diagnostic process.

Leanne and Natalie read literature with Natalie initially taking an online test, with Christine stating that she was fairly ignorant prior to her assessment. The first person to mention anything to James was his mother at seven years of age and it was not until he started working with service users in his job as a social worker that he began to recognize traits in himself.

What is interesting is that each participant has a very different perception of themselves and autism. Natalie initially thought that there was something wrong with her and then discovered this whole other perspective of difference and was cross at the negative medical perspective, where as Russell came to the conclusion that there was something wrong with him. These aspects highlight a potential way forward and a positive purpose for diagnosis, which is helping the individual changing their perspective to a more positive paradigm.

Expectations and reflections

The expectations relate to how participants thought the process would proceed and the reflections are both interpersonal about these but also reflective of looking back at that moment in their lives. All participants were seeking answers, they all wanted yes or no answers and they expected that the process would be like most medical procedures, simple, affirmative and authoritative. Participants were also seeking an explanation for their life history and experiences with a main worry that they would not reach the criteria, highlighting issues in relation to diagnostic criteria.

Christine hoped that she would be helped to gain a better understanding of herself and that she would be helped to cope better in the world. Jack was apprehensive and Natalie was quite frightened as she was worried after she read damming things about parents that she would have a visit from Social Services, which is ironic with James working within that sector. Leanne was similarly worried regarding the same aspects as Natalie, which ties in with the quote in the literature review concerning past issues with witchcraft.

Pre assessment

This section relates to the day of the assessment and just before 'the event'. Jack, James and Christine reported anxiety in not knowing what to expect, with Natalie inferring this. Rachel was not apprehensive due to knowing the Doctor, while Russell does not explicitly state anxiety but infers relief at being referred to a specialist in autism. These aspects highlight the need to be informed of what is going to happen and also knowing the assessor helps to alleviate anxiety, which may not be as highly reported by the medical profession if these components had been in place. Additionally, emotions pertaining to anxiety may also affect the answers being provided, so in these cases having the clinician reassure them long before the interview process may have provided clearer answers, especially with Jack having to travel vast distances for his assessment.

Diagnostic interview – practical and interpersonal

The following charts the actual diagnostic interview from both a practical perspective (what happened) and the interpersonal perspective (how the person felt), with very variable differences in experiences. With Christine having to attend assessment twice and having such different experiences, highlights that there are differences in professional approaches and conduct and that this is not due to participants' variability within themselves.

Critically, Christine's first experience was very positive due to the Psychologist knowing what she was looking at (thinking difference disability), highlighting the value of use of presenting the individual with more positive models of autism. The process only lasted for 45 minutes and although Christine states that she was nervous and there were real feelings of regret about age of her identification, this first process appears to have been very positive by a professional who seemingly instinctively knew what she was doing.

Compare this experience to her second experience with a mental heath team within the NHS in which she felt overwhelmed, humiliated, mocked and stressed with a negative impact on her family as a whole. Additionally, the questions asked were prejudicial with an arrogance such that they could not or would not acknowledge that their evidence was faulty, suggesting that this is common or even good practice among professionals; illustrating that research and how autism is understood and reported is seriously open to question. With this second process, Christine acknowledged her differences in sensory perception, but this was not tested and the professionals were not looking at autism from the point of view of an adult woman, highlighting issues pertaining to the foundation of healthcare in willingness at a very basic level of knowing and understanding the patient.

Regarding instruments and approaches used, Natalie's experience involved reading a children's book, simulating the brushing of her teeth and being asked questions about Star Trek while being made to feel a nuisance. Leanne's assessment also included the use of a diagnostic tool for children (which she believes was downloaded from the Internet), even though a person working in elderly mental health was assessing her. It was not stated which instrument was used with other participants, or if any instrument was used at all. None of the participants stated that they were provided with a sensory evaluation despite Christine, Leanne, Russell and Natalie clearly identifying with sensory/processing differences.

From the data provided, Jack, Isaac, and James all had more enlightened experiences, with Isaac explaining that it was very in-depth and that the questions were not probing and that they were the right questions; Jack stating that the clinician came across as very caring/understanding and explained the process; with James the questions were not loaded and appeared to take into account processing differences by allowing time to answer. This does seem to be an issue with under recognition of diagnosis in females as highlighted by Krahn and Fenton (2012) and Rivett and Matson (2010), for which these differing experiences between the sexes would explain to an extent, although Russell's experience was that he was asked questions too bluntly and that they were too personal. He was quite nervous, upset and crying. This could highlight feminine qualities in some males in addition to sensory aspects!

All participants except for Christine did not have their parents present at the diagnostic interview confirming that this need not be a factor in order to obtain a diagnosis. Jack, Isaac and James had their wives in attendance in order to obtain an every day observational perspective. However, if there is some marital difficulties this could effect assessment. Leanne, Rachel and Natalie all appear to attend the interview on their own. An important element to consider regarding parents who are in attendance at the interview, is that although parents can report on childhood and development, unless the individual is living with a parent there is no way to assess current issues the individual may be facing. Furthermore, the process itself could affect family dynamics. An additional consideration is that as part of the process participants were taken back to their childhood experiences. With no follow-up support and the fact that reliving these experiences are likely to be traumatic for most, this should be seen as highly unethical.

Rachel's process appears to be the most positive as she said that it was a quick process whereby the groundwork had already been completed with earlier sessions surrounding mental health issues. It would appear that a major factor within this more positive experience was that Rachel had known the professional over a period of time and they had therefore both grown to know each other and trust was built within this process.

Suitability of environment

Christine, Leanne, Russell and Natalie all explicitly highlighted sensory issues. Participants were not formally evaluated for sensory processing differences as highlighted by Owen, et al. (2013), Chang, et al. (2014) and Tavassoli, Hoekstra and Baron-Cohen (2014). The environment where Christine had her first diagnostic experience was clearly very positive, as it had been designed to be low arousal and was suitable for serving autistic people. Her second experience was at a local hospital where it was not a supportive environment with a maze of corridors. This again highlights that that with the same person in different settings will produce different responses, making the behavioral/Psycho-social modal invalid for assessment purposes.

Amongst participants' experiences, there were huge variations between different environments and perceptions of suitability. There appears to be a distinct variability between the environmental experiences of those who attended a private consultation (which were positive) and an NHS consultation (which were negative). Only James stated that he was asked if the environment was suitable and if any adjustments were necessary. Location and parking was also a factor, as stated by James, Rachel, Jack and architecture as highlighted by all of the participants.

If the environments were suitable then participants' 'symptoms' may not have manifested to the extent that they have, alternatively, there should be uppermost regard for the individual's health and wellbeing as well as an accurate assessment. As Christine states *"I think that the team assessing me didn't realize the building was going to produce some of the behaviour they were observing"*. This creates a problem for the assessment process, as environmental factors are likely to find their way into reports as part of 'the condition', which is one of the main problems with symptom-based assessments as outlined by Insel (2013).

Suitability of professional

The same dynamics can be applied to professional conduct and suitability of the individual clinician/diagnostician, even if training has been provided in the various instruments used in assessment. In many ways, the professional is the voice of authority in how the individual perceives himself or herself and understands there past experiences and their future potential.

As stated by the participants, very well known and well-respected professionals in the field of Autism assessed Christine 1 (Psychologist) and Jack (Psychiatrist) through private consultation. Christine 2 by a mental heath team; Isaac, Jack, Rachel and Russell by Psychiatrists; Natalie and James by a Psychologist and Leanne by a person working in elderly mental heath care. An interesting observation is the considerable variation between participants in 'knowing' with confidence whether or not they were the right professionals. Additionally, participants all have a different view of how they relate autism to themselves in terms of which lens this is viewed; a view that the clinician would have imparted.

With the range of different theories and the spectrum of professional opinion, PNT professionals may have vast amounts of training and knowledge, but if there is a lack of the innate quality of interpersonal qualities needed to work with people, such professionals ought to reflect upon the possibility of a lack of empathy or/and Theory of Mind regarding the autistic person (Beardon, 2008; Milton, 2012 & 2014) and seek to understand how this is affecting their conduct.

4.2.5 Matrix of Themes 3: Post-Diagnostic Perception

Practical Perception	Participant Quotes	Personal perception and identity	Participant Quotes
Post-assessment	Christine 1: *"I got an answer...it didn't solve the issues in my life but it did give me a explanation of what was going on...My understanding of autism has developed over time."* (P) Christine 2: *"The NHS diagnosis concluded that as I was depressed. I couldn't also be autistic, so didn't offer follow on support on autism."* (N) Isaac: *"I knew there was a problem there; I couldn't do anything about it but it answered a lot of questions."* (N) Jack: *"I felt that I had achieved something, which is extraordinary, but I now jumped a hurdle."* (P) James: *"Immediately afterwards I thought the diagnosis was a solution or an identity, and I then thought what do you do with it! So what!"* (P)	Sense of self	Christine 1: *"I felt great...this explains what's been going on in my life...it's taken a long time to get to grips with living with different aspects of autism."* (P) Christine 2: *"I felt literally punched in the stomach; I felt angry, confused, mishandled, cheated and humiliated and that the door to services was being slammed in my face."* (N) Isaac: *"There were no pills so if you've got it you've got it. You've got to make the most of what you've got."* (N) Jack: *"you become a little philosopher, and this kind of gave me a tick and a star which said here is a tunnel to go down, which was brilliant, that was the immediate reaction."* (P) James: *"I asked myself, where does this leave me; who am I? Can I work from this? I didn't have any euphoria. I thought that this is a solution and then I suddenly realized that it isn't."* (P)

Leanne: *"I thought when they told me that they were going to tell me that I had mental health problems or something terminal; it was awful and I was so pleased and relieved when it was Asperger Syndrome; but I also knew at the same time that if I had this Asperger Syndrome, then my family are going down like skittles; then they did; first it was my sons, then my niece, then my brother and family in Australia that I have never even met; it's amazing."* (N)

Leanne: *"I was shitting myself that I had Munchausen Syndrome and with my son I didn't want to look for something to be wrong with myself...I was happy to have the label; I was really happy not to be mentally ill any more; I was really happy not to have to cope anymore; I was really happy not to have anything wrong with me anymore."* (N)

Natalie: *"It was almost like jumping through hoops to get it on paper. When I self diagnosed it answered a lot of questions... it does concern me the next time I have to visit the GP and when it comes up on the screen, does that mean that are not going to believe me when I'm not well, because GP's, I don't think have a very good knowledge of the condition."* (N)

Natalie: *"The diagnosis? That was when I self diagnosed. I went through a range of emotions. There was no doubt in my mind. I completely fit the pattern. With the formal diagnosis I wasn't surprised at all as I was so sure I was right.... I was still a little bit worried about if it would have a negative impact on my family...having it on your medical record as a disorder, I am still uncomfortable because I don't view it as a disorder."* (N)

Rachel: *"It didn't seem to be that much of a big deal to be honest. I guess it was something that I have lived with for some time before."* (P)

Rachel: *"Just getting a name to it and just confirming that I had Asperger's after all; it also put my partner's mind at rest at the same time as well."* (P)

Russell 2: *"I purposely didn't read up on it, but after diagnosis I found out quite a lot about it and joined support groups and things like that. I was happy and felt that perhaps that I could do something about it."* (P)

Russell 2: *"I felt happy that I had discovered what it was and eager to find out more about it... It was pretty instant but I felt relief and happier."* (P)

Language and interpretation	Christine 1: *"I did not want people at work seeing this, so I asked for the report to be changed…neither report explained autism; they weren't documents that I could use to explain autism to people like employers."* (P) Christine 2: *"The one from the NHS was just patronizing and I am trying to get it removed from my medical records."* (N) Isaac: *"I think it was the Relate counselor who said that Asperger's people just have a different outlook on life; we look at things differently to what somebody else does."* (N) Jack: *"The way I read it was that I could put myself in her chair and see me through her eyes without any difficulty because she didn't use difficult language…I was actually pleased by the humanity and the human approach of how she conducted the whole thing. I think I would have objected to a lot of medical terminology, so she didn't give me that."* (P) James: *"It highlighted evidence; as far as she was concerned to say that I fitted the criteria. It didn't have an emotional effect as we just read it through without experiencing emotions."* (P)
The report	Christine 1: *"the report was not something I wanted to show anyone…. I was surprised how badly drafted the report was, poorly written and in its tone and content."* (P) Christine 2: *"I was not asked to sign it off, I was not asked for my opinion, I was being fobbed off with a diagnosis I didn't agree with."* (N) Isaac: *"There was no follow-up, no letters, nothing…I don't believe that I had access to my written diagnosis."* (N) Jack: *"it was sent to me in the post; it was two sides of A4…There were no amendments made…It was not so much of a clinical report in my recollection; it was much more a professional judgment of recognition of a condition."* (P) James: *"She sent it through the post with a request for it to be signed and returned. No amendments or changes were requested or made."* (P)

Leanne: *"The language was ok and fine...I read it all because it wasn't very long"* (N)	Leanne: *"The first word I remember thinking was 'vindicated'.... I didn't know what to expect"* (N)
Natalie: *"I had another meeting where I had to go in and discuss it...I went back to the meeting and I said that 'no, I love my friends', she said 'that's not what you said', and I said 'no it isn't'! That's interesting isn't it...I just signed it and said there you go. She just sat and watched me read it, she did try and hurry me up."* (N)	Natalie: *"It was very formally written...I was horrified actually with some of the bits...I thought my god I sound like an android...I thought that I sounded so uncaring...I would like to see more as – we've established that have a different neurological type, and that's really exciting.* (N)
Rachel: *"he just sent the letter off through the post...He might have mentioned a couple of reasons. It was one sheet of A4... There were no recommendations either verbal or written."* (P)	Rachel: *"It was ok, there wasn't a problem at all because it was what I expected. I felt good that I have got this on paper.... the Language was fairly formal, but that's what I would have expected in a letter from a Psychiatrist."* (P)
Russell: *"I just got sent his report, which was copied to my GP. I think that the report consisted of about 8 pages...I was advised to learn more about it."* (P)	Russell: *"I was a bit annoyed that the clinician got something wrong; it was stated that I had raised a family, which was incorrect. It wasn't a big mistake and of no great consequence, so I never did anything about it."* (P)

Interpersonal Impact	Christine 1: *"diagnosis was the starting point on that journey for me to understand whom I am and to try and un-learn all the stuff I had been told throughout my life, which was well intentioned nonsense."* (P) Christine 2: *"I felt very patronized by that process and voiceless over and over again... It caused strain in my relationship with my parents."* (N) Isaac: *"It upset her more than it upset me...I wish there was follow-up and advice for the two of us, me and the wife to help cope with this problem – strategies for both of us."* (N) Jack: *"I went through an identity crisis (participant crying), which I still find painful, and actually that is at that point that I needed help."* (P)
Practical Impact	Christine 1: *"It has confirmed to me the truth about who I am. I'm autistic, this helps me understand myself; I'm not guessing I'm autistic, it is a fact, the truth about who I am."* (P) Christine 2: *"The diagnostic team confused symptoms with cause; it was incompetent."* (N) Isaac: *"It was very in-depth; there was nothing that upset me about the diagnosis; none of the questions upset me...Without follow-up it did have a negative affect on my marriage."* (N) Jack: *"I feel better for knowing myself than I did before...I now can understand it and I can manage it so much better now, and I can account for it so much better now. The thing that really hit me was when I just explained to just a few people...the wonderful consistent story that came back was that, yea we noticed that you were a bit withdrawn at times or a bit awkward, but that's you."* (P)

James: "This is something I am still trying to work out. I am realizing that I am different and that my brain works differently and that there is nothing wrong with that and that I am more than an individual than I was as I was trying to be like everyone else." (P)

Leanne: "If people would just look at us as a culture, and we live in a multi-cultural society and people can embrace other cultures; it's a culture, and that's an easier thing to understand than a disability." (N)

Natalie: "I suppose that I always knew I was different, and it's very peculiar actually, I remember in my teens when I was depressed I thought I must be nuts, and that's not a very nice way to feel about yourself, so it's nice to know that I'm not nuts." (N)

Rachel: "It's made quite a significant impact. It's made things a lot easier in terms of my marriage because my wife knows now that I have Asperger's specifically and we are both more accommodating of each other because she is disabled too." (P)

Russell: "People have commented, with one person saying recently that I appear to be a lot more confident." (P)

James: "It has taken a long time for me to be who I am. I am still having problems conforming as I am not allowing me to be myself." (P)

Leanne: "My life has begun to make sense…Since my diagnosis, I have been put in a position where I can really help other people to be able to communicate with their children, to be able to understand themselves. (N)

Natalie: "It's filled in the final piece of the puzzle for me as to why I'm different. (N)

Rachel: "I think it's put things in to context a bit more about how, for example I try and avoid particular situations' now, like avoiding supermarkets during busy periods." (P)

Russell: "I feel a lot different now. I think that because of my diagnosis and my need to improve." (P)

The past and the future	Christine: *"It has surprised me how long it has been...I just feel that most of my life has been wasted and I'm still on the journey of trying to put together things that most people work out as teenagers to be honest."* (P+N) Christine 1: *"I still try and allow myself to be myself and try and find things that work for me, and find ways of trying to hold relationships together that work for me, and not feel that I have to be what everyone else is; and that is still something I don't feel I am able to do at age 40, which is ridiculous."* (P) Christine 2: *I had not recognized then that my depression was a lifelong issue, and that I was depressed because I was struggling to live with an undiagnosed disability... What I am now trying to do is get my medical records changed...In short, I have been completely messed around by a system I didn't understand and that my GP didn't understand, and found that the road to services was blocked rather than opened up to me as a disabled person. So here I am, a woman with a communication disability made to fight a nonsensical system."* (N)
On reflection	Christine: *"It's been a long journey....I had these two diagnoses; one which I very much believed because it was from a leading clinical psychologist and matched my experience of life and one from this local hospital which claimed to have some specialism in autism, but was really appalling."* (P+N) Christine 1: *The process with the psychologist was good but in terms of robust evidence it could have been stronger."* (P) Christine 2: *"if I had realized that the NHS assessment was a mental health assessment then I would have refused to attend, and neither I nor my parents would have been interviewed...I don't think the diagnostic process for autism should go anywhere near mental health services or actually for that matter any kind of medic or the health service at all."* (N)

	Isaac: *"I believe my sister had an Autistic problem…It has gone further because some of the grand children have got ADHD, so it's coming down through the line…I recognize the pushiness of society and competition compared to when I was younger when I never had that."* (N) Jack: *"I don't think people understand the re-living that I had to do, and I'm sure that I can't be on my own of going back on things in life."* (P) James: *"I have had a work problems assessment with occupational health and they have taken my diagnosis into account but until recently they haven't acted on it and no one has ever taken the diagnosis, such as the clinical depression component and put any recommendations into practice; they have just looked at it and then the process if finished. My diagnosis did not change anything regarding the workplace; everything went on as it did before; they just said 'so what'."* (P)
Isaac: *"That's me, I can't change it, you can't change it; we just have to get on with life. I just plod along, I'm happy with my life…I would like to see support for the people and the families, because there's nothing out there."* (N) Jack: *"How do you change the condition from a medical one to a community one?…I would have liked a pathway of enlightenment…it had a structure to it, a wide structure, probing structure…Bad, is just this lack of what a diagnosis should be, it should be the start of a journey, a journey of understanding."* (P) James: *"In retrospect I see my diagnosis as the right thing to do. I feel different on reflection now, although I am still looking for who I am, fully, I do feel different because I have an outside view of myself now, where as I didn't have one before."* (P)	

Leanne: "I had already been masticated in the jaws of all these systems and processes before...the first time I stepped into a psychiatrist office I was 9; you are brought up with it... it's helped me to recognize who I am...Its allowed me to be who I should have been or who I was meant to be; I like who I am." (N)

Natalie: "I have realized why the negative things have happened to me...I have just started this group where I want to help and enable others if I possibly can and I think it's been positive...I would like it to be viewed as a positive and for people to be shown how to move forward, how to use their strengths, as apposed to being a social deficit and communication issues. It just feels all a little bit insulting." (N)

Rachel: "I like to socialize with specialist groups. A lot of our friends are either involved in the LGBT or through my Asperger's group, or through the church." (P)

Leanne: "I do feel different now on reflection because I've had a few years to get used to the idea that I'm autistic.... it could have been done better...I think it's shit when you get diagnosed as an adult...What makes people think that you don't need help! I can talk; I am really fucking good at pretending to be normal...You get a diagnosis follow up should be mandatory" (N)

Natalie: "if someone goes along and they haven't done a lot of background work, they are going to think that they have some awful detrimental condition, and that they are disabled, and I don't think that is the right perception; that's not certainly not how I feel about it for myself and my family." (N)

Rachel: "What would have been better is some follow-up in terms of advice and support afterwards." (P)

Russell: *"I do believe that the professional who diagnosed my Asperger's should consider the co-morbid elements to give some idea of what else might be a problem and point the individual towards other professionals in whatever field is appropriate; but with me, they didn't seem to look at other problems…Post-diagnosis, there isn't a lot out there."* (P)

Russell: *"my marriage broke up, I lost my post at work, I found out that I was very intelligent; all this happened within the space of two to three years…I wish that I was diagnosed earlier and that my intelligence didn't covered up my learning difficulties and my learning difficulties didn't cover up my intelligence…I feel a lot better about myself and a lot more worthy and not as rejected by other people; I feel loved by some people now; I feel a lot closer to people; my girlfriend's family is great."* (P)

4.2.6 Discussion of Matrix 3

Post assessment and sense of self

This section describes participants' reactions and thoughts directly after the diagnostic interview. Despite very different experiences of assessment, the overall picture as to how the individual felt afterwards is overwhelmingly positive, with a variety of expressions and feelings; as well as concerns and worries about others' perceptions of the label. For the individual, the process is by this sample, an identification process rather than just a diagnostic one as *"this is the generation that missed the opportunity to be identified and understood"* (Attwood, 2008, p.10). This is evident in the initial statements: Christine 1: *"I got an answer"*, Isaac: *"It answered a lot of questions"*, Jack: *"I felt that I achieved something"*, James: *"I though the diagnosis was a solution or an identity"*, Leanne: *"I was really happy not to have anything wrong with me any more"*, Natalie: *"I went through a range of emotions"*, Rachel: *"It also put my partner's mind at rest as well"*, Russell: *"I was happy and felt that I could do something about it"*.

There are however issues which also became apparent for participants, such as what to do about it (Russell, Isaac, James) and the aspects that Natalie raised about negative impact on family and how this diagnosis would be viewed by different professionals which is very valid and justified given the evidence of professional understanding and behavior within the medical profession, such as with Christine 2 which shows in stark terms the effect of having the diagnosis of autism taken away. *"Autism is a lifelong condition"* (NICE, 2012, p.18) and as such, for this to be removed shows potentially more sinister motives not dissimilar from the findings revealed by Kennedy (2013) where professionals feel able to simply remove the diagnosis and/ or not provide one because of their perception of changes within the American diagnostic criteria. Professionals who feel they can play around with these labels will now be made aware of the ethical consequences of performing such an act and will, it is hoped, make this an unacceptable and stigmatizing practice.

The Diagnosis Report – Language and interpretation

The report is the only true indicator and evidence, which may reveal the perceptions between the individual and the assessor. This is a very important document as it will be a communication tool, which will inform and develop understanding in others about that individual. Participants reported mixed results, with Christine saying on both occasions that it was not something she felt she could not show anyone. There are also inaccuracies within the various reports as evidenced by Christine, Natalie and Russell. Isaac did not have access to his report. Language used in the reports was also variable with Christine and Natalie reporting negative use of language and Jack, Leanne and Rachel reporting good use or expected use of language. Natalie was the only participant who had the opportunity to amend the report, which is a sign of good practice; however the perception of both parties in this case shows a clear lack of perception on behalf of the clinician. Reports also varied in length, with Jack and Rachel's being 2 pages and Russell's being 8 pages. There is clearly a need for recommendations (which will follow in the next chapter) regarding report writing as it reflects both the understanding and competence by the clinician of the autistic individual. It also highlights the importance reporting is for the individual in being accurate and relevant.

Practical and interpersonal impact

The following charts the lasting impact of the process with the timeframe commencing after the initial thoughts of the end of the process up until the present day and the lived experiences during these intervening years. The overwhelming response is that the diagnosis has informed participants' identity and enabled them to view their life experiences through a different lens; therefore the following from the literature review seems appropriate, *"If the doors of perception were cleansed everything would appear to man as it is: Infinite. For man has closed himself up, till he sees all things through narrow chinks of his cavern"* (Blake, 1790, p.14).

Although there has been the acceptance of the diagnosis of autism by all participants, some of these may not be accepted in the way that the clinician would have the individual believe. For example, difference rather than disability (disabled by society), however the process from receiving the diagnosis to the present understanding of themselves has involved many different external and internal factors and in many cases having no post diagnostic support or follow-up from professionals has led finally to different approaches as to how they have used their experiences.

Leanne has been able to help support and work with others in a similar position to herself; Jack, although he went through an identity crisis has been accepted by his friends; Leanne confirms that she is not nuts; Rachel says that the diagnosis has made things easier in her relationship and now recognizes her sensory difference and thus avoids particular situations; Russell is more confident. With Isaac, having no follow up did have a negative effect on his marriage and Christine may have avoided the need to seek out mental health services if she had the post-diagnostic support.

On reflection/The past and the future

All participants have concluded that the diagnosis of autism has had a major life-changing effect, especially in the domains of identity, perception and life experiences. One of the saddest aspects is the vast amount of time participants have felt they have lost due to believing things about them, which were untrue. This could be where the real impact of the witchcraft mentality in society as highlighted by Quarmby (2011) how others react to difference and the effect this has on those who eventually become aware through the formal identification process. It seem amazing that such a perceived negative phenomenon can have such positive outcomes when identified.

What might be able to help participants with these negative experiences is if they are paid to help and guide other people through the process. Many of the professionals seem to lack understanding to facilitate the diagnostic process and the health system does not seem adequate enough to cater for it.

CHAPTER 5

Conclusion/Summary of Recommendations

5.1 Introduction

The following chapter highlights selective recommendations, which are based on the evidence presented thus far. This summery is primarily based on the research sample, as residing within the community but elements may be just as relevant for institutional settings. This will be followed by the conclusion and a reflexive account.

5.2 Summary of Recommendations

One can confirm from these findings is that there are many components which make up the identification process of autism and that these processes do affect how the individual will perceive themselves as well as their future wellbeing. This will also include power dynamics within families as well as in every section of the wider community. It is therefore pivotal that these matters are given the upmost consideration for implementation. The following recommendations are selective and not exhaustive.

Recommendations regarding the pre-diagnosis stage

- Individuals should be provided with more information directly by the clinician prior to the assessment in order to alleviate anxiety, which may affect the assessment.

- Consider choice of professional, which should be made transparent. Would an individual prefer to be assessed by a Psychiatrist with minimal knowledge of autism who needs to use diagnostic tools, or a diagnostician with over 20 years experience and has an in-depth knowledge of autism as a human condition?

• GPs should have on their computer a list of clinicians and diagnosticians in the area, which outlines their approach, experience and views. This can then be viewed and discussed with the patient as to who is the best choice for them. Following diagnosis, the patient could anonymously write up a 'document of experience', which can be emailed to the GP and added to the system, which could inform future patients and add to research as to outcomes. This would also make the process more transparent in line with the Autism Act (2009) and hold professionals to account.

Recommendations regarding the diagnosis stage

• There are no objective tests to diagnose autism. Clinicians use a manual, which is a list of descriptors. It is vital within any one individual to examine and differentiate between difference (thinking difference), disability (social model of disability) and illness. Rather than take any one standpoint, there needs to be greater clarity to differentiate between all three. Difference, as a lifelong component should be explored and enhanced, disability should be accommodated as part of neurodiversity, and illness should be appropriately diagnosed and treated, as autistic people are human beings and like anyone else, can become ill. One cannot put everything under one banner. Where does one draw the line between these components and how does the investigator into the individual understand the interactions between these components in relation to the environment/experiences both past and present? With participants very different experiences at the hands of very different professionals this does call into questions regarding cognitive based functioning labels (high and low/mild) within the very short timeframe of assessment and how over the course of a day and even a week these very much fluctuate.

- Sensory and processing aspects should be the first line of enquiry and should be the foundation of assessment. As the medical model focuses on treatments and interventions for these 'differences' there should be consideration that environment and social circumstances will play a pivotal role in the areas of cognitive functioning and indication of impairment suggesting that autism should not be within the medical model at all. Also given that many adults would not reach the new autism criteria, a new approach to identification is required. For example, regarding sensory aspects and Baron-Cohen's checklist, how can a person report about their sensory way of being when they have nothing to compare it to experientially. The viability of this should be one of the branches of research, which follow on from this study.

- Consider a spectrum of approaches that match the needs of the individual and that identification is conducted with the individual's full knowledge and expectations from the outset. It should be their choice of pathway.

Choices could be:

- Identification through a community care assessment so the individual can be assessed in natural environments rather than a few hours in a clinical office, especially as one does not require a formal diagnosis in order to receive a community care assessment. This approach could also better inform gaps in research and provide the clinician/diagnostician with a more rounded view of the issues by becoming more familiar with the person, assisting him/her in becoming more competent and compassionate if this is lacking. This will also accurately identify better and more humane approaches to assessment and cognitive functioning can be better assessed alongside sensory aspects through an environmental audit, as these are unlikely to be apparent within a clinical setting.

- The way forward is a positive purpose for diagnosis, which is helping the individual change the perspectives and perceptions of themselves to a more positive paradigm.

- Conduct an audit of the different environments where diagnosis takes place. People seeking a diagnosis could be sent pictures of the environment before attending in order to judge suitability.

- With regards to additional diagnoses, such as with Russell who in addition to Autism, underwent assessment of Dyslexia, Dyscalculia, Depression, Stress and Anxiety which were all confirmed and diagnosed separately but around about the same time, the presence of one assessed neurological difference should automatically trigger further testing and evaluation of others. An individual should not have to access many different professionals to access all these assessments as an educational Psychologist can test for the learning differences which can then inform the identification of autism and add evidence to the report.

Recommendations regarding the post-diagnosis stage

- To quote Jack: *"I would have liked a pathway of enlightenment"* (Appendix F). Although a world-renowned clinician assessed Jack, he could not find anything post-diagnosis despite accessing many different organizations.

I went through an identity crisis (participant crying), which I still find painful, and actually that is at that point that I needed help, and I got it from working with you; I wouldn't have got it any other way; I would have been as frustrated as hell trying to get the knowledge and understanding that I did by working with you; I don't think it would have been possible, and I would have ended up with a very poor understanding, and then I would have given up on it and then just dismissed it, where as I have found that being able to relate thought processes to being Autistic has been enlightening, and interesting and I have had the power and the knowledge to be able to put it in its rightful place and feeling the right way about it. (Jack, Appendix F)

The autistic author of this research has been the only professional who has been able to assist Jack in his post-diagnostic journey. This demonstrates the effectiveness of identified individuals working together and is recommended here as part of the post-diagnostic process providing this is handled with common sense and sensitivity especially with who works with whom. This also demonstrates the effectiveness and value of autistic professionals, who should be remunerated and employed by service providers as a way forward. Recognition ought to be ascribed towards this dynamic, as it will address many inequality issues while promoting equality in line with the Equality Act (2010).

- One of the perplexing aspects in relation to identity is that why is it that identified individuals identify themselves as being different (neurodiverse), and others as having a condition, illness, disorder, disease and so on! It would seem from this research that the professional who undertakes the assessment in addition to what the autistic person reads will directly influence how and what the person identifies with themselves and also the identity they promote to others. Although everyone has a fundamental human right to identify with themselves how they wish, Autistic individuals should be informed of the many different ways autism is viewed so there is choice for the individual in how they identify with themselves and others.

- Practitioners need to be aware that the reports they write will be a communication document that the individual will expect to use as a communication tool, which explains the diagnosis to others, a communication tool between the practitioner and the end user (employers, family, friends, other practitioners etc.), which describes the nature of differences. Reports will have multiple audiences and needs to be written so. A recommendation is that practitioners have standardized templates, one overarching master document and smaller ones for different groups of people where selected data could be copied into the smaller documents, thus providing a range of communication tools which describes the individual in a manor that can be understood.

- The individual should be sent a draft copy of the report, which has to be agreed upon by both parties to be signed off and should be considered a 'living document', which can and should be updated as the individual develops.

- Professionals ought to reflect upon their own lack of empathy or/and Theory of Mind regarding the autistic person (Beardon, 2008; Milton, 2012 & 2014) and seek to understand how this is affecting their conduct. A recommendation is that diagnosticians seek feedback from clients and GPs, including feedback regarding the report, and adjust their work in line with such feedback.

Over-arching recommendation(s)

- This thesis has focused on the current modes of the identification of autism, however, there should be a move towards a more positive paradigm of identifying autism. For example, an Australian Psychologist by the name of Tania Marshall (2014) has recently published a book that focuses on the positive aspects of autistic females and is to publish more books regarding males as well. The books are not diagnostic tools in themselves, however, they can be used in a constructive way to also focus on the positive aspects of being autistic and enable diagnosticians to (i) be more aware of the positive aspects of autism, (ii) to also seek this in the people who go to them as well as acknowledge this with the client(s), and (iii) make sure this is also reflected in the report. This will enable a more positive shift in identifying autism as well as give the people being recognized as being autistic something to work with; leading to a better valuing of oneself and one's identity. Additionally, by researching adults this will also better inform how to approach autistic children. Consider testing on the basis of sensory, processing, working memory etc. to build up a picture if the individual from the inside out.

- These participants were diagnosed within a variety of different configurations but although there were differences in experiences, and taking into account the very different professional experiences and the different tools, a recommendation is that multi-disciplinary teams should not be used in the process of diagnosis of autism in adults.

- Do not make assumptions about families, and we should be talking about families as well as individuals where assumptions, stereotypes and stigmatization are eradicated. A recommendation is that family as well as individual identification should be considered good practice especially with the genetic familial link so prevalent, avoidable power dynamics and stigma need to be addressed which should be based on choice and considered on a case-by-case basis. (Natalie, Jack, Leanne)

- The development and implementation of a code of ethics for professionals formally attached to the Autism Act (2009) including a licensing scheme specifically for working in autism.

- A review of multi-disciplinary teams as to their effectiveness, especially with the recorded in fighting amongst professionals within such teams (Kennedy 2013).

- For professionals who practice diagnosis, a licensing scheme whereby any individual would need to undergo specialist training to a particular standard. This is to address the issues raised by participants regarding other professionals accepting a diagnosis by another practitioner.

- Regarding the disappearance of Asperger's – the DSM states that "anyone with a good diagnosis of Asperger's Syndrome should be given the new diagnosis of ASD", so it would follow that clinicians/diagnosticians could continue to use the DSM IV criteria for Asperger's and use both terms (Asperger's and ASD) especially as the literature on Asperger's maybe more relevant to an individual post-diagnosis. Although in the UK, the ICD-10 is used, at the time of writing it is unclear if this will follow the American system.

- Isolation needs to be tackled in this group.

- Koegel, Kim, Koegel and Schwartzman (2013) highlight a possible recommendation regarding including special interests in aiding social engagement, which should be seen as a way forward.

- As with Natalie, parents ought to identify more with their child rather than this thing called autism.

- Diagnosticians should seek feedback from clients and adjust their approach in line with such feedback.

- Mental heath teams or mental heath professionals should not be used in the diagnosis of autism. New approaches ought to be researched regarding mental health where autism is present.

- Consider the inclusion of a code of ethics within The Autism Act (2009).

- Following on from this research, there should be a further study using the same approaches taken here, but with professionals' perceptions of diagnosis in contrast with the perceptions of the individuals they have assessed to see the differences in perception between Clinician and patient.

- Consider developing guidelines for the use of neuroimaging techniques more alongside traditional methods to supplement the identification of autism, especially as these techniques will continue to develop with the many different research programs underway at this time.

- A copy of this report (and the appendices) to be sent to the World Health Organization (WHO) committee(s) overseeing the development of ICD-11 in order to develop relevant criteria(s) for adults and females and to consider the relevance of Asperger Syndrome as the deletion of this is likely to deny many adults and children the right to an accurate diagnosis.

- In light of the sensory issues highlighted here and their effect on behavior and health (both mental and physical), Local Authorities should allocate appropriate housing stock to take into account these differences.

5.3 Conclusion

The processes used with this thesis, including the use of matrices within the main body, clearly demonstrate the viability and value of visually comparing different perceptions within this format and it also enhances the discussions and the recommendations. The limitation of this research and methodology is that it does not take in to account the professionals' perspective and how they viewed the participant(s). The main problem is that not enough resources are directed towards this kind of research, for example this kind research takes up a lot of time and was carried out by one person. The strengths of this thesis are very much tied to the ethical practices carried out by the researcher. For example, original sources of research were attained and read through, the most current research has also been included, the process(es) of data collection were made as accessible and emancipatory as possible for participants, and with the use of full transcripts as appendices in an un-edited form enabling the reader with different ways of reading this material to engage with it in as transparent as manner as possible. Though please note, the transcripts were sent to participants to re-read, meanwhile some did make changes and this was accepted so as to take in to consideration aspects of being autistic, they were then signed off by the participants and sent back to the researcher. Researchers who have processing differences could also be allocated assistants to type up transcripts, furthermore, when a researcher also has mental health difficulties and researches this area it can be quite dangerous for the researcher. Hence, universities also ought to be sensitive to researchers' differences. Further research could include say two professionals, one being autistic and the other being non-autistic, who are paired up together to carry out projects; enabling researchers to learn with each other and to become more enlightened together. Academia has a wider role in terms of emancipatory and advocacy research.

5.4 Reflexive Account

I feel that having undergone this process(es) of research I have become more enlightened regarding ethics, research and autistic persons' perceptions regarding identity and the diagnosis process. Every stage of the research process has been thoroughly thought through and actions have been carried out as ethically as possible.

LIST OF REFFERENCES CITED

American Psychiatric Association (APA) (1952). Diagnostic and Statistical Manual of Mental Disorders, Washington, DC: *American Psychiatric Association.*

American Psychiatric Association (APA) (1968). Diagnostic and Statistical Manual of Mental Disorders, *2nd ed.* Washington, DC: *American Psychiatric Association.*

American Psychiatric Association (APA) (1980). Diagnostic and Statistical Manual of Mental Disorders, 3rd ed. Washington, DC: *American Psychiatric Association.* Pages 86-92

American Psychiatric Association (APA) (1987). Diagnostic and Statistical Manual of Mental Disorders, 3rd ed, rev. Washington, DC: *American Psychiatric Association.*

American Psychiatric Association (APA) (1994). Diagnostic and Statistical Manual of Mental Disorders, 4th ed. Washington, DC: *American Psychiatric Association.*

American Psychiatric Association (APA) (2013). Diagnostic and Statistical Manual of Mental Disorders, 5th ed. Arlington, VA, *American Psychiatric Association.* Pages 50, 51

Asperger, H. (1938). The mentally abnormal child (training lecture held on 9th October 1938) Translation by Herbert Murbach 2013

Asperger, H. (1944). The "autistic psychopaths" in childhood, Habilitation thesis submitted to the medical faculty of the University of Vienna, published in *"Archiv für Psychiatrie*, Bd. 117", 76-136, Translation by Herbert Murbach 2013

Attwood, T. (2008). The Complete Guide to Asperger's Syndrome. *Jessica Kingsley Publishers.* Pages 10, 36

Autistic self advocacy network. (2013) [online]. ASAN statement on Frien study on autism and "recovery". http://autisticadvocacy.org/2013/01/asan-statement-on-fein-study-on-autism-and-recovery/#_ednref5 (Accessed: 30.2.2014)

Bagatell, N. (2007). Orchestrating voices: autism, identity and the power of discourse. *Disability & Society.* Vol. 22, No. 4, pp. 413-426

Baines, A. d. (2012). Positioning, strategizing, and charming: how students with autism construct identities in relation to disability. *Disability & Society.* Vol. 27, No 4, pp. 547-561

Baron-Cohen, S. Leslie, A. M., Frith, U. (1985). Does the autistic child have a "theory of mind"? *Cognition*, 21, 37-46. MRC Cognitive Development Unit, London. Pages 39

Baron-Cohen, S. Hammer, J. (1997). Is autism an extreme form of the "male brain"? *Advances in infancy research*, 11, 193-217. Pages 8, 12, 17

Baron-Cohen, S. (2000). Is Asperger Syndrome / High Functioning Autism Necessarily a Disability? *Development in Psychopathology*, 12, 489 – 500. Cambridge University Press.

Baron-Cohen, S. (2006). The hyper-systemizing, assertive mating theory of autism. *Progress in Neuro-Psychopharmacology & Biological Psychiatry*, 30, 865-872. Page 865

Baron-Cohen, S. (2009). Autism: The empathizing-Systemizing (E-S) theory. *A year on cognitive neuroscience*, New York Academy of Sciences, 1156: 68-80. Pages 71,

Beardon, L. (2008). 'Is Autism Really a Disorder Part Two – Theory of Mind? Rethink How We Think'. *The Journal of Inclusive Practice in further and higher education, Issue 1, Pages 20*

Beardon, L. (2013). Diagnosis. Unpublished chapter of a book provided to the researcher in a tutorial session. Pages 1-13, Page 1

Beardon, L., and Chown, N. (2013). West Midlands Adult Autism Identification Pathways, Principles and Practice. [Lecture handout]. From Project report and good practice showcase event lecture, held on 18th November 2013, *Autism West Midlands, Regent Court, Birmingham.* Pages 13

Beardon, L. Edmonds, G. (2007) [online]. ASPECT consultancy report: A national report on the needs of adults with Asperger Syndrome, *Sheffield University.* http://www.sheffield.ac.uk/polopoly_fs/1.34791!/file/ASPECT_Consultancy_report.pdf (Accessed: 12.5.14). Pages 4, 19, 23, 27, 33, 36, 43, 45, 50, 62, 76, 77, 113, 266, 267, 271, 322, 324, 334, 335, 336, 341, 342

Beardon, L. (2014). University Academic, Sheffield Hallam University. *Response.* Email to the author, 2 June. Personal communication.

Beardon, L., Martin, N, and Woolsey, I. (2009). What do students with Asperger syndrome or High-functioning autism want at college and university? In their own words. *Good Autism Practice.* 10(2), 35-42

Blake, W. (1790) [online]. The Marriage of Heaven and Hell (first edition). http://thesorcerersapprenticeonline.files.wordpress.com/2010/04/no-24-the-marriage-of-heaven-and-hell1.pdf (Accessed: 03.01.14) Page 14

Blake, W. (1700s/1994). The Works of William Blake. *The Wordsworth Poetry Library*; Hertfordshire, UK. Page IX

British Psychological Society (2013) [online] Behaviour and experience in relation to functional psychiatric diagnoses: Time for a paradigm shift, DCP Position Statement, *British Psychological Society*
https://www.bps.org.uk/system/files/user-files/Society%20Member/cat-1325.pdf (Accessed: 12.05.14) Page 1

Casanova, M. (2014). Ludwig Wittingenstein debunks theory of mind in autism
http://corticalchauvinism.com/2014/04/21/ludwig-wittgenstein-debunks-theory-of-mind-in-autism/ (Accessed: 12.05.14)

Chang, Y. et al. (2014). Autism and sensory processing disorders: shared white matter disruption in sensory pathways but divergent connectivity in social-emotional pathways. *PLOS ONE*, Vol. 9 Issue 7. Page 1

Cornwell, M. Beardon, L. (2007/2008) Description of the term Predominant Neurotype, from 'Asperger syndrome and perceived offending conduct: a qualitative study', Page 181

Cox, D. J (2012). From interdisciplinary to integrated care of the child with autism: the essential role for a code of ethics. *Springer*

De Jaegher, H. (2013). Embodiment and sense-making in autism, *Frontiers in integrative neuroscience.* Volume 7, article 15, Page 14

Duffy et al. (2013) The relationship of Asperger's syndrome to autism: a preliminary EEG coherence study. *BMC Medicine*, 11:175, Pages 9, 10, Image courtesy of BioMed Central as original publisher

Feinstein, A. (2010). A History of Autism: Conversations With the Pioneers, *Wiley-Blackwell*, Pages 179

Fisher, K. (2012) [online]. Bad-Science + Observational Bias, Image courtesy of Karla Fisher at Karla's ASD page on Facebook (Accessed: 03.01.14)

Gaugler, T., et al. (2014) Most genetic risk for autism resides with common variation. *Nature Genetics*, Volume 46, Number 8, 881-855

Glaser, B. Strauss, A. (1967/1999). The Discovery of Grounded Theory: Strategies for Qualitative Research. *Aldine Transaction*, Pages 1-6

Guest, G. MacQueen, K and Namey, E. (2012). Applied Thematic Analysis. *SAGE*, Pages 6, 9, 10, 12, 17, 96

Great Britain. *Autism Act 2009: Elizabeth II. Chapter 15.* (2009) [Online]. Available at: http://npl.ly.gov.tw/pdf/7063.pdf (Accessed: 12.05.14)

Great Britain. Department of Health (2010) Implementing "Fulfilling and Rewarding Lives" Statutory guidance for local authorities and NHS organisations to support implementation of the autism strategy [Online].

Available at: https://www.gov.uk/government/uploads/system/uploads/attachment_ data/file/216129/dh_122908.pdf (Accessed: 12.05.14) Page 16

Great Britain. Department of Health (2014) Think Autism Fulfilling and Rewarding Lives, the strategy for adults with autism in England: an update [Online]. Available at: https://www.gov.uk/government/uploads/system/uploads/attachment_data/ file/301492/Think_Autism_-Autism_Strategy-colour_contrast_version.pdf (Accessed: 12.05.14) Pages 4, 46, 47

Great Britain. Equality Act (2010). Chapter 15, Crown Copyright [online]. Available at: http://www.legislation.gov.uk/ukpga/2010/15/pdfs/ukpga_20100015_en.pdf (Accessed: 12.05.14)

Great Britain. National Institute for Clinical Excellence (2012) Autism: Recognition, Referral, Diagnosis and Management of Adults on the Autism Spectrum [Online]. Available at:

http://www.nice.org.uk/nicemedia/live/13774/59684/59684.pdf

(Accessed: 12.05.14) Pages 18, 21, 22, 23, 24, 25, 131, 132, 137, 138

Happe, F. and Charlton, A. (2011) [online]. Aging in Autism Spectrum Disorders: A Mini-Review, *Gerontology*, Behavioural Science Section/Mini-Review, 58(1), 70-78.

Pubmed Available at: http://www.ncbi.nlm.nih.gov/pubmed/21865667 (Accessed: 30.05.14)

Hurlbutt, K. and Chalmers, L. (2002). Adults with autism speak out: perceptions of life experiences. *Focus on autism and other developmental disabilities*, volume 17, number 2, Pages 103-111

Insel, T. (2013) [online]. Director's Blog: Transforming diagnosis. *National Institute for Mental Health,* http://www.nimh.nih.gov/about/director/2013/transforming-diagnosis.shtml (Accessed: 05.02.2014)

Jaci, C. Hews, J. C. Roberts, S. Jones, P (2008) Diagnosis, disclosure, and having autism: An interpretative phenomenological analysis of the perceptions of young people with autism. *Journal of intellectual and developmental disability*, 33:2, 99-107

Kanner, L. (1943). Autistic Disturbances of Affective Contact. *Nervous Child*, 2, Pages 217-250

Kennedy, A. (2013) [online] Autism diagnosis survey in the United Kingdom: Anna Kennedy Online. *Teesside University.* http://www.tees.ac.uk/docs/DocRepo/Research/Autism%20Diagnosis%20Survey.doc (Accessed: 12.05.14) pages 7

Koegel, R. Kim, S. Koegel, L. Schwartzman, B. (2013). Improving socialization for high school students with ASD by using their preferred interests. *Springer, J Autism Dev Discord*

Krahn, T. M, Fenton. (2012) [online]. The extreme male brain theory of autism and the potential adverse effects for boys and girls with autism. *Bioethical Inquiry*. 9: 93-103 http://philpapers.org/rec/KRATEM (Accessed: 12.05.14) pages 99, 100

Marshall, T. (2014). I am Aspiengirl: The Unique Characteristics, Traits and Gifts of Females on the Autism Spectrum (on Kindle) *http://www.amazon.co.uk/Aspiengirl-Unique-Characteristics-Females-Spectrum-ebook/dp/B00L5QH952/ref=sr_1_1?ie=UTF8&qid=1409586316&sr=8-1&keywords=tania+marshall+aspiengirl*

Michael, C. (2014). Horizon: Living with autism. Asperger United. *National Autistic Society*, Edition 79, July 2014, Page 11

Milton, D. (2012) [online]. On the ontological status of autism: the 'double empathy problem'. Disability and Society, 1-5, *Routledge* http://www.tandfonline.com/doi/abs/10.1080/09687599.2012.710008#.U7ALIRb_Duc (Accessed: 12.05.14) Page 2

Milton, D. (2014) [online]. Autistic Expertise: A Critical Reflection on the Production of Knowledge in Autism studies. *SAGE Publications* http://aut.sagepub.com/content/early/2014/03/17/1362361314525281 (Accessed: 12.05.14) Page 7

Molloy, H. Vasil, L. (2002). The social construction of Asperger Syndrome: The pathologising of difference? *Disability & Society.* Vol. 17, No. 6, pp 659-669

Moore, M. Beazley, S. and Maelzer, J. (1998). Researching Disability Issues. Buckingham, UK; Open University Press.

Mottron, L. Dawson, M. Soulieres, I. Hubert, B. Burrack, J. (2006). Enhanced Perceptual Functioning in Autism: An Update, and Eight Principles of Autistic Perception. *Journal of Autism and Developmental Disorders,* Vol. 36, No. 1

Murbach, H. (2013). Translator of Hans Asperger's writings. Retired School Teacher. Statement on qualifications. Email to the author, 13th June 2013. Personal communication.

Nadesan, M. H (2005) Constructing Autism: Unravelling the truth and understanding the social. *Routledge*, Pages 2, 10, 210

Nicolaidis, C. (2012) What can physicians learn from the neurodiversity movement? *Virtual mentor: American medical association journal of ethics,* Volume 14, number 6: 503-510

Owen, J. et al. (2013). Abnormal white matter microstructure in children with sensory processing disorder. *Neuroimage: Clinical 2.* 844-853 page 844

Pellicano, L. Dinsmore, A. and Charman, T. (2013) [online]. A Future Made Together: Shaping Autism Research in the UK. *University of London*

http://newsletters.ioe.ac.uk/A_Future_Made_Together_2013.pdf (Accessed: 12.05.14) Page 22, Image 'Autism Research Funding by Research Category', design by Daniel Sinclair, courtesy of CRAE: @CRAE_IOE.

Piven, J and Rabins, P. (2011). Autism Spectrum Disorders in Older Adults: Towards Defining a Research Agenda [Online] *The American Geriatrics Society*, 59(11) 2151-5. Article from: *Pubmed* last accessed 30 May 2014 at: http://www.ncbi.nlm.nih.gov/pubmed/22091837

Quarmby, K. (2011). Scapegoat: Why We Are Failing Disabled People. *Portobello Books*, Pages 32, 34, 88, 89, 176

Rivet, T. Matson, J. (2010). Review of gender differences in core symptomatology in autism spectrum disorders, *Research into autism spectrum disorders*. 5: 957-976, Page 964

Russell, G. Norwich, B. (2012). Dilemmas, diagnosis and de-stigmatization: Parental perspectives on the diagnosis of autism spectrum disorders. *Clinical child psychology and psychiatry*, 17(2) 229-245

Singer, Judy. (1999). Why Can't You Be Normal for Once in Your Life? From a 'Problem with No Name' to the Emergence of a New Category of Difference. In Mairian Corker and Sally French, Eds., *Disability Discourse. Buckingham, UK: Open University Press*, 59-67, Page 64

Tavassoli, T. Hoekstra, R and Baron-Cohen, S (2014). The sensory perception Quotient (SPQ): development and validation of a new sensory questionnaire for adults with and without autism. *Molecular autism,* 5:29, Page 1

United Nations. (1948) [Online]. The Universal Declaration of Human Rights. http://www.un.org/en/documents/udhr/ (Accessed: 03.04.2014)

Waltz, M. (2008). Autism = death: the social and medical impact of a catastrophic medical model of autistic spectrum disorders. *Popular Narrative Media*, 1.1. 2008, 13-24.

Waltz, M. (2010). Reading Case Studies of People with Autistic Spectrum Disorders: A Cultural Studies Approach to Issues of Disability Representation, *Disability & Society*, 20:4, 421-435

Waltz, M. (2014). Worlds of autism: across the spectrum of neurological difference, *Disability & Society,*

Wing, L. & Gould, J. (1979). Severe impairments of social interaction and associated abnormalities in children: Epidemiology and classification. *Journal of Autism and Developmental Disorders*, Vol 9, No 1, pp 11-29. Pages 11, 12, 13, 14, 27

Wing, L. (1981). Asperger's syndrome: a clinical account, *Psychological Medicine*, 11, 115-129, Cambridge University Press. Pages 115, 117, 124, 125

Wing, L. (2002). The Autistic Spectrum New Updated Edition. *Constable & Robinson*, Pages 21

Wolff, S. (1996). The first account of the Syndrome Asperger described?
European Child & Adolescent Psychiatry Volume 5, Issue 3, pp 119-132 © Steinkopff Verlag 1996, DOI 10.1007/BF00571671, Pages 119 – 132

World Health Organization (2010) [Online]. *ICD-10 Version2010, F84: Pervasive Developmental Disorders,* Geneva, *World Health Organization,* http://apps.who.int/ classifications/icd10/browse/2010/en#/F84 (Accessed: 03.04.2014)

World Health Organization (1993) [Online]. *The International Classification of Diseases, Tenth Edition, Classification of Mental and Behavioural Disorders, Diagnostic Criteria for Research.* Geneva, *World Health Organization,* http://www. who.int/classifications/icd/en/GRNBOOK.pdf?ua=1 (Accessed: 03.04.2014)

World Health Organization [Online]. *The International Classification of Diseases, Tenth Edition, Classification of Mental and Behavioural Disorders, Clinical Descriptions and Guidelines*. Geneva, *World Health Organization*, http://www.who.int/classifications/icd/en/bluebook.pdf?ua=1 (Accessed: 03.04.2014)

Wylie, P. Heath, S. (2013) [online]. Very late diagnosis of Asperger's Syndrome 2013 UK survey report, http://www.shropshireautonomy.am55.co.uk/__sites/45/survey-report/late-diagnosis-survey-v7.pdf (Assessed: 03.04.2014)

Yu, K. et al. (2010). Can Asperger syndrome be distinguished from autism? An anatomic likelihood meta-analysis of MRI studies, J Psychiatry Neurosci. 36(6): 412-421, pages 419

APPENDICES

Research Particulars

Appendix A: Masters in Education Program Ethics Sub-Committee Checklist

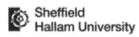 Sheffield
Hallam University

SHARPENS YOUR THINKING

APPENDIX 1

**Masters in Education Programme
Enquiry Based Project**

Ethics Sub-Committee - Student Checklist

		Yes	No	See comments
1.	Is there sufficient information presented to enable a decision to be made re ethics.			✓
2.	Are all significant Ethical issues identified?			✓
3.	Are there any ethical implications that make it inappropriate to undertake the project?		✓	
4.	Are all ethical issues addressed appropriately? *e.g. Arrangements for voluntary consent, confidentiality and right to withdraw; consideration of power issues and conflicts of interest*	✓		
5.	Does the project involve any staff or service users, parents or carers in NHS or Social Care? *If yes, which of the following applies:* *a) The application must go through the NHS or Social Care ethics committee* *b) You have attached written confirmation from your employer / placement that the project can be classified as a local audit or evaluation*		✓	
6.	Has the correct and unaltered form been used?	✓		
7.	Has the form been authorised by your supervisor?	✓		
8.	Are sample consent letters/information sheets attached?	✓		
Are the following included on the consent letters/consent form/information sheets:				
9.	Supervisors contact details	✓		
10.	Right to withdraw	✓		
11.	Arrangements for confidentiality	✓		
12.	How the data will be used and disseminated	✓		

Appendix B: Invitation for Participants

Invitation to Participate

I would like to invite you to participate in a research study investigating the identification of autistic adults' perception of their own diagnostic pathway. The research is voluntary and therefore you have no obligation to participate, however if you are interested in taking part please read the following for more information.

I will be conducting research as a Masters degree student at Sheffield Hallam University under the supervision of Dr. Luke Beardon.

With the Autism Act (2009) calling for clear pathways to diagnosis and referrals to identified post diagnostic services, local authorities are now required to identify and/or clarify such pathways. Although local authorities are required as part of their statutory duty to offer transparent diagnostic pathways with clear diagnostic protocols, the only guide is that of the NICE guidelines. However, research on the process of diagnosis and its impact appears very limited at present. This is especially true of adults living within the community.

The research will require you to partake in an informal recorded conversation, which will include questions regarding your experience of the diagnostic process. It should take no longer than an hour and a half.

You have the right to withdraw from the study at any time and for up to two weeks after participation. If you wish to take part the research requires that you are an adult who has received a formal diagnosis of Autism/Asperger Syndrome.

All your data will be kept confidential and anonymous and only used for the purpose of the study. The data will feature as part of a Masters thesis with your identity being securely protected.

Data will only be accessible to the researcher and their supervisor and will be stored in a secure location at the University (on the supervisor's computer) and by the researcher (on a personal computer), and after formal acceptance of the thesis will be destroyed.

If you have any queries relating to this invitation to participate please contact me through the following details.

Rod Morris

Masters in Autism Student

Faculty of development and society

Sheffield Hallam University

Email:

Supervisor

Dr. Luke Beardon

Senior lecturer in Autism

Faculty of development and society

Sheffield Hallam University

Email:

Appendix C: Information for Participants

The purpose of this research is to identify autistic persons' perception of their diagnostic pathway. I, Rod Morris, would like to have a conversation with you about:

(i) What led you to get a diagnosis?

(ii) What was your perception of the diagnostic process itself?

(iii) What impact has this had on you with regard to understanding yourself?

(iv) Any other factors you would like to outline?

Whether or not you participate in this study is your choice.

If you do decide to participate then I would like to have a recorded conversation with you. It will last for no longer than an hour and it can take place in a location that you prefer.

Please note that:

1. You will remain anonymous (e.g. given a pseudonym), our conversation shall be confidential and the information shall only be used for the purpose of this research.

2. Please inform me if there is anything prior to interview you want me to do to make sure the process is as easy for you as possible? This may include alternatives to the formal interview process such as an online process.

3. If you have any questions before our conversation, or after it, please feel free to ask me.

4. During our conversation you have the right to decline answering any question you might be uncomfortable with.

5. You also have the right to withdraw your participation at any time during or after our conversation. Withdrawal will mean that any information will not be used and will be destroyed.

6. Any information you provide will be kept in a secure location.

7. When we meet, there will be additional time set aside at the beginning and the end of the interview process.

If you decide to withdraw after our conversation, or if you would like to add or take out information, then please let me know via e-mail or phone:

E-mail Address:

This sheet is yours to keep. Please do not lose it, as you may need the above information at some point or another.

Appendix D: Consent Form

Name: (will not be formally used or published)

Gender:

Age:

Additional information, e.g. communication differences and support/adaptations required for this:

Consent

I have read the "Information for Participants" sheet.

I understand my rights including rights to anonymity, confidentiality, withdrawal and the safekeeping of data and I give my consent to take part in this piece of research.

Signature (please initial or mark to indicate consent):

Date:

Appendix E: Protocol for Semi-Structured Interviews

Aims: To examine the perceptual experiences of autistic adults on:

d) Why participants sought a diagnosis

e) What participants felt about the diagnostic procedure

f) What impact the diagnosis has had on the understanding of who they are

RM: I would like you to know that when having our recorded conversation I will initially ask you about the process of diagnosis you experienced, i.e. at the actual time of the process, and will then later ask you to reflect upon the process knowing what you know now. Is this okay?

P: Yes

Rod: Thank you. I would like to remind you that our conversation will remain confidential and anonymous. Are you okay with me recording?

P: Yes

RM: Thank you. So please tell me a bit about yourself…

Preliminary Information:

Current age

Age when diagnosis was conducted

Current social and economic situation

What are your official diagnoses by name

Pre-Diagnosis:

1. Why did you seek a diagnosis?

   - Probing question: How long did it take for you to seek a diagnosis?

   - Probing question: What knowledge of autism did you have prior to your assessment?

2. How did it come about?

3. What were your expectations prior to attending?

Diagnosis:

4. Can you take me through your diagnosis as you perceived and experienced it then?

   - Probing question: What were you thinking/feeling at the time?

   - Probing question: What was the environment like? Was it suitable? Did they make adjustments to the environment?

   - Probing question: Did you feel that you were receiving a 'full profile' assessment?

   - Probing question: What level/type of professional conducted your diagnosis? Was this suitable?

Post-Diagnosis:

5. How did you feel directly after the diagnosis procedure?
   - Probing question: How or/and when did it hit you?

6. Did the clinician/diagnostician ask you to read and sign your diagnosis off?

    -   Probing question: Did you read it all? How did you feel when reading it?

    -   Probing question: Were you given the opportunity to preview your report and comment on it before it was finalized?

7. What did you think of the language and the perspective in the report?

8. What were the recommendations on your assessment for a way forward?

On reflection:

9. What is your perception now?

    -   Probing question: Do you feel any different now, on reflection?

    -   Probing question: In hindsight, how could your diagnosis have been done better? What was good about the process? What was bad?

10. What impact has your diagnosis had on the understanding of who you are?

11. Is there anything you would like to add?

Thank you for your participation. I will send you what I transcribe so that you can check it and confirm whether it is an accurate record. Furthermore, if you would like a copy of the final study report please let me know.

Appendix F

Interview Data

Christine Interview Data

Preliminary information

Current age: 40

Age when diagnosis was conducted: 32

Current social and economic situation: *"I'm out of work I am applying to go back to university but I need funding to do that. I am in quite a vulnerable economic situation: having had a very disheartening experience in trying to find disability support in the workplace, and having left that workplace where I was unhappy, and now wanting to go back to university in middle life. I have years of experience and good qualifications but don't see myself being able to cope in a mainstream workplace, I need to do other things with my life, but economically I feel, no I am very vulnerable."*

What are your official diagnoses by name: Asperger Syndrome (Diagnosed as dyslexic as a child, aged 6)

Pre-diagnosis

Why did you seek a diagnosis?

"I have been aware all my life that there was something different about me that I couldn't explain, and I was very confused about why other people found it easy to make friends and I didn't, and why other people were coping at work, and I wasn't; I just couldn't explain this. I felt like a complete failure as a human being and I hadn't put two and two together at all. It was somebody who I knew socially who had a mental health background, and who had observed me in a number of social

situations who said to me one day, after a great deal of thought because she was quite worried about saying it, she said, 'I think you might be on the Autism Spectrum.' It's not the type of thing you blurt out to somebody but I was grateful to her that she said it and I do regret not having a diagnosis earlier than the age of 32, because I think that if I had had the right support in my life in adolescence then growing up would have been a less depressing experience; a much less overwhelming experience and I wouldn't have put myself in situations which were very stressful situations and failed to cope, as an adult I was still choosing the wrong situations like jobs, for example.

Anyway after the friend said that she thought I was on the spectrum I said to my disability adviser at my workplace (she was already supporting me with dyslexia and had worked in a number of other organizations with autistic people) that this friend of mine said that I may be on the spectrum, and she didn't consider it to be an out-of-the-world suggestion that I could be on the spectrum, and it was she who arranged my diagnosis, which my workplace paid for, and I was seen by a very well-known clinical psychologist and that was a very constructive experience.

The center where I was diagnosed had clearly been designed to be a low-arousal environment, I thought that I was treated with respect; I was interviewed; the interview did look at some of my childhood behavior, but it also talked about who I was as an adult and the psychologist, when she gave me her report, had recommended reading so I could go and find out more about autism, and she knew that I would be going back to the workplace with the disability adviser who had referred me and could follow this up.

That was reasonably supportive as an experience, but my particular case is a rather messy one because I then went to my GP and said I needed mental health services, which were relevant to autistic people, and the local hospital where such services are delivered kicked up a fuss and said oh no, we only treat people we have diagnosed ourselves, which I thought was totally ridiculous because people could of course move into the neighborhood, and why is one diagnosis different from another? But I went along with this because they were the only service provider in my area, so I went for an NHS diagnosis at this local hospital; it wasn't set up to be a supportive environment for autistic people; I found the diagnosis process quite overwhelming, quite humiliating, stressful; my parents had to be involved, they found it to be very confusing; I felt mocked by the person doing the interview as if he thought my religious beliefs were very silly; I was interviewed at one point by someone who had English as a second language, who was supposed to be assessing my social skills.

The whole thing was ridiculous because I didn't know that it was a different type of assessment; I didn't realize that this was a mental health team who were only looking at autism as a possibility if they couldn't consider me to have some type of mental health condition; and being an adult woman of 32 of course they could easily assume that my symptoms were something else and they said I was not autistic.

So, I had these two diagnoses; one which I very much believed because it was from a leading clinical psychologist and matched my experience of life and one from this local hospital which claimed to have some specialism in autism, but was really appalling. I tried to complain about the NHS diagnosis but the complaints procedure was ineffective; I went back to my GP and said that I want a second opinion, and because autism was classified as mental health, they said that they couldn't refer me out of borough and that the second opinion would have to be with the same people who did the first diagnosis at the hospital, (at that time you could only have second opinions out of borough for physical conditions), I didn't want a repeat of the first NHS diagnosis so said no thank you, and then my paperwork sat with the Primary Care Trust for about 3 years, they had to approve funding for an out of borough assessment and after 3 years Primary Care Trusts were abolished, and the Primary Care Trust had done nothing, no matter how many times my GP phoned them up.

What I am now trying to do is get my medical records changed. DSM (Diagnostic and Statistical Manual of Mental Disorders) has changed its definition of autism and my diagnosis Asperger Syndrome no longer exists. So I need the clinical psychologist who did my workplace diagnosis to confirm that I am still on the spectrum, and I want her letter to replace this hospital report on my medical records.

In short, I have been completely messed around by a system I didn't understand and that my GP didn't understand, and found that the road to services was blocked rather than opened up to me as a disabled person. So here I am, a woman with a communication disability made to fight a nonsensical system, and I think one of the reasons why I wanted to do this research with you Rod was just to say how stupid my experience has been; and it was eight years ago but I don't think much has changed at the local hospital; it's still run by the same idiots.

I know that without my dyslexia diagnosis I would not have got any support I needed in the workplace, and that the same would be true for autism, no diagnosis no services."

Probing question: How long did it take for you to seek a diagnosis?

"From the point that my friend said to me that she thought that I could be on the spectrum, through to seeking a diagnosis; it wasn't very long at all, it was almost straight away that I went to see the disability adviser at work. It didn't take very long for my workplace to refer me for a diagnosis. The part that took time was my employer approving the funding, but once it was approved it didn't take more than a month or so. It was fairly straightforward as far as I remember; it was eight years

ago. With the NHS I was on a waiting list for some months, but that's how the NHS works."

Probing question: What knowledge of autism did you have prior to your assessment?

"Not much really; I had heard of it; when I was at primary school, the class I was in when I was 11 years old included an autistic girl. It was a small village school in the Yorkshire Dales; she coped in that class but didn't go to a mainstream secondary school. She could be described as fairly severely autistic, although I don't like that phraseology. She was the only person who I really knew who had the diagnosis of autism. I didn't see myself as being like her.

I had family members who were part of that generation who were never diagnosed, and I had known them all my life. My grandfather, his daughter -my aunt, and I was very aware of our family's politics where the behavior of these family members was odd and had never been explained. So it was quite a negative thing for me to identify with them.

In terms of autism itself, I didn't know very much about it; I started to read about it and so re-defined myself. I wish I had known earlier that I was autistic, that my behaviour followed an autistic pattern and that there are other people like me. I knew I was different because of my dyslexia but I also knew that I wasn't exactly like other dyslexic people. I knew that there was something about me that I couldn't explain. I had grown up with some autistic people who were not necessarily a very positive part of my family life; I hadn't joined all the dots, but when I read a books on autism I began to piece things together.

This reading began mainly after diagnosis; I read some of the books recommended to me on my diagnostic report and then over the years found other things. I think that

I was fairly ignorant prior to my assessment and if I had understood autism's messy history with the mental health profession and how diagnosis worked before I asked my GP for diagnosis I would not have allowed my GP to refer me to a mental health team or even used an NHS service at all, but because I didn't have this knowledge diagnosis was mishandled and I was blocked from accessing services."

How did the NHS diagnostic referral come about?

What were your expectations prior to attending?

"That I would simply be diagnosed as Autistic, that the diagnostic process would make sense, that I would be able to get some form of support as a result of diagnosis; I was quite naive regarding the types of support that were available. I thought I would be helped to gain a better understanding of myself and helped to cope better in the world."

Diagnosis

Can you take me through your NHS diagnosis as you perceived and experienced it then?

Probing question: What were you thinking/feeling at the time?

"I was nervous about the actual process, and I think the overwhelming feeling I have about this experience, although I can't really remember what I was feeling eight years ago, was that I wish that someone had told me that I was autistic as a teenager, and I had gone through my high school years knowing the truth about myself, and that so many years of my life had been wasted, the unproductive, depressed years where I didn't understand myself, the years when I knew there was something wrong but

didn't know what it was when I was receiving silly advice from well meaning people but was feel a failure because I couldn't cope in the way other people expected me to none of these years need have been wasted and I needn't have been so depressed and alone and stressed out. Why did no one tell me I was autistic before?"

Probing question: What was the environment like? Was it suitable? Did they make adjustments to the environment?

"For the diagnosis with the clinical psychologist the environment was suitable, but the local hospital didn't have a clue. To get from the place where you could have a cup of tea to the room where I was actually seen was just a complete maze of corridors that badly needed a lick of paint; the whole place was a depressing, rabbit warren of a place; it clearly hadn't been designed with autistic people in mind at all. It was ghastly; the whole set-up made me feel really, really tense. It may have affected the assessment, but I think in their mind they didn't even recognize sensory overload as relevant when diagnosing autism. I think that the team assessing me didn't realize the building was going to produce some of the behaviour they were observing."

"With my first diagnosis, the one with the clinical psychologist they had clearly set out the building so it was a low-arousal environment, and they knew exactly what they were doing in terms of serving autistic people. I feel that the first assessment was an interview with me as an adult about my life, which was handled by someone who knew what she was looking at (thinking difference disability); able to ask the right questions; the interview went on for 45 minutes, then the psychologist had the information she needed and she could draw a conclusion. The local hospital said that their test was better because it asked more questions and involved more people – like my parents, but actually I don't think they had the right skills; they were looking at everything from a mental health perspective and I don't think they understood

learning difference, although they claimed to have better expertise in autism, they clearly didn't have a clue about how to handle or communicate with autistic people; I felt patronized, and I felt miss-handled by them. They didn't really know what they were doing, and their questions seemed irrelevant, and they said it was a full process but actually they weren't looking at autism from the point of view of an adult woman; they didn't look at sensory issues (they weren't a diagnosis criteria at the time but anyone with autism expertise would have seen that I was overwhelmed by my environment); they asked questions which were prejudicial to the process because they were looking at everything from a mental health perspective.

My parents were in the same room for part of the NHS diagnosis and part of the time they were interviewed separately. Goodness knows what went on in that room when I wasn't there. I can only guess that my parents either said that there was nothing wrong with me because they didn't spot the signs when I was a child or they didn't remember what happened 30 years ago or they didn't understand what the questions were getting at. I don't know what went on in that room.

The hospital were so inexpert they couldn't see that their evidence was faulty. I don't think they realized what I realize now, which is that my mother grew up in a home where she was parented ineffectively by someone who hadn't had their autism diagnosed. My mother's social role modeling was odd and she learnt to cope with a dysfunctional home by avoiding confrontation. I now think she is on the spectrum to a degree herself. So she would not spot or challenge an irrelevant line of questioning, I don't think she understood the questions.

The idea was that my parents could talk about my childhood, but it was 30 years ago and they were trying to remember something they weren't looking for at the time, signs of a disability they hadn't even heard of in the early 70s. Signs that my particular mother was likely to miss. I really wanted my sister to be interviewed for my diagnosis because she's emotionally astute and has worked with disabled children and would have been able to articulate something relevant. But I was told it had to be parents. I should have put my foot down and said that my parents wont be involved. I wish that I had simply been assessed as I am now as an adult it's more relevant and less stressful, I know now that involving parents puts family relationships under a great deal of stress. If I'd been more socially astute (non-autistic) I would have seen that my mum didn't want to acknowledge that autism exists in my family so could not participate in an autism diagnosis. Whereas my sister is part of the new generation and more open minded.

Looking back, if I had realized that the NHS assessment was a mental health assessment then I would have refused to attend, and neither I nor my parents would have been interviewed. In a mental health assessment someone is diagnosed autistic only if their symptoms cannot be explained as features of a mental health condition, which is like concluding that someone can only be dyslexic if they are not depressed. My parents thought they were answering questions on autism not my mental state in general. They have no understanding of autism or mental health and no ability to spot when a question has a hidden agenda. Also, I've never talked to my parents about things like being bullied at school, they didn't know about my mental wellbeing in childhood and youth or the incidents that point to autism that occurred outside the home. The stressful time of diagnosis was not the time to try and start a different relationship with my parents.

The mis-diagnosis that was the out come of the NHS assessment was confusing for my parents. I was said to be depressed, which isn't the whole story, I am also autistic. My parents felt guilty about letting me down as a child. They felt they had caused the depression. But however, they had parented me I'd be autistic and there is nothing for them to feel guilty about.

I deeply regret getting my parents involved at all: they felt guilty about the way they parented me, they felt confused by the process; they were confused by the fact that I had two reports with different conclusions, and that led to a lot of tensions in my relationships with my parents; and it's only now that my sister's three year old has been diagnosed as being on the spectrum that my parents understand that autism isn't something that is going to go away in our family; my mum wants to run away from it. Even though my mum is a retired primary school teacher and has had autistic children in her classes, she is quite negative about autism and I found that really difficult because I needed to find a positive voice for myself as an autistic person.

The first assessment was me as an adult talking to a clinical psychologist who understood learning difference, the second one was an NHS mental health assessment involving my parents talking about my childhood, and I found it very patronizing, they just wanted to fob me off saying I was depressed. I had not recognized then that my depression was a lifelong issue, and that I was depressed because I was struggling to live with an undiagnosed disability. The diagnostic team confused symptoms with cause; it was a incompetent."

Probing question: Did you feel that you were receiving a 'full profile' assessment?

Autism is part of a constellation of neuro-diverse conditions. I was assessed separately for dyslexia and autism. It ought to be possible to have one assessment that picks up all kinds of issues like, dyspraxia, dyscalculia, attention deficit hyperactivity disorder and so on. Many people have traits of more than one form of neuro-diversity.

At the same time that diagnosis was to limited in its view (just autism and not neuro-diversity as a whole), it was also to broad, it included looking at irrelevant conditions.

It is wholly inappropriate to see autism as a form of mental health condition and to diagnosis autism only if someone's bahaviour cannot be explained as a mental health condition. An assessment of a neuro-diverse person's mental health needs, and their big needs, must come after their diagnosis of their thinking differences.

Probing question: What level/type of professional conducted your diagnosis? Was this suitable?

A clinical psychologist did the first assessment. She knew about autism and from a background of seeing it as a thinking difference. She did not know about other forms of neuro-diversity.

The second assessment was carried out by a mental health team conducting a general mental health assessment in which they would only diagnose autism if my behaviour and difficulties could not be explained as a form of mental health condition. They had the wrong view of autism, the wrong training and experience. They did the assessment as tick box exercise without understanding how autism presents in adults and in females. The subtleties of my social expression were assessed by a junior team member who did not have English as her first language. The team leader was a psychiatrist I am not even sure what training the other team members had. I was also given an IQ test by a junior team member and do not know why this was relevant or what her qualifications were to deliver this test or assess the results. I have had an IQ test every time I have had my needs as a dyslexic person assessed at work and I spent the whole test explaining that I'd done all the tasks before and asking whether that would affect the outcome. The team member was clearly too junior to know.

Since my assessment I have spoken to others who have been seen at this hospital, the community mental health team have said to me that they have been surprised that some people they have referred to this hospital have been assessed as not being autistic, the hospital has a reputation for not thinking women can be autistic, and I have heard that they treat another form of neuro-diversity, ADHD with mental health drugs. I advise other people in my area not to go to this hospital for diagnosis or treatment, which is tricky as they are the locally funded service.

Post-diagnosis

How did you feel directly after the diagnosis procedure?

"With the first diagnosis I felt great, I got an answer; this explains what's been going on in my life; it didn't solve the issues in my life but it did give me a explanation of what was going on. With the second one I felt literally punched in the stomach; I felt angry, confused, mishandled, cheated and humiliated and that the door to services was being slammed in my face for no better reason than the NHS does not want to spend money on people. It caused strain in my relationship with my parents, the friend who said to me that I could be on the spectrum couldn't believe the outcome and I was left wondering what on earth I was going to do."

Probing question: How or/and when did it hit you?

"I don't know because the diagnosis was so many years ago. My understanding of autism has developed over time and it's taken a long time to get to grips with living with different aspects of autism. Three years ago when I left my job, I had space in my life to make some changes and that's when I went on a dairy and gluten free diet. The NHS hasn't understood how important that is for autistic people and I have been refused gluten free bread on prescription – and it's expensive, I have also had poor advice from a nutritionist who simply dismissed the diet out of ignorance. It took me a couple of years to adapt to getting the diet right and that's just one thing that has

helped me. It took a long time for me to adapt to my diagnosis as a whole, I had to read up on it; I needed to know how to ask for support at work; I needed to meet other autistic people; I needed to change my diet and all this took several years."

Did the clinician/diagnostician ask you to read and sign your diagnosis off?

"The psychologist didn't really know how to write a report that was suitable for the workplace. Some of the evidence for my diagnosis, incidences of being bullied at primary school, were going to be seen by my employer. I did not want people at work seeing this, so I asked for the report to be changed. The psychologist wanted the evidence left in for clinical reasons so the solution that the disability advisor at work came up with was she (the disability advisor) would write a summery report for my Human Resources records which just talked about my needs at work as an autistic person and didn't go into detail about my childhood or negative experiences in my adult life.

With the hospital report, I was not asked to sign it off, I was not asked for my opinion, I was being fobbed off with a diagnosis I didn't agree with; I tried to complain about how the diagnosis had been carried out as well as the conclusion. The hospital complaints process was useless; it simply involved asking the clinicians what had gone on; they clearly weren't going to say that they'd made a mistake. No, I wasn't asked to sign that off and I felt very patronized by that process and voiceless over and over again afterwards, because I was refused a second opinion due to autism being misclassified as a mental health issue, (at that time second opinions were only funded out of borough for physical conditions so I was offered a second opinion at the same hospital that came up with the first NHS opinion, which I refused) and then because the Primary Care Trust sat on my case an refused to come to a decision about referring my out of borough for a second opinion and this went on for three years until PCTs were abolished and because inaccurate information is stuck on my medical records to this day.

Probing question: Did you read it all? How did you feel when reading it?

"I felt that while it was very useful to have a diagnosis, the report was not something I wanted to show anyone; it talked about difficult instances in my life (the evidence for the diagnosis), the one from the psychologist, talked a little bit about autism but neither report explained autism; they weren't documents that I could use to explain autism to people like employers, this is what it means to be me. (This might not be their job)

The one from the NHS was just patronizing, and I am trying to get it removed from my medical records, but there isn't a process to have it removed from my medical records, so even though I know it's nonsense, I cant have it taken off my medical records and replaced by the psychologist's report because the psychologist's report is not an NHS document, so I feel really stuck. It seems to be a system designed to give people who can't communicate effectively a real runaround, and we as a nation waste a lot of money not giving people the support that they need to live their lives."

I knew what to do with a diagnosis of autism because I had already asked for disability support at work for dyslexia, but most people are diagnosed as autistic and there is no follow up support. No counselling, no information on autism, no information on where to meet other autistic people, no signposting to accurate information on benefits and how to read between the lines (that non-autistic skill) of the forms if you have a disability that isn't a medical condition, no information for family, friends, employers. There's just nothing and going back to your GP won't help because you'll have to educate them about what autism is. (Which you might already have had to do to be referred for diagnosis in the first place).

This is a big problem, diagnosis is handed to people by medics, and they are the last people who should be telling someone that they are disabled. Disability is not something medics can fix, like flu, it's something disabled people live with in society and the health service doesn't really understand the social model of disability or disability empowerment at all.

Probing question: Were you given the opportunity to preview your report and comment on it before it was finalized?

"Not by the NHS, and with the psychologist that was something I had to ask for and not something that was offered to me, and I had to say not to send it to my employer. I was surprised how badly drafted the report was, poorly written and in it's tone and content totally unsuitable to be sent to someone's employer."

What did you think of the language and the perspective in the report?

"I think in order to be of any use to anyone who is newly diagnosed and to be useful to the people that person will need to share the report with, the people writing the reports need to be very clear about terminology. Reports need to be accessible to lay people, they need to be in plain English, they need to be written in a professional tone. I didn't need people in my workplace to start questioning my diagnosis and looking at the evidence, they simply needed to be informed that I was on the spectrum. I think that clinicians aren't necessarily very skillful in terms of writhing reports, knowing they are going to have different audiences, that GP's and family members and autistic people themselves, as well as employers are going to have to make sense of this document. I think that what psychologists need to produce is simply a document that says, 'I confirm that this person is on the autistic spectrum', and then perhaps a fuller report for the actual person on the spectrum saying 'this

is the evidence I have considered and why I reached the conclusion I came to', so that psychologist are not put in the role of having to produce legal evidence which isn't their skillset, or evidence which is going to be mangled by someone who doesn't really understand."

There is also an issue with using medical terminology like 'disorder'. Reports must make clear what is being diagnosed but not leave the person the report is about feeling that they are a broken version of an non-autistic person. We don't diagnose men as having a masculinity disorder which means they are defective compared to a female norm. It's the same with autism, it is perfectly valid to be autistic.

What were the recommendations on your assessment for a way forward?

"With the psychologist's assessment I was simply being referred back to my workplace, yes I was autistic and so needed support. The psychologists expertise wasn't in what support I would need in the particular job I had. She recommended some reading so I could understand autism, which was a start for me to understand my diagnosis and advocate for myself at work. The report may have made one or two comments about the workplace but I think that the report was just being handed back to HR at my workplace who would then have brought in experts on autism to have my workplace needs assessed. I've met some inexpert experts on autism in the workplace and the needs assessment process is hit and miss, but that can't be resolved by the diagnostic report writer.

The NHS diagnosis concluded that as I was depressed I couldn't also be autistic, so didn't offer follow on support on autism. Even in terms of my mental health needs it didn't refer me to anyone who could look at the different areas of my life, how I was coping with work? How was I coping with housing? How was I coping socially?

I am now on a steering committee with the local council and clinicians locally are feeling under pressure not to give an autism diagnosis if support is not available locally. I think that there is a fear that if it isn't written in the report, you don't get the service, but this means that people get neither the diagnosis they need or the services they need.

My view is that it is not the job of the person assessing whether someone is autistic to do anything other than judge whether the person before them is either autistic or not. Assessment for support must be a separate process or it is too easy for a low tax economy to close its eyes to what it refuses to see and fail to diagnose autism. It's the clinician's job to give the diagnosis, and if local services are not there then that is a separate issue, which does not determine the outcome of the diagnostic assessment. Rather better assessment identifies the need for different services: ones that meet the need that is there not the needs assumed to be there by misdiagnosis. I can't bare it that it is people with communication disabilities who are subject to these idiotic assessments where the availability of support determines whether someone's autism is recognised or not.

Even if someone is diagnosed it should not be the person carrying out the diagnosis who assesses their support needs. Psychologists are being asked to make recommendations for situations like housing and workplace needs which are outside their area of expertise.

After diagnosis those found to be autistic need a separate needs assessment and signposting to local services. As someone's needs will include issues like employment support this assessment needs to be more than a typical social services assessment. Social service teams need to ensure that their assessments are carried out by people who understand autism, make assessments on the basis that an autistic person will have life-long needs – a person coping well with support has not has not learned to cope with being autistic and will no cope if support is removed, and understand that autistic people need specific types of support and cannot be slotted into general services. All the confidence building in the world won't help someone who can't read social situations spot that they are being bullied at work.

At the moment, where I live, all needs are being looked at in one big assessment and this includes mental health needs. There is an assumption that if someone's mental health needs are not looked at during diagnosis then they won't be picked up at all. Diagnosis can only be conducted effectively by psychologists because it is they who understand autism, because it is they who have experts in learning difference. I will say again that autism cannot be diagnosed by mental health professionals or as part of a general mental health assessment – such assessment processes tend to miss rather than identify autism.

Having made a diagnosis the autistic person then needs to be offered a separate assessment of their mental health needs. Autistic people often have profound mental health needs and will need a response, which is appropriate for an autistic person. For example, an autistic person's mental health issues will not be episodic, parking someone on anti-depressants for a few months (on pills which were not tested on autistic brains) is not the answer. Autistic people have long-term mental health needs, which are a disability in their own right and need to be addressed appropriately, the talking cure needs adapting for those who communicate differently.

Another issues which has come up at the steering group is that many NHS services use multi-disciplinary diagnostic teams. Teams can be made up of a few people who know about learning disability and a few people who know about mental health, simply because these are the people available to be co-opted onto the team. They don't have the right training to look at autism, which is neither a mental health issue or restricted to those who are learning disabled. Among those with training on autism, each person has a different training. Some are psychiatrists some psychologists. There is a different mix in every team and this is replicated all over the country no two autism assessments alike.

Multi-disciplinary teams suffer from an unacknowledged internal conflict. It is not clear what training on autism is needed to work in the team or what approach to autism is being used by the team. Teams cannot just muddle on through with ideas on autism from both mental health and learning difference being referred to side by side. The service these teams offer is inevitably poor, it lacks a theoretical framework, and clear standards of professionalism.

I think those people who set up the these teams are themselves not clear what expertise is appropriate for the task of diagnosis or are unsure how to find enough psychologists, as well as being motivated by saving money, or feel they are trapped with budgets tied to existing out-moded provision.

So those mental health 'experts' who have made a mess of autism in the past are being allowed to go on doing so. It muddies the waters so much having them involved in diagnosis at all. It's hard for someone being diagnosed by a multi-disciplinary team to spot whether their assessment is a mental health assessment or not, or to tell quite what it is. I suspect it's a mental health assessment which is merely dressed up as something more modern.

A third issue we have faced on the steering group is that there seems to be all sorts of very complex routes to diagnosis involving GPs, speech therapists, occupational therapists; it's bazar. This leads me back to the root issue. That autism needs to be seen for what it is. It is not a mental health issue. I really think that autism needs to come out of the DSM not just be redefined in the new edition and the new edition passed to a whole range of professionals. Autism needs to come out of a book of mental health conditions because it is not a mental health condition; it doesn't belong in there anymore than dyslexia does; you can't tick all the boxes have autism and not schizophrenia instead, because the people doing the diagnosis don't even know what they are looking at.

Here's what I'd like. An assessment by a psychologist which looks at all forms of neuro-diversity. So you don't have to go for a separate assessments. It is a pain to have to have separate diagnostic processes for dyslexia – not NHS, and autism – NHS. And then once someone's had their neuro-diversity conditions diagnosed then there needs to be another assessment which looks at their mental health in a way that's relevant for someone who is neuro-diverse – which recognises that dyslexia means issues at work, which leads to depression but that xyz treatment won't work because the person is autistic – you get the picture. Both assessments are needed but they are different things. At the moment autism is being assessed alongside what it is not, mental health conditions, and not seen as part of a cluster of conditions it is like – other neuro-diverse conditions. And no-one has realized that if autism isn't identified that mental health treatment for other issues will be inappropriate.

So I'd like one test for all types of neuro-diversity and the psychologists would sit down with someone and say yes, you are dyslexic, yes you are autistic, we've done one test, here you are, these are your results, this is where you are in terms of neuro-diversity as a whole, and it doesn't have to go near a medic, because no form of neuro-diversity is a form of brokenness and medics see a diagnosis as brokenness.

People manifest neuro-diversity in different ways; there are overlaps between different conditions so the assessment might say that this person has issues of motor co-ordination, they have issues of short term memory, they have issues of putting things in a sequence, they have issues of being overwhelmed by sensory needs.

The diagnosis would show how someone had features of different conditions. I'd like to avoid a tick box approach where someone has enough traits of autism for a diagnosis but only a few dyslexic traits so misses out on a diagnosis of dyslexia. The report would have to describe someone's diversity as a whole and see how different traits affect and compound each other.

I'd like to avoid each individual having their own diagnosis with no one in society knowing what any of it means and everyone getting lumped together as neurodiverse somehow, and people not knowing whether a neuro-diverse person they meet has sensory needs or if this person is on a particular diet We still need to words autism and dyslexia but we also need to be clear what these words mean. I face a lot of because people don't really know what the word autism means and I think we need a very clear message to the public that this is what autism is and it's difficult because each autistic person is different, but that doesn't mean we can't be clear about what it is.

So what is autism? It's a perfectly valid way to see the world. This whole deficit, disorder kind of language is really unhelpful, and there needs to be an understanding, especially among those conducting diagnosis, that someone can be really disadvantaged in society simply by being different but that doesn't mean there is anything wrong with the difference; people who are black are not running down to the doctors saying 'quick, give me bleach therapy, I'm suffering from being black'."

Rod Morris

On reflection

What is your perception now?

Probing question: Do you feel any different now, on reflection?

"It's been a long journey; it has surprised me how long it has been, because I already knew about disability rights when I was diagnosed as being autistic and yet even so it has been a long journey of learning to understand myself, taking the time needed to research autism, getting involved with groups of other autistic people, learning to communicate with other people who are like me which was a novel experience because I hadn't met people who were like me before, and you need to turn off your coping mechanisms for the neurotypical world and actually adopt your mother tongue; I realized that accessing services was very difficult, that I was being messed around by mental health professionals who didn't know how to treat depression in an autistic person. I went on to do a masters degree and researched how psychotherapists work with autistic people. I could tell you a few tales.

It's been a long process of working out who I am; can I cope in a workplace? What's going to work for me? Changing my diet. It's taken years and years to try and adapt and I still don't have all the answers. I didn't find out I was on the spectrum until middle life, eight years later I am still trying to put the pieces together, so this has been a very long journey.

There is so much shit written about autism. We are a community of people who do not have a lot of money and yet there seems to be an industry producing expensive, shitty books about autism. Here we are as people with a communication disability and yet trying to information on autism which is well researched is something of a challenge as is finding information which is from the autistic person's point of view or useful information about how autistic people can actually live our lives. Newly diagnosed, you could easily walk into the trap of believing any old snake oil about autism you find on the internet. And the world wide web is the wild wild west when it comes to autism there are some dodgy so-called treatments out there. Chelation anyone?

There is a generation reaching young adulthood now who were diagnosed as children and who have had their understanding of autism shaped by their parent's reaction to their diagnosis, usually a negative reaction. I worry for them. There is an industry producing negative information on autism for panicky parents and it is so much harder to find the material which is the positive voice of autistic adults. You'd never think that autism runs in families. If the parents listened to the positive adult voice they'd stop panicking.

Diagnosis is going to affect more than the person being diagnosed. Each family member need to be helped to see autism in a positive way, by which I do not mean the naïve nonsense on disability seen on day time TV.

It would have been very helpful for my diagnosis to have been presented to my whole family in a group counselling session. In my family; my aunt does not want to go near diagnosis although everyone else in the family is convinced she is autistic; my mum wants to bury her head in the sand and is quite negative about what's going on as facing the fact that there is autism in our family means facing things about her childhood that she does not want to deal with; my sister is very positive about being a parent of a three year old who is autistic but she is going through a real battle with social services trying to get him into the right kind of school. Her husband has had to get used to marrying into a family where there is autism; my other sister is considering starting a family; she and her husband have had to consider what it will mean if they have autistic children; lots of people with very different points of view;

some of us have lived with autism for years (without knowing it) and others are completely new to the subject.

On the other hand, no matter how old you are when you are diagnosed, you have to form an identity as an autistic person, you have to find out who you are for yourself. I think if my diagnosis had been handled simply within the context of my own family, it would have been harder for me to form a positive identity. This is not just because I was diagnosed as an adult. My dyslexia was spotted in childhood but I had to find my own identity with dyslexia because the identity I was handed by parents and teachers was ignorance, disappointment, low-expectation or naïve nonsense about being positive about difference which didn't look at the barriers I faced in my life.

Rod: How about diagnosis on an individual basis, but also on a family basis as well?

"I think that is so, so true, and I think there would have been far less doubt about my diagnosis if staff in the NHS had seen me within the context of my family, (met my aunt), and I think that we as a family we would have been able to respond better and needed fewer support services if we had been able to sit down as a family with someone who could have told us what autism is and how if affects people and how it affects relationships in families and this is how we could get on better. I think my mum would have found that very helpful; my aunt may have crawled out of the woodwork and admitted she was on the spectrum too and we'd be able to talk about how to support her without doing it behind her back and we'd have been able to sit down with my aunt and say some of your behavior needs to be addressed and we didn't have the guts to tell you before because you are so stinky about being criticized but actually you can't go on upsetting people and so some very useful things would have come out of it."

Rod: It can be really hard as a single person to convince other family members!

"You need your family to be there for you so you are not in isolation; you need them there even when the rest of the world doesn't understand. It's hard when your own family don't understand and my diagnosis was so badly handled it made relationships in my family worse."

Rod: How diagnosis is conducted at the moment will affect research; so if there are issues with diagnosis there will be flaws within research!

"Which means in turn that we don't get the services and we don't get the understanding because services and attitudes are built on is this muddled thinking. And it's really difficult to undo it because whole professions are saying don't saw off the branch we are sitting on because changing things after the event is really hard. Even with Freudian psychoanalysis; if Freud had been alive today with the scientific knowledge we have about the brain, he would have come to some very different conclusions about the mind, but actually trying to re-work understanding of psychoanalysis is really hard because so much has been built on what we didn't know a hundred years ago."

Probing question: In hindsight, how could your diagnosis have been done better? What was good about the process? What was bad?

"The process with the psychologist was good but in terms of robust evidence it could have been stronger (more examples from my life about ways I behave and things I find hard) and in terms of a useful document at the end which I could have shown to people without shame it could have been better; in terms of signposting of services apart from the workplace it could have been better.

For the NHS diagnosis, I don't think the diagnostic process for autism should go anywhere near mental health services or actually for that matter any kind of medic or the health service at all. In the same way that the Jobcentre is not run by medics, the state's diagnostic service needs to be based in the community. There needs to be a straightforward self-referral process (like walking into a diagnosis shop), the diagnosis needs to looks at neuro-diversity as a whole, and the people doing the diagnosis need to be professionals who have expertise in neuro-diversity. Diagnosis should be a simple process of looking at how someone thinks and copes now as an adult so your family circumstances won't block diagnosis – and lets face it autistic people are highly likely to have problems in their family relationships. Most of all diagnosis needs to be empowering and not shaming, this means not only ensuring that the person diagnosed is offered information on where to go for support, like local groups where you can meet other autistic people, but someone at the diagnostic service befriending the newly diagnosed person so that they have someone to go with them to their first group meeting.

Finding the autistic community should not be daunting. It should be like walking into a pub and finding the locals are friendly and will chat and that actually they are your long lost family. Which is how I imagine gay people feel when they first come out and go to a gay bar and meet other gay people.

So diagnosis should be a very empowering process and not medical or condemning in any way."

What impact has your diagnosis had on the understanding of who you are?

"It has confirmed to me the truth about who I am. I'm autistic, this helps me understand myself; I'm not guessing I'm autistic, it is a fact, the truth about who I am. My own further reading on autism has helped me to understand who I am, so diagnosis was the starting point on that journey for me to understand whom I am and to try and un-learn all the stuff I had been told throughout my life, which was well

intentioned nonsense and to try and put in place things that will work for me and to change the way I think about myself and that is a surprisingly difficult thing to do; I still try and allow myself to be myself and try and find things that work for me, and find ways of trying to hold relationships together that work for me, and not feel that I have to be what everyone else is; and that is still something I don't feel I am able to do at age 40, which is ridiculous; I just feel that most of my life has been wasted and I'm still on the journey of trying to put together things that most people work out as teenagers to be honest."

Is there anything you would like to add?

No

<u>Isaac Interview Data</u>

Preliminary information

Current age: 65

Age when diagnosis was conducted: 55 (2003)

Current social and economic situation: *"I'm retired now. I had to give up work for medical reasons, not because of Asperger's. I was a postman."*

What are your official diagnoses by name: Asperger's

"I had tremendous difficulty in obtaining a diagnosis because some of the places wanted my parents input, but my parents were deceased. I had it done at a hospital in Birmingham."

Pre-diagnosis

Why did you seek a diagnosis?

"We were having problems with the marriage and we went to Relate and one of the Relate councilors, who wrote books on Asperger's and she could see Asperger's in me. I had never heard about Asperger's up until that time. Even my GP had not heard of Asperger's and had to use the computer to look it up. That was the first time I had heard of Asperger's and that was in in 2002/2003. It did take me a while to get a diagnosis."

Probing question: How long did it take for you to seek a diagnosis?

"First place I went to was a place in Cambridge, but they couldn't do it without my parents being there, then I went to a well known charity and they gave me the name of the hospital in Birmingham where I saw a doctor which is where I had the diagnosis done. It took under a year (months)."

Probing question: What knowledge of autism did you have prior to your assessment?

"None at all"

How did it come about?

"I went through my Doctors to get a diagnosis. I had to get a referral to the hospital and it was straight forward."

What were your expectations prior to attending?

"I just wanted an answer; had I got it or hadn't I got it, but according to this councilor at Relate she saw the behavioral patterns. I was nervous, as I didn't know what they were going to come up with. Most people with Asperger's have other problems as well, and I think I have Dyspraxia because I'm very clumsy and can get disorientated. That's just my thinking; I have not formally been diagnosed with Dyspraxia."

Diagnosis

Can you take me through your diagnosis as you perceived and experienced it then?

"They wanted to know about my childhood more than anything, how I got on/treated at school, the family background."

Probing question: What were you thinking/feeling at the time?

"I had a good childhood, it was hard because my father hadn't a well-paid job but I was treated alright. I kept thinking what are they going to find; have I got more than this. It was in-depth, it lasted over 3 hours. The female doctor passed me onto

someone else, he was asking most of the questions. There were 2 people involved in the process at the same time; a main consultant who asked me most of the questions and the other only asked me a few. It was NHS based."

Probing question: What was the environment like? Was it suitable? Did they make adjustments to the environment?

"Yes, it was all right. I was made to feel comfortable; the questions weren't probing and were quite easy to answer. No adjustments made to environment, which was just an ordinary consulting room."

Probing question: Did you feel that you were receiving a 'full profile' assessment?

"It was in-depth, it went right back through my childhood, school and work; I have always worked and have never had a problem in finding a job. My wife was with me so some of the questions they asked us both together, others were with me on my own. At the end, the doctor and me and my wife were told that with the information we have you have Asperger Syndrome."

Probing question: What level/type of professional conducted your diagnosis? Was this suitable?

"Yes, to me, the questions he asked were the right questions. I believe it was a psychiatrist. I get thrown when people say Asperger Syndrome isn't a psychiatric problem, and then someone else says it is a psychiatric problem, so if it isn't a psychiatric problem why do they get a psychiatrist to do the diagnosis. It throws you a bit. I, myself don't see it as a psychiatric problem, if it was a psychiatric problem, you wouldn't have done what you'd have done would you, you'd have been having

happy pills in a Psychiatric hospital. Some people say, you're not normal, and I say what is normal. I view Asperger's as a difference. To some people it is an advantage, to others it is a disadvantage."

Post-diagnosis

How did you feel directly after the diagnosis procedure?

"That was all right with me, because I knew there was a problem there; I couldn't do anything about it but it answered a lot of questions."

Probing question: How or/and when did it hit you?

"At the time when it was confirmed. There were no pills so if you've got it you've got it. You've got to make the most of what you've got."

Did the clinician/diagnostician ask you to read and sign your diagnosis off?

"That I can't remember. There was no follow-up, no letters, nothing."

Probing question: Did you read it all? How did you feel when reading it?

"I don't believe that I had access to my written diagnosis. They just told me that I've got this problem."

Probing question: Were you given the opportunity to preview your report and comment on it before it was finalized?

N/A

What did you think of the language and the perspective in the report?

"Everyone has a different view on it, haven't they; there is not one general view on it. There are loads of people who have different ideas on what it is and this is what throws you. I think it was the Relate counselor who said that Asperger's people just have a different outlook on life; we look at things differently to what somebody else does."

What were the recommendations on your assessment for a way forward?

"This is what upset the wife; it was just a case of just go away and live with it. There was no follow-up or suggestions. It upset her more than it upset me. It was just the case of if you'd got the diagnosis, there's nothing else we can do for you; that's your life now. Without follow-up it did have a negative affect on my marriage. I just get on with things; I'm what you would call a plodder, I just plod along and just carry on with things."

On reflection

What is your perception now?

Probing question: Do you feel any different now, on reflection?

"No, I've just got on with life."

Probing question: In hindsight, how could your diagnosis have been done better? What was good about the process? What was bad?

"It was very in-depth; there was nothing that upset me about the diagnosis; none of the questions upset me. I wish there was follow-up and advice for the two of us, me and the wife to help cope with this problem – strategies for both of us."

What impact has your diagnosis had on the understanding of who you are?

"That's me, I can't change it, you can't change it; we just have to get on with life. I just plod along, I'm happy with my life. To me, there is more people who have actually got is than have actually been diagnosed, because you see people in the street and you thing he could have it because he is doing some of the things that you do, and you see other people doing it."

Is there anything you would like to add?

"I would like to see more done for Asperger people, but according to a friend of mine, in the DSM they are going to group it all together under Autism. I believe my sister had an Autistic problem (she died when she was 70) because in the 1950's she was sent to a boarding school for children with learning problems; two of her children have learning problems and they were sent to a special school. It has gone further because some of the grand children have got ADHD, so it's coming down through the line. This grandson, they were going to send him to a special school, but they have had second thoughts and are going to send him to a mainstream school. I am poor at math and it was my worst subject at school. I don't suffer with anxiety or depression but I have memory problems. On my father's side they are ordinary working class; my mothers side there's a couple of millionaires. I believe that every Asperger person is different; no ones the same, you can see odd things, but everyone's different. I have always worked apart from with medical problems, and I see many in Autism groups who have never worked. I have a friend I have known since I was nine, and another friend (dead now) who I had known since fifteen. I recognize the pushiness of society and competition compared to when I was younger when I never had that. Post diagnosis, I would like to see support for the people and the families, because there's nothing out there. If you are a parent

with a child, there is support. The window cleaner came yesterday and his son had Asperger's; he is an 11 year old who has been in a Psychiatric Hospital, and he has ADHD as well now. They keep throwing bloody pills down kids. I believe this should all be done on a family basis, with the genetic link. You don't need loads of back up, but some. Someone to just listen to you or your partner with the problems that you face and see if they have any ideas."

<u>Jack Interview Data</u>

Note: Ethically, the author of this thesis declares he has known this participant for many years, but this does not interfere with the content as the experiences presented here occurred long before first contact.

Preliminary information

Current age: 70

Age when diagnosis was conducted: 65 (2008)

Current social and economic situation: *"Both good; It's something that I've always known was important to me and I have worked on both of them all my life; I have a strange habit of wanting to stay in touch with people that go back years. I play a lot of sport, which helps me to meet people. The social aspects of my life have always been important to me because when I was young I couldn't relate well to people; I wanted to but I didn't quite know how to engage, so throughout my life I was observant as to how people conducted themselves, and it is a learning process I am still doing."*

What are your official diagnoses by name: Asperger Syndrome

Pre-diagnosis

Why did you seek a diagnosis?

"My daughter, who was a speech and language therapist, worked with some people with Autism and said to me one day 'I think you and I, dad, may have it'. So, that was important for me to find out and at the time I was retired which gave me time to think about it and to negotiate a diagnosis and how to get one."

Probing question: How long did it take for you to seek a diagnosis?

"Probably two or three years. The thought process I went through; at the time, I was reflecting on the aspects of my quality of life, and I was asking myself, do I want

this because I couldn't see what good it will do me now, but then I looked at my quality of life and came to the conclusion that my quality of life I perceive as quite good, so there are no reasons why I shouldn't do it. But as it turned out it became an important question to me, so I decided to go after it. It took about two and a half years from the original concept that I might be, to mulling through it and eventually that I have to find out. It was a further six months before I received a diagnosis after I wanted to find out. I initially requested one from my GP, who said that 'I didn't know about Asperger's or Autism or anything like that, but I will back you'. Because it turns out they had to fund the diagnosis, which turned out to be quite expensive, so I ended up having to pay privately for my diagnosis. The diagnosis cost me £600, which I thought was quite expensive just to have a couple of hours meeting. This was down in London." (Jack lives in Birmingham)

Probing question: What knowledge of autism did you have prior to your assessment?

"None at all, apart from what I knew about myself. It was obvious that I did understand a lot because of all the self-analysis".

How did it come about?

"First of all I found out that there were very few people who were qualified to go through the process; secondly I found that there was no one particularly on my doorstep, and it eventually came to a choice of two, one was a national charity, and the other one was a guy in Sheffield. I wasn't too struck by what I had heard about the guy in Sheffield although somebody did recommend him and so I decided that I would go to the national charity. The lady who assessed me turned out to be a very well respected and well-known clinician in the field of Autism. She was very good at

interacting and making both me and my wife comfortable for why we were there and what the process was about and that some things that she would ask me, she would need verification from my wife, because normally for a diagnosis they normally like people who were around for the whole of your life, well I couldn't provide that."

What were your expectations prior to attending?

"What I was hoping for was a positive diagnosis one way or the other; I wanted confirmation, one way or the other and that is what I was looking for, and I was somewhat apprehensive. I didn't know what it would unveil but it was like waiting to attend your own court case, but I wanted an answer."

Diagnosis

Can you take me through your diagnosis as you perceived and experienced it then?

Probing question: What were you thinking/feeling at the time?

"I was considerably nervous; it was down in London and we had driven down there; we arrived early so therefore I had time to kill and my wife suggested that I have something to eat, but I didn't fancy anything, so we just walked. I was apprehensive, just straightforward apprehensive; I didn't know what to expect, I was nervous of what might come about, but I had this overall mission on getting a positive answer, yea or nea."

Probing question: What was the environment like? Was it suitable? Did they make adjustments to the environment?

"We found it ok, but I had a Satnav and we could park outside her offices, so that was good. The secretary met us and we had to wait for the clinician to arrive. She then

appeared and then we walked up this huge set of stairs and along a long corridor with high ceilings, then eventually into a large boardroom. My wife and me sat to one side, and she sat on the other side. She introduced herself, and she explained the process and I think she came across as very caring and understanding and she actually told me about her work with her colleague which made me feel as though she was qualified. She made me get to the point where I felt that whatever she said was true, so I had faith in her. She had a process that she was working to which she didn't disclose, but she didn't hide that fact that she was doing it either, and she did say that there were times where she would need to ask my wife for verification of something, which was not that she doubted my word or anything. She was very good and she settled me down."

Regarding background history and development and taking into account that his parents were no longer alive, Jack said that *"She did ask those types of questions, and I was able to answer most of them. My initial experience of life was when I was about three years old and my very first trauma was just before I had to go to primary school and I had to wait for my mate to pass and watch him go to school and there was me not able to go to school because I wasn't ready for it and that is an experience that I carry with me, I can re-live that moment. I was able to not remember anything about whether I was bright or not, but the reactions of people and what they told me was that I was very bright and outward going, but absolutely and completely devoid of safety; if there was something to do I would throw myself into it, and I think the first trauma I had in life, I didn't know what it was until we discussed it and it turned out to be one of these little peddle cars that I could cycle up and down the side of our house, but then when I got proficient at it I opened up the gates and started to do fast turns on the pavement. We didn't have many cars around in those days, so it wasn't very dangerous to swing out onto the road either, but it was at that point that my parents confiscated the red car, and I don't think I took too kindly to that. I think there is a scar because of that, because people told me that it was so important and I felt as though I was treated wrongly."*

Probing question: Did you feel that you were receiving a 'full profile' assessment?

"Yes, very much so. She covered an awful lot of things and I was able to give her an honest answer and as with this interview I probably gave more than I was asked for; so she got a good understanding of the truthful upbringing that I had and as it want on, my wife was able to start contributing, because she got to know my mother and my father before they died. We talked about things like clumsiness, how you felt in social situations, lots of things I don't remember, but I do remember thinking that applies to me, that applies to me in part, or no absolutely not. It was those sorts of answers to her questions that I was able to give, but she did cover a lot of ground. She also asked my wife similar questions about me also. It started to get quite interesting and amusing when I was telling her about when we go to see people, and in the car I will always ask my wife what is it I should say and what is it I shouldn't say, and it's more important to know what I shouldn't say than what I should say. I will also talk after such meetings by asking that I didn't know what was going on, and she would explain it. My wife was able to put things into context for me and we got to know each other extremely well and therefore we know each other inside out, so I have always been open with her to the point of bluntness, and she has always understood and accepted me for who I am, and in the main, that's not difficult to live with, but now and again it can be."

Probing question: What level/type of professional conducted your diagnosis? Was this suitable?

"I don't think I could have got anyone better, as she was someone who had dealt with a lot of people on the spectrum over a considerable period of time, along with someone who I was assured was one of the guru's of the subject, and they were

both working together for a long period of time. They didn't agree on everything, but they did agree on the basics and were respectful of each other, but she had her own views and professionalism, and it was a likeable situation and I felt at the end of the time, at the point that she was just about to pronounce that I could have faith in what she said. It was interesting when she got to that point because she said that there are some people who need to have it proven in blood that you have the Triad of Impairments. She said to me that I don't believe that you have the triad and that she said that you don't need all the parts to actually be on the spectrum, and I think you are unquestionably on the spectrum." When asked about a fuller assessment such as assessment provided in the individual's real life setting as we would all do things in private that we wouldn't do in public, Jack believes that *"the clinician wouldn't have learned anything because there are two me's; there's the me that I am and there's the me I portray, and I have become very successful in portraying something that I am not necessarily feeling. People often completely misunderstood me and it's all because they are reading into me things that I am finding difficulty with and they are reading the signs that they believe they are picking up and they are wrong. I think I do portray myself as someone who is far more confident than I really am. I think what the clinician was saying was that the stories that I told and the stories that I could share with her and that my wife could back up, she felt an absolute reflection of what she had seen in others, somewhat to a lesser degree, but reflected the same pattern of progress throughout my life and how you learn to cope with things and we told her a few amusing little stories which were very truthful and open as to the way we were and how my wife had to treat me which was different to what one would expect. I think she understood that I was at a stage in my life where I didn't have much pressure because a) I'm still very happily married for a long time b) the type of job that I had done and the sort of things I have got out of it, the way I interacted and the way I could express myself, it was obvious that I wasn't having a traumatic time, but there were times in my life, which I shared with her, when that going gets tough that's when you need to dig very deep and that's when you find out what your weakness are; that's when you find out that you are not as strong as you think you are and you realize that anxiety and depression set in and all the nasty things that you wish you hadn't experienced, but I could start to see that the two were related, the condition and the actual effect. It wasn't surprising that I had mental health issues, yet nobody would pick them up, nobody would even understand, and that I think is effectively being misunderstood, and its always been very puzzling to me because you don't always know how people with mental health issues actually feel. I knew how I felt; it was different to the way I normally feel, but I had nothing to judge it against. Some people are born with talents and some people are born without talents, and some are born with abilities that are strong, and some people are born with inabilities that get in the way; I had very few inabilities, but the ones I did have were very much of a social nature, and maybe the cause for my need to address the social aspects, because I knew it was a weakness and I didn't want to be weak, I wanted to be strong, so I wasn't shy in addressing the issues, and I used a lot of people in trying to develop my understanding that way, and I felt at the time of the diagnosis that this was all beginning to start to give me an answer as to why I had problems and what were the basic causes which I had never even had hinted at before. There were several occasions where she understood my coping strategies, and she was quite impressed, and found it rather unusual. I think she understood that despite of the extra effort I had to put in, in any situation that I felt was worthwhile that I actually persevered with it, to the point where I was probably working double hard than anyone else, I was working with in order to just keep up."* When informed about the change in the DSM-5 in Autism regarding "behaviors may only manifest when social demands exceed limited capacity" (APA, 2013) Jack absolutely agrees, stating *"I would very much say that, absolutely; when it gets to a certain point I just blow, and I have to retire and shut the world out. I knew how to protect myself; I wouldn't go into areas I was not capable of existing in; If I got to the point where I couldn't take part I would not continue to take part, either through switching off by thinking about other things while conversations were going on, or actually withdraw."*

Post-diagnosis

How did you feel directly after the diagnosis procedure?

Probing question: How or/and when did it hit you?

"Immediately and relieved. I felt that I had achieved something, which is extraordinary, but I now jumped a hurdle. Achievement in that I had confirmation that here was a light that said because of these reasons you are like you are. What do you do when you think differently to other people; why do you think differently; what's right for you, what's right for them, what's right for everyone else, is there an absolute right; you become a little philosopher, and this kind of gave me a tick and a star which said here is a tunnel to go down, which was brilliant, that was the immediate reaction." In relation to the deficit medical model of disability, Jack said *"There are two answers to that because there are two aspects 1) How did it effect me 2) Did I feel I was handicapped in any way, no, I didn't feel that and I have not had any of that sort of way of thinking up until the diagnosis, so I had no baggage; I had no pre-conception of what it meant. So that was my next thought, what does it all mean and lets start the journey. So, from that point of view, no I didn't feel handicapped in any way, but getting to know more about the condition has led me frustratingly to read very many books that haven't meant an awful lot to me, talked to an awful lot of people, most of which hasn't helped very much; tried to seek help from organizations where you'd expect it to be given, and not*

found; really getting quite angry that even though I was regarded as on the spectrum, there was no help, their was no guidance, there was no way of understanding that would be given to you, other than what you found out yourself, and that made me really annoyed. What are these organizations out their doing? They are raising other issues; they don't stick to their original cause and they wander way off."

Did the clinician/diagnostician ask you to read and sign your diagnosis off?

"Yes, it was sent to me in the post; it was two sides of A4, it recalled the process that she engaged in, in order to come to her conclusion; she stated her conclusion, she signed it, and I signed it; she didn't sign it in front of me, she signed it be sending it to me, then I signed it and sent it back. There were no amendments made as I felt that she alluded to the things that we discussed and agreed on, and all she was doing was reflecting the significant agreements. It was not so much of a clinical report in my recollection; it was much more a professional judgment of recognition of a condition, and my need to know where to look in order to understand."

Probing question: Did you read it all? How did you feel when reading it?

"Yes I did; I read it several times and avidly. A) I got what I wanted, which was a confirmed direction. B) Secondly, the words were not delivered in a way….. The way I read it was that I could put myself in her chair and see me through her eyes without any difficulty because she didn't use difficult language; there was no judgmental part to it whatsoever; it was a pure reflection of what we discussed and it was laid out in the sequence and the depth that we discussed it. Whether this is a good way of getting a diagnosis, I have absolutely no idea, and I was actually pleased by the humanity and the human approach of how she conducted the whole thing. I think I would have objected to a lot of medical terminology, so she didn't give me that."

Probing question: Were you given the opportunity to preview your report and comment on it before it was finalized?

"Yes"

What did you think of the language and the perspective in the report?

Already covered

What were the recommendations on your assessment for a way forward?

"There are societies around that you can approach in order to further your understanding of the condition, and this is what I was trying to get into, and then I actually went with my badge of honor as a new found recruit to this condition, and went to a well known charity and said 'what help can you give me?' They basically said 'piss off, there is nothing wrong with you mate, we can't help people like you because we have no time for people like you, we have time for people who are much more heavily affected'; they then expected me to run away, tail between my legs, and I said this was unacceptable and so I pushed and I probed, and they said 'look, I tell you what we can do, we can introduce you to a group that meets on a social basis, come along and see what you think of that'; so I did that and I was absolutely appalled by what I saw; I don't think it was good for the group who was there; I could see there was a lot of difference between the group who was there and me, because I had an awful lot of confidence that they didn't have and I had the ability to express myself and to look people in the eyes and to engage in a way that they appeared not to be able to; however, the amount of rules for the way that they were allowed to conduct themselves was so intense that it didn't allow them any time to express themselves. The rules that were imposed on them as being a member of this group; you couldn't speak for more than a minute; I know the reason why

that is imposed, but that was a rule and they didn't deviate from it, and everybody regarded it as a rule that was being broken if it was exceeded, so they treated them like a load of zombies rather than trying to extract any meaningful thoughts out of them, and to me they were looking for progress, they were looking for areas of how each of them could develop, they felt that the development they were looking for was because it was a social event, how well they socialized, and therefore how well they could stick to these rules and think of others rather than just themselves, and so on. I felt it was like a sword dangling above them, that if they did break it that this sword would slice them apart, and it was so strict and unfeeling that one or two of them actually broke away and couldn't take part any longer and so they were counseled by somebody else which then started to deteriorate because they weren't there around the table taking part and there was only one left doing that and he wasn't particularly skilled in what he was doing, I don't think. The amount of empathy he had, the amount of understanding and reflection on how it would affect him, had he had similar difficulties, was just not present. I was quite disgusted. He was an 'officer' with the charity; I don't think he was clinically qualified or a medical practitioner; I think he was employed by the charity to run these sort of groups. I don't think he was either qualified or knowledgeable, but he did work for the charity so no doubt he did understand the theory that they believe. That session around the table was only the second bit; the first bit, they met in a pub and they knew it was for a discussion and they formed their own social groups, which in the main was one large group which they all sat round and somehow took part depending on the level of their social ability and they also had the job of ordering food, which they did individually and they all paid for their meal and so on, prior to stage two which was this round table thing. The third aspect was you all go back and you all have your meal, depending on where you sit and who you are sat next to, you interact with them. That turned out to be an awful lot better; one girl and one guy in particular wanted to search for the meaning of their life, so we discussed that and that appeared to form a kind of bond between the three of us, and all three of us were expecting that perhaps next time we could take it a little further, but that time never came because they were only showing me and that this cannot be offered on an ongoing basis, and were unable to say that they could in future, again on the basis that they wouldn't be able to offer me anything after my constructive criticism and feedback which was either taken completely the wrong way by not understanding that it was constructive criticism, and nor could they defend or discuss it because they had nothing to say. The two people I was talking to: one was married and was trying to come to terms with his diagnosis and why his wife had to be so understanding etc. The other was trying to get a job and not feeling that she was succeeding."

Rod: It seems that you were looking for commonality in other people, but others you came into contact with after diagnosis was not reflective of your experiences.

"Well, more than that, I felt that if they were running such a thing, then the beauty of being able to help each other should have been fostered, and it actually wasn't, it was frowned upon because I don't know, whether it is because of health and safety or whatever and you could get into the wrong hands; you could be because of your gullibility in being misled, and therefore the charity would be accountable for that, I don't know, but there was so much that they could have got out of taking the three of us that naturally got together and could be empowered; they could have done that, but they didn't. Totally controlling. The point that I wanted to make was that I couldn't find any positive help for somebody who they regarded as competent, and yet the difficulties that I have got, were as real as anybody else in that room, if not more so, because I could understand the implications and the difficulties and the impact; and all of those could actually be very soul destroying."

Rod – I would imagine that if you were put in a position of a mentor within that group, you might have the insight to be able to assist in a more positive way?

"Absolutely, and that was not considered. That was one thing they told me; the other thing I went to was a social evening where we played bowling, and again it was not a social evening at all, it was like a day release for mental patients where we were treated as such, although they were residing in the community and all legally classed as free citizens. It was disgusting. That was very scary; it was also very, very disappointing because what I was looking for, they weren't able to give me; they were possibly able to give me but they didn't have the time. I think that what should happen is that the people who are out there, so called societies to help everybody with the condition; if somebody goes along with a badge saying I am Autistic there should be room for help at whatever level and every level. It's about opportunity and my experiences are that there was none of that whatsoever, and that disappointed me horribly and I realized that on a national basis another charity was equally unfeeling; they had a wonderful resource on the computer which pointed you to various documentation, and they ran various campaigns, which were not actually providing the help that I think a national organization should. I think that most of the research is still based on children. The reason that I feel that I have managed my way through life is that I have a support structure in other people who accept me for who I am and without that support structure being in place on an ongoing basis, and at the end of a phone and/or a knock at the door, or whatever way I want to start a discussion or a chat of any form because something is not right and I want to understand it; I have that support structure in place; for many people who don't have that support structure in place, there is no structure in their social life and that is something that should be recognized and somehow that support structure should be explained, put in place, but enabled by the individual themselves to put it in place; so it is a set of skills that need to be passed over to people who haven't learned

those skills or who find it difficult to understand why those skills are so important, because you need help in the community that is ever present; it's not good enough to run something once a month to meet a bunch of people under strict terms and conditions; what you need to do is have them in their own environment that they are comfortable with and a structure they feel safe with, and understanding people within that structure who understand their condition and their needs. Also acceptance by the community; I don't think that is difficult; there are many people now who have children who their children are being told that they have these difficulties and they are Autistic in nature, and therefore Autism is becoming something that is much more known about; but it is because of the nature of understanding of people at schools and such like, rather than the clinical fraternity who know sweet FA about Autism. I wholeheartedly, unquestionably believe that diagnosis should be conducted on a family basis, because this is what I mean by these networks, and family is the strongest, closest, if it works, a group that should be enabled, and that means that you will find out when you have a diagnosis just how far apart they are, or are not. It is not just about Autism, but how do you care, and how do you provide the care and the understanding for somebody with a difficulty, which is not an illness; if it were an illness then everyone would say that I have a carer etc.; if it were just a difficulty and a social difficulty can actually be really annoying; if it were defined then it would already fit into existing service provision."

On reflection

What is your perception now?

Probing question: Do you feel any different now, on reflection?

"Yes I do; very much so. I went through an identity crisis (participant crying), *which I still find painful, and actually that is at that point that I needed help, and I got it from working with you; I wouldn't have got it any other way; I would have been as frustrated as hell trying to get the knowledge and understanding that I did by working with you; I don't think it would have been possible, and I would have ended up with a very poor understanding, and then I would have given up on it and then just dismissed it, where as I have found that being able to relate thought processes to being Autistic has been enlightening, and interesting and I have had the power and the knowledge to be able to put it in its rightful place and feeling the right way about it. There is a lot of philosophy going on and I don't think that other people will get that, and without that I don't see how their lives would change, and I can see how if, say I was a little deeper into the Autistic Spectrum than I am, I think that I would become very isolated; there were times in my life where I just had to be isolated, but I think I would have withdrawn, and I chose as a coping strategy that the only way out of this was an affirmation of my previous decisions to have friends that I would trust and friends who would trust me; their availability at the end of a phone or whatever; people who have their different roles, so that social network that is missing from most Autistic people's lives; it is that in my opinion that has to be addressed, and you shouldn't be talking in terms of carers, you should be talking in terms as part of your social structure; you are part of this world, and you provided the Autism knowledge component to a wonderful extent; Maybe the role of charities, rather than provide*

social groups is to provide a network of similar people so they can be hooked up, but you need a group and a mentor in that group and you need them to sign up to an understanding of what a group is about, what it delivers and defined roles. I have seen many individuals, who when isolated they are not in a good place mentally, when they felt they had something to contribute that people valued, they became different people, and this is what groups and structures and groups would do and acceptance and bringing out those skills, and their role in giving as well as receiving."

Probing question: In hindsight, how could your diagnosis have been done better? What was good about the process? What was bad?

"I would have liked a pathway of enlightenment, like we have discussed; as I say, I don't think people understand the re-living that I had to do, and I'm sure that I can't be on my own of going back on things in life, turning points in your life when you made a decision a certain way and then you analyze and think, well, that was a good decision, or that was a bad decision, why did you make those decisions, and now you can start pasting over what you did know at the time, the additional knowledge of what it is like to be on the spectrum, and then you become a little bit more enlightened. Until you have relived your life, you can't actually put that down. With regrets and me, I was fortunate because I think I have made an awful lot of right decisions, they haven't always been good for me in terms of not making my life easier, but they have been good because at the end of it I have felt improved as an individual and as such it has all been worth it. It may not have been worth it for the effort I had to put into it but I think that goes with the job as it were; it goes with the condition. I think my wife and me work very well together but I don't think you can receive help without wanting to give it; it's a two way process and as much as I receive help from her I think she receives help from me. She is obviously of a very nervous disposition naturally, but not many people would guess that; she is

quiet but she always thinks things through and she always contributes and I think she has become more assertive as we've lived together longer. She just lacks self-confidence, which is a trait in her family. It is interesting that her lack of confidence helps us to complement each other and empower each other; we are still happy with how the relationship is working. We have always analyzed things because I have always had to be that analytical in order to obtain confirmation, which helps in social skills by ensuring an understanding of each other's thought processing. So, it is having the right type of support which is not something that is once every month, but hopefully and ideally is everyday and is continuous, twenty four hours a day, seven days a week. This won't be derived from service provision, but on the basis of family and/or community, with services initiating that. You need somewhere to have this discourse, and if you have a group of you, forget about the costing of money due to the travel and so on, but there are expenses involved and it does cost money to get from one side of town to the other if you do that where as if you introduce one neighbour to another, or being able to provide the skills so that you can do it for yourself which is the end result.

Coming back to the process, good about the process is that it had a structure to it, a wide structure, probing structure and at any point I felt free to be able to go in there and probe it even further. Bad, is just this lack of what a diagnosis should be, it should be the start of a journey, a journey of understanding, and they have no one to hand you over to, they have got no ideas that they are giving you to take the next step; how do you get to understand it enough to be able to be able to understand what it means to you as an individual and so on; what's the point of a diagnosis if you don't have a path to do something about it. Looking in books, you can put your own interpretation on it and it ends up with no one saying it didn't mean that at all, what it really means is da di da de da and I can't learn unless I get that clarification, so it is a process, particularly in areas such as socializing, which is the fundamental issue in many ways to all of what we have been talking about, and I think that the difficulty is that empowerment, the ability to start the process off so that you've got the rest of your life to improve your skills in that, and I didn't get any of that. It's not to do with trying harder, it's about enlightenment; how do you get benefit out of a diagnosis, when you have no medicine to take; there has to be a way of pointing people down their pilgrims route that they then need to start addressing, and not only that, there is this need for other people to take that journey with you; it's a very lonely journey and it's an impossible journey. Another aspect is that diagnosis doesn't assess how your brain works and there is this aspect that when everyone is assigned the same label, it is assumed that everyone is the same where as we are all unique individuals and that doesn't come across to me from the professionals at all. I think that they are looked on as a Doctor who looks on a patient, and therefore it is a type of parent/ child relationship, and actually you need to have it on an equal basis; somehow you need to create an environment where you can be equals in what your relationship is, and I think that is absolutely critical, and how do you go from a diagnosis to an understanding of what that means to you, how do you get your proper understanding, what does that mean to you and how can that affect your life."

What impact has your diagnosis had on the understanding of who you are?

"Tremendous; I feel better for knowing myself than I did before because there were parts of me that I didn't understand that I understand much better now because if there is something that I didn't understand, I re-thought through it, you know, why did I react like that? I now can understand it and I can manage it so much better now, and I can account for it so much better now. The thing that really hit me was when I just explained to just a few people, because I initially thought that I would have to go around and tell everyone I was Autistic, and I spoke to just a few people close to me and they were good enough to understand why I was talking to them and why I

needed them for a couple of hours and we went for a walk and discussed it, and the wonderful consistent story that came back was that, yea we noticed that you were a bit withdrawn at times or a bit awkward, but that's you."

Is there anything you would like to add?

"How do you change the condition from a medical one to a community one? How do you change these charities and do gooders through a stage beyond understanding to one that we have just discussed that is a community, integrated type of resolution; realizing that there are many people out there who can contribute, could contribute if, and if treated right would contribute in a way that we just don't benefit from at the moment; and if you had that, the word benefit is an interesting one because at the moment they do get benefits and are actually written off and warehoused whereas what they should do is just understand a little bit of enlightenment to give people part of the game of socializing and that the give back they will give will enhance them as individuals and it's an ever increasing set of skills and it's not only a self-learning process, but it should be a natural self learning process, where as it is not a natural process to Autistic people because they are so wrapped up in the intricacies of trying to understand themselves that there is no time to understand others, and so they do need to be given a good education and what it really is that's going on and that will enlighten them and then they need the support structure around them to help them move from one position to another. I can't see any health organization, any charity or anything going on in the community whatsoever to enlighten people with the condition and all those with them. How do you achieve that? Because it doesn't cost money."

James Interview Data

Preliminary information

Current age: 59

Age when diagnosis was conducted: 57 (2011)

"Current social and economic situation: "I'm trained and work as a Social Worker. I'm comfortable being in the community and believe myself to be middle class, but not sure. I own my own house, am married with no children but I have two relationships with wife's children and am financially not too bad."

What are your official diagnoses by name: *"Asperger Syndrome (at the top of the scale, she said)"*

Pre-diagnosis

Why did you seek a diagnosis?

"It was quite a strange set of sequences. The first person to mention anything of the sort was my mother when I was 7 years old, I was a person who didn't fit in; strange; on the wrong end of everything; problems persisted even when working unless it was very precise and very ridged I couldn't do it. When I went to university to study social work, I met mothers of children who were Autistic, and prior to that I had worked with some service users who were Autistic and had Asperger's Syndrome, and subsequently became a subject I became engrossed with. Going to University expanded on that interest. I ended up transferring that knowledge to University and ended up doing a presentation on it and whilst working with service users I started noticing traits in myself, but was unsure but it became more apparent the more research I did, so I had arguments in my head, am I inducing this or is it me, with everything going all over the place, I just couldn't put it together. I was having

problems with concentration at University and ended up teaching most of the stuff to myself. I couldn't cope with University, getting around and getting there. I did more research and when things were getting difficult at work, so I talked to my GP about it, and she referred me for an assessment at the hospital, who contacted me and said the earliest appointment was in 18 months time, but I didn't know if I could last that long, so we decided to go private, with my wife paying."

"When we went for the assessment I was thinking we'll solve it, am I trying to solve anything, I'd lost who I was; that was one of the reasons I wanted the assessment was to find out who I was, so I can put it quite clearly, maybe this is just behavioral or it's just the way I think, I don't know. We went through the tests and I was looking for something, trying to explain why life had been so peculiar and so difficult all the way along. My wife was very supportive and she was with me throughout the assessment. I was looking for an identity, as I didn't think I ever had one. I needed to know whether someone professionally agreed with my thoughts."

Probing question: How long did it take for you to seek a diagnosis?

"My wife organized it and researched over many months to seek the most professional, respected and qualified person instead of seeking anyone out who would just give a diagnosis. We discounted anyone who would give a diagnosis as long as you paid them. So, it was a couple of months. All my GP just said that if anyone cancelled then I could be seen quicker; by that time I was desperate so it only took a couple of months of raising the money and finding someone. Under the NHS I think I would have been diagnosed by a Clinical Psychologist, it wouldn't

have been a multi-disciplinary team, it would have just been a straight forward assessment."

Probing question: What knowledge of autism did you have prior to your assessment?

"I had a basic knowledge; enough to do a presentation on the Triad of Impairments. I didn't have an in-depth knowledge of exactly what goes on. I had an interest; I had suspicions but I wasn't self-diagnosing. I knew Autism existed and Asperger's Syndrome but I wasn't clear what the difference was. It was an interest but I was reading anything too in-depth about it."

How did it come about?

Already answered

What were your expectations prior to attending?

"I thought it might have given me a reason of who I am, also I was apprehensive about where do I go if it isn't. I wanted an answer and for somebody to explain but I also wanted someone who could professionally do that, not just patting me on the head and saying you're on, because That's what happens to a lot of people I've seen since. My expectations were to have a resolution as to whether I was right or whether I was wrong, or another reason as to why I was having such difficulties in such simple areas. I've always had a concept as to why can't I just pick it up and do it like they do. I was just trying to put my life back on track so I could go in a straight line as apposed to going round in circles, which is something I was doing at the time. Regarding the diagnostic procedure, I knew it needed to take into account background. I work in an environment where a CP (Clinical Psychologist) has to do a depression assessment, you go in, you

go out, you meet the criteria and it's all quite simple. I knew that the assessments for Asperger Syndrome were far more concise; there was a lot more traits to be taken into account. I was aware that it was to do with childhood; it was a lifelong assessment rather than just what is happening now. I was aware that any chronic issues happening around me now were not going to be connected to the assessment; everybody's opinion including my wife's would be taken into account. I feel it was a bit awkward not having my parents there for assessment, as they were dead. I knew it wound involve tests and involved both verbal and observation components."

Diagnosis

Can you take me through your diagnosis as you perceived and *experienced it* then?

"The Clinician did not take into account early developmental history, as my parents were dead, but they did take into account later developmental history and the opinion of my wife. The Clinician asked about certain social situations and what the outcome was, did I have difficulties, were there any specific social issues that arose. She put the questions in a way that I could only give a direct answer to. There wasn't any loaded questions."

Probing question: What were you thinking/feeling at the time?

"I was numb. I was apprehensive prior to going. I was quite worried and scared and questioning whether I have done the right thing; is this a good idea? Maybe we'd better forget it."

RM: "What was behind the fear?"

"I was trying to find a solution and it might not be there, so where do I go, what do I do after that. I was trying to put that out of my head. I talked about it with my wife; is

prior knowledge a good thing or a bad thing; maybe you shouldn't seek a diagnosis if you have already got suspicions! That is what brought the anxiety up. When I got there, she was very specific in what was going to happen. I was told that 'no matter what happens in here, you are going to be the same person when you get out; you're not going to be a different person.' (These alleviated my anxieties and worries that I had prior) Once it started, it was just a series of questions, which wasn't so bad; she gave me plenty of time to answer the questions so it took a long time. It got easer as the process went on. She was very straight with the questions; there was none of this 'what do you think'. There were time-limited tests, which were all very structured. She wouldn't say they were time limited until I was about half way through and if I was struggling where there was an expectation. She also interviewed my wife, both separately and together. She asked what my interests were and to what degree. She quoted the DSM and said that 'all her observation and evidence has to fit certain criteria; that it's not just based on her opinion, it's based on fitting the criteria and if you don't fit the criteria, you don't get the diagnosis.' She was a very frank person, which I view as good. I got less anxious as it went along. When it ended, she went to make her assessment and I was notified later on through the post."

Probing question: What was the environment like? Was it suitable? Did they make adjustments to the environment?

"She did ask, 'is the environment ok?' and if there was anything that needed adjustment, to which I said there wasn't. It was quite a small environment; it was comfortable, there wasn't anything getting in the way. There wasn't anything influencing me from the outside and didn't cause any bother; it was a nice small room; the lighting was ok as it wasn't bright; it wasn't a clinical environment and it was quite a small place. It wasn't a huge building which was good. Parking was easy also."

Probing question: Did you feel that you were receiving a 'full profile' assessment?

"I had a series of tests; I don't know how detailed an assessment is supposed to be; I knew it involved my life as a whole and the ability to do certain things. I didn't know how detailed those things were supposed to be; I was leaving it up to the professional as I didn't know enough to say 'you haven't done that bit', because obviously the younger you are the easer it is. At my age there wasn't any school reports to reflect back on. She went down the sensory profiling road and asked about that. Sensory issues causes me a lot of problems, such as the sensation of shaking hands and how that sensation affects me and not that I just don't not like shaking hands. She asked about other issues such as smells and similar issues and social interaction and asked if there were any issues with that and his wife backed this up from an observational, independent point of view, reflecting on particular instances that she observed and didn't know what was going on and that most of the interaction between me and my wife wasn't reciprocal at all. So, all these issues were covered; the sensory issues were covered which is something that I wasn't aware of at that particular time. As far as I was aware, from a Psychologist point of view, she covered everything at that particular moment in time. I believe that if I had been younger, there would have been more tests, although I don't know what the test for children are."

Probing question: What level/type of professional conducted your diagnosis? Was this suitable?

"Under the GP, I think a Clinical Psychiatrist would have diagnosed me. It wouldn't have been a multi-disciplinary team as it was just an assessment. My occupational health doctor knew the clinician and this gave me more confidence as he said that she is an extremely competent person who he has known for quite a while. The

person who diagnosed me was an MSC Health Psychologist, councilor for a charity, diploma in casework and supervision. That is her title. She does counseling in the subject as well specializing in Asperger Syndrome over a 10-year period, 1st class honors degree etc. I do believe that with the knowledge I have, that she was suitable. I don't know if a professional has to have a particular title before you can diagnose but she has many years of experience; she was well known and thought of by my occupational health doctor who thought highly of her. I assumed if she wasn't of a high standard or sufficiently positioned, she wouldn't have been able to give a diagnosis, or wouldn't have been allowed to. She seemed very detailed; I don't know if any of the other processes are any different. I didn't think at any time that it could have been any more in-depth, because I was an older adult and there were fewer resources to go on, but she seemed thorough. He doesn't know whether her title enables that."

Post-diagnosis

How did you feel directly after the diagnosis procedure?

Probing question: How or/and when did it hit you?

"It is still hitting me. Immediately afterwards I thought the diagnosis was a solution or an identity, and I then thought what do you do with it! So what! That in itself doesn't solve any issues; that is when I asked myself, where does this leave me; who am I? Can I work from this? I didn't know if anything was going to hit me out of the blue such as like that solves everything now. It explained a few reasons but it didn't give a pathway toward the future either. What do you do with it? Do you tell people? My wife told her sons and they said we don't know whether to say whether that's good or not. What do you do with a diagnosis, and a hidden one? A diagnosis made me feel better, but I wasn't sure how anyone else was going to react to it; its taken me

57 years to get to this stage; how long is it going to take everybody else. I didn't have any euphoria. I thought that this is a solution and then I suddenly realized that it isn't. It's like somebody giving you a new name; is that going to change your life! Well no, its not going to change your life, you're still going to be who you are; you can't cure it, cant do anything, just got to work with it, then I'm going to need support to work with it and I know that people say that you should work in your special interest areas, but that wasn't working at work; I didn't think it was going to solve anything at work; if I had lost a leg it would have been a lot easer. I thought I might have euphoria, but I didn't; it was a non-event."

Did the clinician/diagnostician ask you to read and sign your diagnosis off?

"Yes, she did. They signed it later after she did it. She sent it through the post with a request for it to be signed and returned. No amendments or changes were requested or made. My wife read through it as well and didn't see the need for any amendments."

Probing question: Did you read it all? How did you feel when reading it?

"I did read it all. I found this a difficult question to answer as I didn't know what I was expecting to see in the assessment such as how technical it was supposed to be, but there were different quotes from the DSM criteria and how many I had to fill to reach the diagnosis, and what it would mean. It highlighted evidence; as far as she was concerned to say that I fitted the criteria. It didn't have an emotional effect as we just read it through without experiencing emotions."

Probing question: Were you given the opportunity to preview your report and comment on it before it was finalized?

"Yes"

What did you think of the language and the perspective in the report?

"It was all objective. It was understandable; she explained why she had reached her decision. She would pick out different criteria in the DSM and why I fitted it. I was happy with the language."

What were the recommendations on your assessment for a way forward?

"She went through my medical history, social interaction, childhood development, social interests and routine; she mentioned something called the AAA, communication, imagination, and motor co-ordination. She said that I was also displaying other traits. She advised me to read more about the syndrome in an effort to increase the understanding of myself and the effect it has on my communication and interaction with others. I was advised to avoid becoming over stressed, which will cause more Asperger traits; I need to have a place that I can retreat to in order to enable me time to process and get things back into gear. I find it difficult to express emotions etc. She didn't offer any specific groups and there are not any groups where I live. She just advised me to do some more research. There were no specific recommendations other than carry out more research for self-knowledge. The onus was on me."

On reflection

What is your perception now?

Probing question: Do you feel any different now, on reflection?

"It has taken a long time for me to be who I am. I am still having problems conforming as I am not allowing me to be myself. In retrospect I see my diagnosis as the right thing to do. I feel different on reflection now, although I am still looking for who I am, fully, I do feel different because I have an outside view of myself now, where as I didn't have one before. Before, when things were going wrong, I didn't know why, but I now feel that I have a bit more control of how I react to others and how they react to me, and although I don't feel more confident, I feel more informed of what to do and how to do and that if an issue comes up, how I can cope with it. Whether or not you like it, you have to fit in; so I think it was worth it as it has resolved some doubts in my head and I was encouraged and boosted by the fact that the occupational health doctor new this person very well and had a lot of respect which gave me more confidence in her assessment. Some of the tests are quite intricate but are for people who are much younger. I am confused about what I have learned normally as an adult in life, and that I had coping mechanisms, which I hadn't realized were coping mechanisms in situations where I panicked and had to leave; and I didn't know what that was about; I thought it was about blaming me. I am not blaming myself as much as I used to. I am still hiding my differences, but I see that as good as it is for the benefit of other people. I have seen people speak and they say 'if you don't like it then get out', but that's the way I am; I don't tend to do that because I am still trying to fit in and projecting a character that I haven't got. I am still having difficulty coming to terms with that and having a hard time saying to people this is how I think due to the responses of them saying what are you going to do about it then. There are still a lot of problems and conflict at work as there is

still an expectation that I can change and be able to do what everyone else does. I am frustrated by my workplace in that they don't understand Asperger's Syndrome and that it is my problem and that I can change and that is my responsibility. I have difficulty with situations where there are issues with metalizing on both sides, with the Burdon being firmly placed on me, such as being told that I must fit in etc."

Probing question: In hindsight, how could your diagnosis have been done better? What was good about the process? What was bad?

"If there were more family members it would have been more convincing for me, and if it had of been done sooner. I don't think there was anything bad about it. I don't know if I should be re-referred and that one assessment is enough. I have had a work problems assessment with occupational health and they have taken my diagnosis into account but until recently they haven't acted on it and no one has ever taken the diagnosis, such as the clinical depression component and put any recommendations into practice; they have just looked at it and then the process if finished. My diagnosis did not change anything regarding the workplace; everything went on as it did before; they just said 'so what'."

What impact has your diagnosis had on the understanding of who you are?

"This is something I am still trying to work out. I am realizing that I am different and that my brain works differently and that there is nothing wrong with that and that I am more than an individual than I was as I was trying to be like everyone else. I still find it difficult to concentrate and to keep focus."

Is there anything you would like to add?

"No"

Leanne Interview Data

Preliminary information

Current age: 51

Age when diagnosis was conducted: 44 (2006)

Current social and economic situation: Has two jobs but are both part-time, both term-time, doesn't have a salary. *"I'm in a scary financial position, because my youngest son is 19 he is still in full time education for the next few weeks. In September the child benefit will stop and so will the child tax credits and family tax credits so I will be about £200 a week worse off, which is scary." "The last few weeks since my dad died, my boy has been brilliant and helped loads, he's answered the phone when I can't talk to anybody and he just tells everybody to go away; he has coped fantastically; I don't know what I'd have done without him and he doesn't get any recognition for that and he shouldn't have to have that responsibility but it's just the way it is."* Leanne has two sons and a daughter; *"both of my son's have been diagnosed but my daughter hasn't although this doesn't mean she is not on the spectrum."*

What are your official diagnoses by name: Asperger Syndrome

Pre-diagnosis

Why did you seek a diagnosis?

"I can't think of a short answer to these questions, so please be patient with me. My young son who was in a special school and, the short answer is that I was doing research because a couple of people independent of each other said the he had traits of Asperger Syndrome/Autism. One was a teacher at an infant's school that he had been permanently excluded from and I can't remember who the other person was; he ended up going because he was permanently excluded fro three infant schools; that's pretty good going, so he ended up going to a special school, it was an EBD (educational and behavioral difficulties) school; he ended up being

sent their because I had tried for a long while to get help because there was clearly something going wrong with the lad, he wasn't coping in school so we went through two CAMHS (Child and adolescent mental health services); where I live, we live on the boarder between two counties so if you get a doctor referral it could either be from one county or the other; it's just the way it works when you're on the county boundary, so we got sent to CAMHS in one county and then in another county and we saw various other people and it was all very difficult when you have a child on your own isn't it. I took him back to mainstream where they were holding back on it and I was saying can you look into it, and they were saying that 'he couldn't be autistic because he could talk', then when going all through that, 'it's not easy bringing up a child on your own, is it?' So, I did some research and I went on to a number of websites and I recognized the symptoms, so I self-diagnosed, went along to the doctors with loads of information and books because they wanted to put my son into a mainstream school and I really wanted to make sure he got the best provision, and because two people in his educational process had suggested that he had traits of Asperger Syndrome or Autism, so I wanted it pursued especially as my previous attempt had fallen short when I saw an educational psychologist who said he couldn't be autistic because he can 1: talk 2: he could understand words like patronizing. It was funny because about a year ago I was telling son about this and he said 'who's ed Psych? I thought there is no better example of somebody being on the non learning-disabled end of the autistic spectrum. It's just perfect, isn't it! I did some research, I self-diagnosed, I went to the doctor with all the research I got and he asked 'why do you think you have Asperger Syndrome?'"

Probing question: How long did it take for you to seek a diagnosis?

"6 months"

Probing question: What knowledge of autism did you have prior to your assessment?

How did it come about?

"I told him that I was researching on behalf of my son, then I recognized the symptoms/traits in myself, then I went to my GP and she referred me"

What were your expectations prior to attending?

"This is where very personal, family history comes in. I was actually convinced that I did actually have Asperger's Syndrome, but I also have memories going back to my childhood of my mum saying 'why do you always have to have something wrong with you?' Why can't you just be normal?' 'Why can't you just be the same as everybody else?' "Why can't you be more like your sister?' 'Why do you always have to have something wrong with you?' 'Why do you always have to be center of attention?' and so on, very negative things and I was just thinking, maybe I'm just making it up' maybe I just have to have something wrong with me. I was arguing with myself, but hold on a second, I wasn't looking for something to be wrong with me; I was looking for an answer for my son; I was being a proxy and it wasn't about me it was about my son; I wanted to know what is the right thing to do for him, I wanted the right way forward, I want to know what his issues are. So, that was where I was coming from. Apart from this, I can't remember having any expectations prior to diagnosis."

Diagnosis

Can you take me through your diagnosis as you perceived and experienced it then?

Probing question: What were you thinking/feeling at the time?

"I think the overriding thing was how do I be autistic? When I realized I brought three books. I couldn't have picked three better books because they did what they said on the tin; yea, that's what it's like. So now I've got to learn how to be autistic; I spent so many years pretending to be normal, which didn't fucking work, but I don't know how to be autistic at all, so I was thinking crazy mad things." "I was thinking there was an interesting line in the skirting board; it was plastic skirting board and somebody made a really bad join and I was just looking at it all the time and she was wearing stripy trousers and ankle boots; I can't remember anything about what she looked like; I can just remember this wrong join in the skirting board in this little windowless office."

Probing question: What was the environment like? Was it suitable? Did they make adjustments to the environment?

"No, I don't think they did not. It was like they made a little office out of a bigger place, and they had not done the skirting board right and I was staring at it all the time thinking that was just wrong, and I cant answer any better than that. From what I have read since, I think the environment was very low arousal."

Probing question: Did you feel that you were receiving a 'full profile' assessment?

"Yes, at the time. Since then I have realized they didn't have a fucking clue how to do it."

Probing question: What level/type of professional conducted your diagnosis? Was this suitable?

"It was a person working in elderly mental health care and she must have downloaded this questionnaire off the Internet. She did the GADS test, which is aimed at children. So I have a Pervasive Developmental Disorder, but I was 44. You know what, they didn't have a fucking clue; they just pulled somebody off elderly mental health care; I was only 44, you know; it's a joke."

Post-diagnosis

How did you feel directly after the diagnosis procedure?

"Being diagnosed was a bit of a relief, because I knew a little bit about Munchausen Syndrome; it was something that was mentioned some years prior to me being diagnosed. Can you remember Beverley Allitt; She had Munchausen Syndrome by proxy; it was still a very recent memory and Munchausen Syndrome by proxy is apparently when you hurt people to bring attention to yourself where as Munchausen Syndrome is where you hurt yourself to attract attention to yourself, so I was shitting myself that I had Munchausen Syndrome and with my son I didn't want to look for something to be wrong with myself; it was to do with helping my son to get him the right schooling, so I was relieved that there was nothing wrong with me. I thought when they told me that they were going to tell me that I had mental health problems or something terminal; it was awful and I was so pleased and relieved when it was Asperger Syndrome; but I also knew at the same time that if I had this Asperger Syndrome, then my family are going down like skittles; then they did; first it was my sons, then my niece, then my brother and family in Australia that I have never even met; it's amazing."

Probing question: How or/and when did it hit you?

"Yes, because I was happy to have the label; I was really happy not to be mentally ill any more; I was really happy not to have to cope anymore; I was really happy not to have anything wrong with me anymore."

Did the clinician/diagnostician ask you to read and sign your diagnosis off?

"I can't remember; I think she said the 'I am 95% sure you have Asperger Syndrome'; with the percentages she said that 'we always like to leave a little bit of room for doubt, just incase it's wrong' so they can say the we were 5% right. I don't need to say anymore, do I?"

Probing question: Did you read it all? How did you feel when reading it?

"I read it all because it wasn't very long. The first word I remember thinking was 'vindicated'."

Probing question: Were you given the opportunity to preview your report and comment on it before it was finalized?

"I don't think it was applicable."

What did you think of the language and the perspective in the report?

"The language was ok and fine. I didn't know what to expect; so, they told me I had Asperger Syndrome and I recognized that I had Asperger Syndrome; they told me that I probably had Asperger Syndrome with a 95% probability, so I was fine with that; I was a bit disappointed that I failed in getting 100%"

What were the recommendations on your assessment for a way forward?

"There was nothing in writing, but she said that she wasn't going to put me forward for any counseling because (to the best of my memory) 'you've got through all these things without any help; you should be fine'. At the time I didn't argue with it but in hindsight I would argue with it a lot; I think it should come as standard; if it had been a health issue; oh, congratulations Leanne, you have cancer; no, if it were a health issue, if it were any other sort of issue, you would be put forward. 'You've got through this far', right, you've had a broken leg all your life, you were born with a displaced hip; there's no point, is there. I wasn't even given a contact number; I think it's shit when you get diagnosed as an adult, and I was a mature adult of 44, I had got married, had three children, I own my own house, I've worked and had jobs etc. What makes people think that you don't need help! I can talk; I am really fucking good at pretending to be normal. When you go there should be a follow up which should be mandatory. You get a diagnosis follow up should be mandatory; it doesn't matter whether its physical, mental; what's the difference; why would there be any difference between cancer and neurological difference."

On reflection

What is your perception now?

Probing question: Do you feel any different now, on reflection?

"Yes I do feel different now on reflection because I've had a few years to get used to the idea that I'm autistic. My life has begun to make sense. Before I got my diagnosis I recognized that I had been hurt a lot, and I just want to say that if my hurt can help somebody else to hurt a little bit less, then my life has been a life worth living. Since my diagnosis, I have been put in a position where I can really help other people to

be able to communicate with their children, to be able to understand themselves. One student who I work with recently said that I like working with you because you know what it's like, and that's a really good thing. By helping other people it gives us community. I've said this before, if people would just look at us as a culture, and we live in a multi-cultural society and people can embrace other cultures; it's a culture, and that's an easier thing to understand than a disability."

Probing question: In hindsight, how could your diagnosis have been done better? What was good about the process? What was bad?

"In all honesty I had already been masticated in the jaws of all these systems and processes before; it could have been done better; I wasn't expecting anything except to be sitting in an office talking to somebody; that was my expectation; I was 44; the first time I stepped into a psychiatrist office I was 9; you are brought up with it."

What impact has your diagnosis had on the understanding of who you are?

"Its vindicated me; there is nothing wrong with me; it's helped me to recognize who I am; it's helped my children and other people I am close to; its given me a job, well kind of. Its allowed me to be who I should have been or who I was meant to be; I like who I am. I liked that fact that my dad was very positive about it."

Is there anything you would like to add?

"I was going to say something about gender; as a child I had three ambitions:

1. *To read as well as they did on Jackanory*
2. *To be funny*
3. *And to be a boy*

I managed two out of three; I'm still working on being funny."

Natalie Interview Data

Preliminary information

Current age: 39

Age when diagnosis was conducted: 38

Current social and economic situation: Married with 5 children. Currently a qualified Science teacher and stay at home mum. Runs an autistic group.

What are your official diagnoses by name: Asperger's syndrome (no additional diagnoses)

Pre-diagnosis

Why did you seek a diagnosis?

"One of my children (6 at the time) was having some problems at school and I researched his particular type of behavior and suspected that he fitted onto the autistic spectrum, specifically Asperger's Syndrome. I took him for a diagnosis with a really long list of attributes, he was seen by a speech and language therapist, pediatrician and an occupational therapist, he was diagnosed with ASD(Asperger type). I decided to research different things that would help him at school because the school were awful, and through that process I found more and more things that were actually relevant to me. So, I knew that I was the same, and I procrastinated for about a year whether I wanted to be diagnosed, and in the end I decided yes because I didn't want him to feel alone. I wanted to be able to tell him that mummy's the same; it's fine, I'm fine, you're fine and you can have a good life, because I found that the whole clinical side of it was very negative and I don't feel it needs to be negative."

Probing question: How long did it take for you to seek a diagnosis?

"A year"

Probing question: What knowledge of autism did you have prior to your assessment?

"An awful lot of knowledge I've developed from research from various sources. I read all and anything I could about AS, including information specific to women."

How did it come about?

"I went to my GP after I had just had my youngest child for a post-natal chat, and I had the most stressful time getting there. Everything went wrong and I was running late, I hate being late, so I went in and she did the talk about how do you feel about having your baby, and I said that I'm a bit stressed. Then I just burst into tears and said oh, I think I may have AS, and she said 'it's alright dear, you're probably just a bit depressed', and fobbed me off. Three months later I went back in a more coherent form and saw another doctor, and just described what I was like as a child, and said that my son has been diagnosed, and I just want to know. I feel that I didn't need anything, but I would like to know so I could tell him that you're the same as mummy, and she sent me to a hospital, which has a specialist Asperger's unit. I saw a speech and language therapist first who made me do AQ10, which is a shortened AQ test, and asked me lots of questions to make sure I wasn't depressed or having psychiatric problems. I must have passed because I then went to a clinical psychologist a few months later, who put me through an official diagnosis, and told me at the end that I have passed the test and that I do indeed have AS. This was all based where I was living."

What were your expectations prior to attending?

"I expected it to be quite clinical and quite formal. With the speech and language therapist it was actually quite nice, she was friendly and I felt quite relaxed and she was quite chatty. With the clinical psychologist, she was far more formal, but she believed in the whole neurodiversity angle because she was very positive, which surprised me as I wasn't expecting that. It was pretty much what I expected, not one of the tests though because it was a children's test, which was a surprise. I had to read this children's book, and it felt slightly patronizing as I had to mimic brushing my teeth and things which made me feel a bit of a wally."

"I suspect that the speech and language therapist is probably paid less than the clinical psychologist; she's probably the one who screens you to see if you're on the right track and I think it's the psychologist who does the real diagnostic work. I think it's a bit of a buffer to make sure you have gone to the right place. That was my perception of it."

Diagnosis

Can you take me through your diagnosis as you perceived and experienced it then?

1. Diagnosis of self: *"That was a strange experience. I took the AQ test online and got 37 and I thought my husband would do worse, and he did it and performed fine, and that's a real shock. I thought there's something wrong with me, I'm defective and I felt quite depressed, then I did some more reading and research and then I realized that I am just different, and I was just quite cross about the clinical things I have read and the negative things I have read, and then discovered this whole other ethos, and then I just felt extremely positive. I wanted to bring my children up to be positive*

and also to reach out to other people and really dispel the whole myths of us having something the matter with us, so ultimately I feel very positive and very empowered, but also very frustrated. This positivity comes from me realizing that all my life I have been in these situations where people were really negative and I just didn't know how to deal with it. I felt that I was somehow useless and really blamed myself whereas I was just dealing the negative social behavior of other people who should have been well enough behaved not to have manifested it, so I suddenly realized that none of this is my fault. I have a different kind of brain, I'm smart, not defective and I just find the whole thing really interesting. I quite like learning for real that I am different rather than this horrible suspicion that I've had all my life, and wondering why the hell I don't fit in. So I approached it from that kind of angle."

Probing question: What were you thinking/feeling at the time?

2. Diagnosis by the psychologist: *"I was quite frightened because I had read some quite damning things about people with Asperger's as parents and I was quite worried that because I was being diagnosed that someone would tell social services and they would come snooping around my family with all these awful suspicions, so I was quite paranoid and a little bit worried. Before the diagnosis I cleared that up and asked if this diagnosis could be used against me, am going to be judged? Actually I'm not, they don't do that, and once she had reassured me that no, because I have never done anything wrong, that wouldn't happen, I went through the process and it was almost, well, I didn't really feel anything at all, I didn't really feel anything at all other than lets get to the end of it and you can just tell me and I'll have my piece of paper and that's that and I can move on."*

Probing question: What was the environment like? Was it suitable? Did they make adjustments to the environment?

"I don't think they take on board that some people have sensory issues because they had buzzing strip lights. I can deal with it, it annoys me but there may be others with worse sensory issues than me and I felt that was a strange thing to have in a place where you were conducting these types of tests. I thought that would be a really obvious one not to have. There were no questions such as "is the lighting ok?" "how did you feel about the level of sound", it was just straight into it as the psychologist wanted to get me out of the way as she had a lot of other work to do, so I felt like I was being a nuisance in some sort of way. I think these people have an air of importance about them and you're just another one who has turned up who is going through the same process. This was done through the NHS and I didn't have to pay for it. We are very lucky as we have this dedicated unit that does diagnosis."

Probing question: Did you feel that you were receiving a 'full profile' assessment?

"No. I wrote them a letter of documentation before I went and mentioned that I clearly had some sensory issues and issues with noise which I self manage, I tend to try my best to just ignore, but deep down I find it quite painful at times although I have learned to live with it. I also have issues with touch and sensations as well. I had written to them about that and when I got my diagnosis through the post it said that no sensory issues have been reported. I guess I have lived 39 years and I've put up with it, I cut the labels out of clothes and people know not to touch me if I'm upset. They did no sensory test. I gave them the information on the day and they didn't bring it up at all. I have issues with taste as well so it's quite clear that I have a different sensory system, I guess that's just fine."

Probing question: What level/type of professional conducted your diagnosis? Was this suitable?

"I had a clinical psychologist. I don't know if she was suitable or not. She decided that I fitted the diagnosis. She said at the beginning of the meeting that she would have to go away and discuss it, and at the end of the meeting she just told me straight out and said that their was no ambiguity she was quite sure that I fitted the criteria, so I guess she was competent. She said that she would have to discuss it with her colleague, she said that "I probably won't be able to tell you today, I'll have to discuss it with my colleagues", and then at the end she just told me, so I guess if somebody is a bit ambigious, that maybe she has to have a conversation with the Speech and Language Therapist. I think sometimes people are invited back for further assessment, but I must be a screaming aspie! I just hanged loose and didn't behave myself or anything. She went and asked me about Star Trek, silly woman…

Post-diagnosis

How did you feel directly after the diagnosis procedure?

"I was still a little bit worried about if it would have a negative impact on my family, knowing in my self and being secret, obviously I'm in complete control of who knows and who doesn't know, having it on your medical record as a disorder, I am still uncomfortable because I don't view it as a disorder, and it does concern me the next time I have to visit the GP and when it comes up on the screen, does that mean that are not going to believe me when I'm not well, because GP's, I don't think have a very good knowledge of the condition."

Probing question: How or/and when did it hit you?

"The diagnosis? That was when I self diagnosed. I went through a range of emotions. There was no doubt in my mind. I completely fit the pattern. With the formal diagnosis I wasn't surprised at all as I was so sure I was right. It was almost like jumping through hoops to get it on paper. When I self diagnosed it answered a lot of questions. I did a lot of work on myself regarding depression and I thought I had eliminated every issue I had apart from being a bit rubbish when people are being hostile and I thought that there's the last little part I need to just sort out, and of course it didn't quite pan out how I expected, I havn't turned into this social guru who knows everything, but I have worked out that I am different."

Did the clinician/diagnostician ask you to read and sign your diagnosis off?

"Yes, she did, and I had another meeting where I had to go in and discuss it. She had a few things – I wasn't entirely sure that she understood some of my answers, but maybe that's part of the issue. I just signed it and said there you go. She just sat and watched me read it, she did try and hurry me up."

Probing question: Did you read it all? How did you feel when reading it?

"I was horrified actually with some of the bits. She asked me to define friendship, especially with a friendship with one of my friends I had known since I was 5 years old and this is a person I love and respect, she is like my sister, and she said define friendship and I said 'well, its more than superficial interaction, isn't it'? she put it on my report, and I thought my god I sound like an android. I did say it; it was the first thing that popped into my head. The fact that it turned up on my letter; I hadn't thought that it would appear, and I thought that I sounded so uncaring. I went back to the meeting and I said that no, I love my friends, she said that's not what you said,

and I said no it isn't, that's interesting isn't it. What would you say to a stranger? would you gush emotion?I generally wouldn't."

Probing question: Were you given the opportunity to preview your report and comment on it before it was finalized?

What did you think of the language and the perspective in the report?

"It was alright. It was very formally written of course. I felt that it had a clinical slant on it, but I guess it is a diagnosis, and that's right. I would like to see more as – we've established that have a different neurological type, and that's really exciting, but it was very much that it was Asperger's Syndrome and I had the following difficulties in childhood blah blah. It felt a bit like we care but not now. It made me feel a little bit uncomfortable but I don't think the GP's even read them; I think they just read the first page."

What were the recommendations on your assessment for a way forward?

"They said that I could go to their social skills training group. I'd like to do that just to see how it's done because I might be able to pick out elements to use with my children, and they asked if I had any interest in joining a women's group, which I did, but they haven't actually sent me the information. It's been about a year now and I haven't chased it up either. They are NHS based groups. They have them at the hospital where all the psychiatric patients go, so I was quite perturbed, like going to a place for diagnostics where they have all the people who are sectioned in there, so it made me feel uncomfortable to be going into that type of environment. You don't see any of it; the place is so quiet, it's dead, I didn't see anybody on my way round, and it's just the department of learning disabilities tucked around the back, but I was concerned and I said to my husband 'oh my god, having it here, I don't want to go in

there because I don't have any psychiatric problems', but I guess for them it was a logical place to put it."

On reflection

What is your perception now?

Probing question: Do you feel any different now, on reflection?

"Having gone through this whole process of discovery? I think I'm very fortunate to have this service near by, because I've heard of people who struggle with diagnosis. I think it's quite backward in its approach, I think the whole clinical approach to it is a bit irritating. After diagnosis it would be very nice for them to give you a talk about what it really means rather than just to give you this label and assuming that you know because if someone goes along and they haven't done a lot of background work, they are going to think that they have some awful detrimental condition, and that they are disabled, and I don't think that is the right perception; that's not certainly not how I feel about it for myself and my family, so I would like to see some changes in that regard. I would like it to be viewed as a positive and for people to be shown how to move forward, how to use their strengths, as apposed to being a social deficit and communication issues. It just feels all a little bit insulting. I have realized why the negative things have happened to me, but it could be someone younger who has been diagnosed, that may not be glaringly obvious to them and they may need to be guided through why they were bullied, what happened, was it your fault? was it the negative behavior of others? and how do you manage this in the future, as apposed

to them just sending you a letter saying you have Asperger's Syndrome. There isn't really anything for adults; I mean there's the social skills group, but I never got an invitation to that, and there's the women's groups that I asked about. They said that there are different sorts of women at the group and that some of them go on go on about their interest, some of them don't talk, some of them have had a hard time, so I just thought that sounds great, you know, you really sold it to me there. I think in terms of actually educating people in terms of what it means for them, they don't want to do anything."

Probing question: In hindsight, how could your diagnosis have been done better? What was good about the process? What was bad?

"I think for me, the speed at which I was seen and diagnosed was very good. I probably would have been seen even sooner but I insisted that I had my appointment in the school holidays so that my husband was off work. So the speed was good, I think it's nice to have a dedicated place to go to. I think the process needs to be pretty much what it is as they are looking for things that are very hard to see so I think giving questionnaires and tests that show up your differences are probably the only tools they have, but I think post-diagnosis, there needs to be more for people."

What impact has your diagnosis had on the understanding of who you are?

"It's filled in the final piece of the puzzle for me as to why I'm different. I suppose that I always know I was different, and it's very peculiar actually, I remember in my teens when I was depressed I thought I must be nuts, and that's not a very nice way to feel about yourself, so it's nice to know that I'm not nuts. I guess for a long time I have decided that I don't really get on with very many people and I never knew why, and now I know why, and I think it is very useful, I have certainly enjoyed the community

where I have just started this group where I want to help and enable others if I possibly can and I think it's been positive."

Is there anything you would like to add?

"No"

<u>**Rachel Interview Data**</u>

Preliminary information

Current age: 39
Gender: Transgender (male to female, currently in transition)

Age when diagnosis was conducted: *"When I went to see the Doctor for depression I think he initially figured out I had Asperger's, I was 28 (2002) at the time but it wasn't until I was 30 (2004) that I saw him again specifically for getting an Asperger's diagnosis from him."*

Current social and economic situation: *"I'm married and we have a mortgage and I'm an IT consultant and run a limited company and I do freelance web design work as well"*

What are your official diagnoses by name: *"I think its Mild Asperger Syndrome. I've not got depression at the moment but did have in 2002. I think the main reasons for that were a mixture of relationship problems with a previous relationship and it was around the first anniversary that my father had died and things were getting stressful at work as well, so with all that going on together it caused depression at that time."*

Pre-diagnosis

Why did you seek a diagnosis?

"Around 2003 to 2004, when I was in the early stages of the relationship with a lady who I went on to marry, she suspected that I might have Asperger's, having noticed some traits within me that she recognized from the son of a work colleague who also had Asperger's, and then she suggested that I should get a diagnosis of it just so there is a record of it."

Probing question: How long did it take for you to seek a diagnosis?

"It was fairly quickly to arrange an appointment; it was only a few weeks as this was done privately, because I had seen him for the depression and that was paid for

by health insurance I had with the company I was working for at the time; I think I probably paid myself for the Asperger's diagnosis. I have a feeling that rather than go through my GP, I went directly to him, as I had already seen him for the depression, although I did get a GP referral for the depression at the time."

Probing question: What knowledge of autism did you have prior to your assessment?

"Yes, I had quite a decent understanding of Autism before then as well; mainly through books and the internet."

How did it come about?

What were your expectations prior to attending?

"I expected that I would most likely have a diagnosis of Asperger's before actually attending."

Diagnosis

Can you take me through your diagnosis as you perceived and experienced it then?

Probing question: What were you thinking/feeling at the time?

"I wasn't particularly apprehensive, so I think it was just going on to see the Doctor and expecting him to say I have Asperger's, but not worrying too much about it. By knowing the Doctor before this prevented a lot of anxiety, because that last time I saw him I was in a lot worse state by a long way. I was in a very bad state of depression, so seeing him again when my mental health was ok; it really wasn't much of a problem. If it had been a stranger I think I would have been more

apprehensive, but because it was somebody I've met before, I didn't have that much fear."

Probing question: What was the environment like? Was it suitable? Did they make adjustments to the environment?

"Yes, it was basically a room at the clinic which is a private hospital in Somerset, so I think it was the same place I had been to before to see him previously. It was a private hospital; the parking was ok; it was in a suburban part and not in the center. In terms of sensory stuff, the kinds of things that trigger my sensory stuff is like a supermarket on a busy day is the type of environment that effects me the most because you've got the bright lights, people getting in your way, lots of noise, all the products of clashing colours on display at the same time. They didn't ask or make any adjustments."

Probing question: Did you feel that you were receiving a 'full profile' assessment?

"No, I think it was because I had figured out about my Asperger two years ago; it was just to rubber-stamp the fact that I had Asperger's. The time I saw him for depression was a more in-depth discussion and he noted that on my records at the time; the second time (for Asperger's) it was a quicker meeting. I was not aware of his inclination of Asperger's when I went to see him for depression. When I went to see him for the Asperger's diagnosis he said at the time the main focus was getting the depression treated and sorted, so he didn't want to cloud the issue with mentioning Asperger's. It was me who approached him for the Asperger diagnosis."

Probing question: What level/type of professional conducted your diagnosis? Was this suitable?

"Yes, it was a consultant Psychiatrist. Very much the right professional with the right qualifications."

Post-diagnosis

How did you feel directly after the diagnosis procedure?

"Good, I think – Just getting a name to it and just confirming that I had Asperger's after all; it also put my partner's mind at rest at the same time as well."

Probing question: How or/and when did it hit you?

"It didn't seem to be that much of a big deal to be honest. I guess it was something that I have lived with for some time before."

Did the clinician/diagnostician ask you to read and sign your diagnosis off?

"No, he just sent the letter off through the post. It was a letter saying that he had reached the conclusion that I had 'mild Asperger Syndrome'. He might have mentioned a couple of reasons. It was one sheet of A4."

Probing question: Did you read it all? How did you feel when reading it?

"Yes, I was ok, there wasn't a problem at all because it was what I expected. I felt good that I have got this on paper."

Probing question: Were you given the opportunity to preview your report and comment on it before it was finalized?

"I didn't ask to, so I guess I didn't in that case."

What did you think of the language and the perspective in the report?

"It just seemed fair enough; there wasn't any issues with it; the Language was fairly formal, but that's what I would have expected in a letter from a Psychiatrist."

What were the recommendations on your assessment for a way forward?

"There were no recommendations either verbal or written. I think that it was because it was a fairly mild case that he thought there was no action to be taken."

On reflection

What is your perception now?

Probing question: Do you feel any different now, on reflection?

"I think it's put things in to context a bit more about how, for example I try and avoid particular situations' now, like avoiding supermarkets during busy periods, because I know that's one of the triggers that freaks me out. Traffic jams as well and I've Never felt like I've fitted in to social situations involving alcohol, pubs and drugs either, so I suppose that kind of makes sense as well. Career wise it makes sense that I have gone down the path of working in IT. That seems like a popular career choice for people with Asperger's. The only times where I have told them at work is when I've made the tea."

Probing question: In hindsight, how could your diagnosis have been done better? What was good about the process? What was bad?

"The good was that it was a quick process and that he had already done the work about two years previously to the diagnosis. There wasn't any hassle in getting the diagnosis. What would have been better is some follow-up in terms of advice and support afterwards, but I guess because I did it off my own back via a private consultation instead of something more structured, this may have been the case. I could have gone back to my GP and asked for more information, but I didn't at that time."

What impact has your diagnosis had on the understanding of who you are?

"It's made quite a significant impact. It's made things a lot easier in terms of my marriage because my wife knows now that I have Asperger's specifically and we are both more accommodating of each other because she is disabled too and she has some mental heath issues including bi-polar and stuff; so we support each other. We know what makes each other tick and what situations to avoid. She knows never to send me to the supermarket in the middle of the day."

Is there anything you would like to add?

"I have good days and bad days. I find that if there are too many things going on at the same time, I find that difficult as well as prioritizing time."

Rod: Diagnosis can bring up issues of the past, which can be a good thing or a bad thing. With poor experiences it can make the person re-evaluate those past experiences and that could be a good thing or it could be a bad thing.

"That was the case with me because in secondary school I was a major target for bullies as I was bullied quite a lot, but at the same time I was bright academically, so I guess I threw a lot of effort into my schoolwork, which helped me."

Rod: Good you had an escape route.

"I was frustrated and board at primary school but found my interest in secondary School which is where I excelled. I left School with GCSE's and A-levels and went on to study chemistry at Oxford, and graduated with a 2.1 and then went on to work in IT not long after graduating. I did see an educational psychologist when I was about 7 because of behavioral issues and they said that I was in the top two percent of the population intellectually and I was put in contact with a national association for gifted children, which ran Saturday morning courses. I don't think I did as well as I expected at University due to difficulties adjusting to the different method of teaching compared to school. The whole gender thing, having transition has made it easer for me to cope with the Asperger's, ironically. I know somebody else who maybe interested in speaking with you. They also think they have Asperger's or something similar and they are in transition as well. The main differences (I believe) between Asperger's and Autism are that most people with Asperger's are good at communicating verbally and contextually, whereas a lot of people with Autism wouldn't be. I was lucky in the third year of secondary school onwards because a lot of the bullying occurred in the lunch hour and in morning break, but from the third year onwards, I used to go to an electronics club that was held in the physics lab in the lunch hour. Although we had electronics taught in the physics classed, the extra lessons made me more advanced in those lessons. The main worries at the moment are mainly financial and needing to find another IT contract fairly soon. Other than that, I think the main pressures have been my wife's ongoing health issues, who was in hospital for most of April with kidney failure and she was in intensive care, she

was that bad. She was disabled from birth with a spinal condition and has to use an electric wheelchair and a hoist, so her health isn't that good compared to most people. The other thing is that my Mother is in a care home with dementia and we are trying to sell her house to pay for care home fees. What gets me is that there is ex amount of people unemployed that don't have any illness or disability; they are not finding jobs, so if you've got an illness or disability, the employers are going to go with those without disabilities first, even though they are not meant to half the time. I don't see Asperger's in my case as any sort of major deficit; I just see it as thinking a bit differently, which ironically has benefited my career. Everybody should be treated with dignity."

Rod: We just socialize differently!

"Yes, I like to socialize with specialist groups. A lot of our friends are either involved in the LGBT or through my Asperger's group, or through the church. At school I found some subjects harder than others, but I just thrown more energy into those I guess. I like Science and chemistry and music. Being given a computer helped me with algebra. People with Asperger's have a much clearer idea of what is really going on behind the scenes and underneath the surface than a lot of NT's fed all the bullshit."

Russell Interview Data

Preliminary information

Current age: 58

Age when diagnosis was conducted: *"I was told unofficially by a psychiatrist with specialism in autism about 10 years ago (48 years old), then 3 years later I had an official diagnosis. (51 years old) I went back as I needed an official diagnosis."*

Current social and economic situation: *"I work full time for BT and I have worked since I was 16, I do work too hard for some of my peers and they don't like how much work I do; at home I am very lazy and I can't be bothered to do anything; I employ a cleaner to do everything; I'm divorced; I was married for 18 years; got divorced, again at age 48; I currently have a girlfriend whom I have been seeing for 8 years, but we don't live together; financially I am ok with no worries; I don't have any friends and I don't go out; If you took away all the professional people I know and my girlfriend, I wouldn't have anybody. I see a councilor and have regular massages. I find it hard to socialize in the normal way; there has to be something keeping us together, like work or school, in the school days. I have no children as I couldn't have any with my wife; I never found out why; we did have IVF for a few years."*

What are your official diagnoses by name: *"Asperger's Syndrome, Dyslexia, Dyscalculia, potential long-term memory problems Which I am trying to get assessed but its like banging my head against a brick wall, Depression, Stress and Anxiety, very poor sleep."* (These were all diagnosed separately but around about the same time – between the ages of 48 and 50)

Pre-diagnosis

Why did you seek a diagnosis?

"I became initially aware that this was a problem through a TV program, which covered a family where the husband had Asperger's; not long after that my wife left me, so all the old problems reared their head such in socializing and trying to find another partner; during that divorce I went to Relate, and for many weeks, it teared me apart; they look into everything, even what colored socks you're wearing, and it was with a view of getting me back together and not the marriage because it was

excepted that the marriage had broken down. One of the things we looked at was my intelligence and my abilities; it was then decided to investigate these things including whether I had got Asperger's, whether I'm Dyslexic and what my IQ was, which was high, where as I always thought I was below average, and I have now ended up in MENSA, which is unbelievable and has given me another interest."

Probing question: How long did it take for you to seek a diagnosis?

"The first one I saw, once he had interviewed me, he asked me why I wanted a diagnosis, and I said that I wasn't bothered about an official diagnosis or having a bit of paper; I just wanted to know what is happening; it has come to me realizing that something is wrong with me; something is stopping me from socializing in the normal way, particularly with women, finding partners and girlfriends. After the divorce I felt that I was back to square one, back to when I was in my teens and no better off, so I wanted to know what it was, and if it wasn't Asperger's then I'll carry on looking. He said that I had Asperger symptoms, so no need to look any further, but warned me that a diagnosis might damage my career, but I said that I wasn't bothered about an official diagnosis, and it was left at that. The reason I went back and saw a different Psychiatrist was that, even though I was working for the same company, I lost my post at work and had to find a new one, and they were trying to force people into call centers, and I knew that there was no way I could work in a call center; so I went to get an official diagnosis to help me with this, so that they would have to treat me as disabled and make reasonable adjustments for me."

Probing question: What knowledge of autism did you have prior to your assessment?

"Not a lot. I always thought of Autism as that of little kids in a world of their own, who don't communicate with people. This was my view of Autism before I knew

about Asperger's. Although I watched the program, I didn't conduct any research thereafter. It was only after the divorce that I was having real problems again that I started looking into it. I am still friends with my ex wife and she came with me to the assessment."

How did it come about?

"I initially went to my GP. He wouldn't refer me to anyone who specializes in Autism to start with; he just wanted me to go to my local mental health unit and be interviewed there. Fortunately, they then agreed to send me to a Psychiatrist who specialized in Autism. The second time I went, I paid for it privately, as I thought the NHS wouldn't be too happy if I went back wanting to go through it all again with the NHS paying."

What were your expectations prior to attending?

"With the first one, when I just wanted to know what was wrong, my expectations were that it was Asperger's and that I was hoping that I was right. I wasn't looking forward to putting in all the work, time and energy trying to find out what it was if it wasn't Asperger's. I was very unsure of myself back then and I didn't know that I was intelligent; I knew that I was different; I felt different; I felt that I couldn't get on with people like other people do, so I was searching for answers, and that with an answer I could do something about it and improve my life. I was nervous going to it. My wife supported me and she accompanied me to the assessment, even though she had announced that she wanted to leave."

"With the second one, I was still unsure because I believed that I didn't have the symptoms that badly, some of the people I have told since don't believe I have Asperger's as they can't see that I have a problem. So, I was nervous the second

time round but this surrounded the question as to whether I was bad enough to have a diagnosis, and I didn't know how this diagnosis thing worked, how bad you have to be to have a diagnosis. I was also worried about my job situation; without a diagnosis they would force me into an unsuitable post, which would make my mental health worse and leave me having to leave the job, and we don't like change."

Diagnosis

Can you take me through your diagnosis as you perceived and experienced it then?

Probing question: What were you thinking/feeling at the time?

"Regarding the official diagnosis, I was nervous going through the interview; I was quite upset, nye on crying; some of the questions I felt were (even for someone with Asperger's) too blunt and out of the blue, very personal questions that were just dropped on me out of the blue which I found very difficult to answer honestly to a stranger about. They were questions to do with my sexual life. My ex wife came a second time but the Psychiatrist didn't see her a second time as he obviously thought he didn't need her input as he had seen enough of me. It was difficult and I was very worried about the outcome, and if I didn't get a diagnosis, what else could I do. Psychiatrists do look back into childhood; unfortunately my parents are both dead and my youngest sibling was 8 years older than me, and they left home when they started work, so they weren't true brothers and sisters that I had, they were more like extra parents to me. I am very sure that one of my brothers has got it and both my ex wife and my girlfriend said oh yes, he's got it. They can see it and I can see it, and he's aware of it; I think that my brother is ignoring it for now."

Probing question: What was the environment like? Was it suitable? Did they make adjustments to the environment?

"The NHS one was very clinical, hospital type environment, the second one where the official diagnosis happened was at a private clinic so it was quite homely. The only problem there was that it was late in the evening so my ex wife was left waiting in a waiting room for the duration of the diagnostic process in a very cold environment with the heating turned off. They didn't ask me if any adjustments were needed to the environment. I have some sensory issues, but there was nothing that bothered me at the time of the interview."

Probing question: Did you feel that you were receiving a 'full profile' assessment?

"I think there could have been a fuller assessment of me and my life but maybe they only probed as much as they felt necessary because, certainly on the second assessment when I was officially diagnosed, I was quite upset, so they might have thought not to push it any further. They didn't discuss my other diagnoses such as Dyslexia, but they focused on what was bothering me, which was the interaction with other people component. This was within the social aspect, personal relationships, work and being asked to look at jobs in call centers as this is to do with people and being in a room full of my peers and dealing with the public. So, it was interaction with people, which was my big problem at the time."

Probing question: What level/type of professional conducted your diagnosis? Was this suitable?

"I think they were quite high up specialists in the field. On both occasions, one person was assessing me. I think they were appropriately qualified as one was a

professor, so they weren't any old local authority Psychiatrist's. They were not local professionals, but they were both psychiatrists, one of which was in Leister."

Post-diagnosis

How did you feel directly after the diagnosis procedure?

"I felt happy that I had discovered what it was and eager to find out more about it then because I hadn't looked into it much before diagnosis because I recognized that when one knows about the subject, even subconsciously, you could be presenting the symptoms that you have read about. So, I purposely didn't read up on it, but after diagnosis I found out quite a lot about it and joined support groups and things like that. I was happy and felt that perhaps that I could do something about it."

Probing question: How or/and when did it hit you?

"It was pretty instant but I felt relief and happier, and once I started reading up on it and going to support groups I almost felt a bit guilty because I saw people in the support groups who were a lot worse off than me, who couldn't get work, who couldn't have anywhere near a normal life. I felt some displacement where I didn't know which camp to put myself in, but I still go to a support group now after all these years, and there are those in the group who have classic Autism and Asperger's Syndrome as well other diagnoses; but I enjoy going because it's structured."

Did the clinician/diagnostician ask you to read and sign your diagnosis off?

"No, I can't remember that happening at all; I just got sent his report, which was copied to my GP. I think that the report consisted of 8 about pages."

Probing question: Did you read it all? How did you feel when reading it?

"I did read it; I was a bit annoyed that the clinician got something wrong; it was stated that I had raised a family, which was incorrect. It wasn't a big mistake and of no great consequence, so I never did anything about it."

Probing question: Were you given the opportunity to preview your report and comment on it before it was finalized?

No (read previous comments)

What did you think of the language and the perspective in the report?

"I thought it was ok; I didn't have any strong feelings about it."

What were the recommendations on your assessment for a way forward?

"To research more about Asperger's and to contact support groups. There was no mention of contacting any particular organization. I was advised to learn more about it."

On reflection

What is your perception now?

Probing question: Do you feel any different now, on reflection?

"I feel a lot different now. I think that because of my diagnosis and my need to improve, as I felt that I must improve to have a happier life, so I was driven to make the most of what I have got and also to try and learn all these skills that other people learn automatically. People have commented, with one person saying recently that I appear to be a lot more confident. I have learned that it's an ongoing thing that I just have to push myself to do things, because if I don't do them, then I will always

be poorly skilled at those things; unless I do them, I won't improve. I do protect myself from some things but the things I want to achieve have a cost associated with them, and that cost is that I have to put in the effort to keep on doing things and to learn from my mistakes in order to gain social skills; and unless I do that, I will just be lonely, depressed and unhappy; so I have to do things which are very uncomfortable perhaps initially, not perhaps in terms of going into a call center, but by joining organizations and groups and going to places on my own to mingle with a bunch of strangers and to try and socialize, and to also to learn the skills which I feel is totally different for example to differentiate between sexual relationships and personal relationships, which is a hard thing to do. I drove to Germany this year, I was prepared to go on my own, but I had someone to go with me, to a personal development workshop, and it's not the first one I have been to that this organization has run, but it was the first one in Germany I have been to. I do try to talk to people more."

Probing question: In hindsight, how could your diagnosis have been done better? What was good about the process? What was bad?

"The bad things were; it took quite a bit of time and I had to go via another health worker before I got to a specialist; I had to travel and it would have been better if there were more local facilities; it would have been really nice if I had some notice of what the questions would have been, as I am not very good at thinking on my feet and some of the questions can be a shock when they are read out to you and you are expected to answer. It could be that it is designed that way to highlight difficulties in answering the questions, if they are that clever. Post-diagnosis, there isn't a lot out there; the initial group I went to is an independent group which has been set up and run by a mother whose husband and son have been diagnosed with Asperger's; that was great to start with, but it has become too popular, too big

and too noisy, so I don't go any more as I don't enjoy it; when it was a really small group I enjoyed it. The second group I went to was one funded by the NHS and run by a Psychologist and that was really structured and like a formal meeting and the Psychologist facilitates the meeting; where as the other group was more of a social group, this was more structured where he made sure everyone had a chance to speak and he would control the ones who couldn't stop speaking and we did practical things such as designing leaflets for hospitals and they had speakers in who would educate us; such as a speaker on psychotic drugs and a speaker on benefits, which was of no interest to me. A lot of the others are on benefits and can't work. We had speakers from organizations who help disabled people into employment. That was quite a good group and it's the only one I still go to. It is no longer funded by the NHS and the group has to now find its own funding; so it's more like a business now, which is not as good because too much of time in the meeting is taken up as a business meeting, focused on who is doing what and where we are going to get funding from, so it's less enjoyable now. The third group I used to go to was run by a charity and every month they would just go out for a meal at various local pubs and restaurants and this was really nice as there would only be half a dozen of us and it was nice and quiet and by having a meal there was something for us to do, if we were just sat there supposingly socializing without a meal, I think a lot of us will just be staring into nothingness, but a meal gives you something to do. I went to this for about a year, but I stopped going because of health conditions related to diet. Those are the three groups I went to."

What impact has your diagnosis had on the understanding of who you are?

"I feel a lot better about myself and a lot more worthy and not as rejected by other people; I feel loved by some people now; I feel a lot closer to people; my girlfriend's family is great. The more people get to know me, the more they can see it in me;

when I first told my girlfriend, her reaction was to dismiss the diagnosis and say there is nothing wrong with me, but now she sees it and I have done and have said things which are inappropriate and she sees that I miss-reads things and take things literally."

Is there anything you would like to add?

"I wish that I was diagnosed earlier and that my intelligence didn't covered up my learning difficulties and my learning difficulties didn't covered up my intelligence (until I was 48). I think that children as early as possible should have their IQ tested, and then if their academic skills don't match up to their IQ then they should be investigated to see why they are not succeeding. It's not just the Dyslexia, Dyscalculia and the memory problems that are my learning difficulties, I think a lot of it is down to the Asperger's in that I have very narrow interests; anything outside that I don't want to know. I don't know whether I have a bit of ADHD, but I can't really read that well; I couldn't read a novel although I can physically read; my mind would be elsewhere, I also have trouble with hearing a little bit although there is nothing wrong with my hearing, it's just that if the environment is noisy, if there is more than one conversation going on at once, then I can't concentrate on what someone else is saying, so that obviously affects learning at school and the fact that by not socializing at school affects learning as well. I am pretty keen in saying that things should change for children; that children should be looked at better and assessed better and if they don't achieve in relation to their IQ level then they should be investigated and helped. I couldn't believe it when I had my IQ tested and I was in tears, I was crying. They told me that I was in the top one percent, and I left school with just a few CSE's. The English CSE, they wouldn't even let me take the exam I was that poor; they wouldn't even let me attempt it. I am a bit annoyed that I could have got a lot of help in the early days, which would have made my life a lot different. My IQ was

tested after going through the diagnosis of Asperger's, but they were all within the same few years. There was the Asperger's, the Dyslexia/Dyscalculia diagnosis, and the long-term memory problems came out, and my marriage broke up, I lost my post at work, I found out that I was very intelligent; all this happened within the space of two to three years. I am not sure whether it would have been helpful to have all these elements tested at the same time because I believe that it is better to see a specialist rather than to see someone who is a jack-of-all-trades; so I am unsure which would be better. I do believe that the professional who diagnosed my Asperger's should consider the co-morbid elements to give some idea of what else might be a problem and point the individual towards other professionals in whatever field is appropriate; but with me, they didn't seem to look at other problems."

Appendix G

Analysis/Coding Level 1 and 2

Christine: Matrix 1 (Private diagnosis)

Current age: 40

Age when diagnosis was conducted: 32 (2005)

Current social and economic situation: *"I'm out of work I am applying to go back to university but I need funding to do that. I am in quite a vulnerable economic situation: having had a very disheartening experience in trying to find disability support in the workplace and having left that workplace where I was unhappy and now wanting to go back to university in middle life. I have years of experience and good qualifications but don't see myself being able to cope in a mainstream workplace. I need to do other things with my life, but economically I feel, no I am very vulnerable."*

What are your official diagnoses by name: Asperger Syndrome (Diagnosed dyslexic aged 6)

Questions	Responses	Analytical memos
	Pre-Diagnosis	
Why did you seek a diagnosis?	*"I have been aware all my life that there was something different about me that I couldn't explain, and I was very confused about why other people found it easy to make friends and I didn't, and why other people were coping at work, and I wasn't; I just couldn't explain this. I felt like a complete failure as a human being and I hadn't put two and two together at all. It was somebody who I knew socially who had a mental health background, and who had observed me in a number of social situations who said to me one day, after a great deal of thought because she was quite worried about saying it, she said, 'I think you might be on the Autism Spectrum.'"*	Christine is talking about difficulties that she couldn't explain and yet it was someone she knew socially who had observed her in a number of situations. Autism is seen to be a social difficulty and yet it was someone she knows socially who recognized the difficulties; it's a paradox. Her mother was a primary school teacher, recognizing Christine as being dyslexic. Why is it that her other diagnoses were not picked up on after Asperger's being in the diagnostic manual for so long?

Christine's main difficulties seem to be with the workplace and her workplace paid for the assessment privately. |

		She does regret not having a diagnosis earlier; because she feels that had she had the right support earlier on it would have been a less depressing and less overwhelming experience.
	"I do regret not having a diagnosis earlier than the age of 32, because I think that if I had had the right support in my life in adolescence then growing up would have been a less depressing experience; a much less overwhelming experience and I wouldn't have put myself in situations which were very stressful situations and failed to cope, as an adult I was still choosing the wrong situations like jobs, for example." "After the friend said that she thought I was on the spectrum I said to my disability adviser at my workplace (she was already supporting me with dyslexia and had worked in a number of other organizations with autistic people) that this friend of mine said that I may be on the spectrum, and she didn't consider it to be an out-of-the-world suggestion that I could be on the spectrum, and it was she who arranged my diagnosis, which my workplace paid for."	
How long did it take you to seek a diagnosis?	"It wasn't very long at all, it was almost straight away that I went to see the disability adviser at work. It didn't take very long for my workplace to refer me for a diagnosis. The part that took time was my employer approving the funding, but once it was approved it didn't take more than a month or so. It was fairly straightforward as far as I remember."	Quicker referral than the NHS.

What knowledge of autism did you have prior to diagnosis?	"Not much really; I had heard of it; when I was at primary school, She could be described as fairly severely autistic, although I don't like that phraseology. She was the only person who I really knew who had the diagnosis of autism. I didn't see myself as being like her."	Some of the participants' views of 'autism' are that of the classically 'autistic' child and or person.
	"I had family members who were part of that generation who were never diagnosed, and I had known them all my life. My grandfather, his daughter –my aunt, and I was very aware of our family's politics where the behavior of these family members was odd and had never been explained. So it was quite a negative thing for me to identify with them."	Family connection is highlighted, like the other participants. She, like others, has recognized generations of her and their family who were never diagnosed. If you grow up in a family whereby 'autism' is not recognized and is accepted as the norm then how does a young child in that family figure out they're 'autistic'?
	"In terms of autism itself, I didn't know very much about it; I started to read about it and so re-defined myself. I wish I had known earlier that I was autistic, that my behaviour followed an autistic pattern and that there are other people like me. I knew I was different because of my dyslexia but I also knew that I wasn't exactly like other dyslexic people. I knew that there was something about me that I couldn't explain. I had grown up with some autistic people who were not necessarily a very positive part of my family life; I hadn't joined all the dots, but when I read a books on autism I began to piece things together."	Maybe she knew far more about 'autism' from lived experiences in her family setting with her grandfather, however, maybe what she wasn't so aware of was the medical view. This aspect of identity comes up, like the others' accounts. Maybe a part of the report has to do with the person's identity. One of the recommendations is that an 'autistic' person is being asked to read what it is like to be 'autistic'.

	"This reading began mainly after diagnosis; I read some of the books recommended to me on my diagnostic report and then over the years found other things. I think that I was fairly ignorant prior to my assessment and if I had understood autism's messy history with the mental health profession and how diagnosis worked before I asked my GP for diagnosis I would not have allowed my GP to refer me to a mental health team or even used an NHS service at all, but because I didn't have this knowledge diagnosis was mishandled and I was blocked from accessing services."	Across a range of participants: some Clinicians recommend books and some don't. A Clinician should have a wide range of literature they are aware of and should recommend books that reflect the individuals' identity.
What were your expectations prior to attending?	"That I would simply be diagnosed as Autistic, that the diagnostic process would make sense, that I would be able to get some form of support as a result of diagnosis; I was quite naive regarding the types of support that were available. I thought I would be helped to gain a better understanding of myself and helped to cope better in the world."	A person who's seeking a diagnosis should have a knowledgeable advocate.

Diagnosis

Can you take me through your diagnosis as you experienced it then?	*"I was interviewed; the interview did look at some of my childhood behavior, but it also talked about who I was as an adult."*	
What were you thinking/ feeling at the time?	*"I was nervous about the actual process, and I think the overwhelming feeling I have about this experience, although I can't really remember what I was feeling eight years ago, was that I wish that someone had told me that I was autisitc as a teenager, and I had gone through my high school years knowing the truth about myself, and that so many years of my life had been wasted, the unproductive, depressed years where I didn't understand myself, the years when I knew there was something wrong but didn't know what it was when I was receiving silly advice from well meaning people but was feel a failure because I couldn't cope in the way other people expected me to none of these years need have been wasted and I needn't have been so depressed and alone and stressed out. Why did no one tell me I was autistic before."*	If Christine had been assessed as a child, she may have been recognized under DSM-I or DSM-II (autistic thinking, although not a diagnostic entity) as her birth year is 1973. Note: This manual at the time was used primarily in institutions.
What was the environment like?	*"The center where I was diagnosed had clearly been designed to be a low-arousal environment."* *"The environment was suitable".*	

Was it suitable?	"They had clearly set out the building so it was a low-arousal environment, and they knew exactly what they were doing in terms of serving autistic people."						
Did they make adjustments to the environment?	N/A						
Did you feel that you were receiving a 'full profile' assessment?	"I feel that the first assessment was an interview with me as an adult about my life, which was handled by someone who knew what she was looking at (thinking difference disability); able to ask the right questions; the interview went on for 45 minutes, then the psychologist had the information she needed and she could draw a conclusion."						
What level/type of professional conducted your diagnosis?	"I was seen by a very well-known clinical psychologist and that was a very constructive experience, I thought that I was treated with respect."						
Was this suitable?	"She knew about autism and from a background of seeing it as a thinking difference. She did not know about other forms of neuro-diversity."						
Post-diagnosis							
How did you feel directly after the diagnostic procedure?	"I felt great, I got an answer; this explains what's been going on in my life; it didn't solve the issues in my life but it did give me a explanation of what was going on."						
How/or/and/when did it hit you?	"My understanding of autism has developed over time and it's taken a long time to get to grips with living with different aspects of autism."						

Did the clinician/ diagnostician ask you to read and sign your diagnosis off?	"The psychologist didn't really know how to write a report that was suitable for the workplace. Some of the evidence for my diagnosis, incidences of being bullied at primary school, were going to be seen by my employer. I did not want people at work seeing this, so I asked for the report to be changed. The psychologist wanted the evidence left in for clinical reasons so the solution that the disability advisor at work came up with was she (the disability advisor) would write a summery report for my Human Resources records which just talked about my needs at work as an autistic person and didn't go into detail about my childhood or negative experiences in my adult life."	
Did you read it all?		So you have a report that you are left with stating that you are 'autistic' yet you can't show anyone the evidence, as the information is too inappropriate.
How did you feel when reading it?	"I felt that while it was very useful to have a diagnosis, the report was not something I wanted to show anyone; it talked about difficult instances in my life (the evidence for the diagnosis), the one from the psychologist, talked a little bit about autism but neither report explained autism; they weren't documents that I could use to explain autism to people like employers, this is what it means to be me. (This might not be their job)"	
Were you given the opportunity to preview your report and comment on it before it was finalized?	"That was something I had to ask for and not something that was offered to me, and I had to say not to send it to my employer. I was surprised how badly drafted the report was, poorly written and in it's tone and content totally unsuitable to be sent to someone's employer."	

| What did you think of the language and the perspective in the report? | *"I think in order to be of any use to anyone who is newly diagnosed and to be useful to the people that person will need to share the report with, the people writing the reports need to be very clear about terminology. Reports need to be accessible to lay people, they need to be in plain English, they need to be written in a professional tone. I didn't need people in my workplace to start questioning my diagnosis and looking at the evidence, they simply needed to be informed that I was on the spectrum. I think that clinicians aren't necessarily very skillful in terms of writhing reports, knowing they are going to have different audiences, that GP's and family members and autistic people themselves, as well as employers are going to have to make sense of this document. I think that what psychologists need to produce is simply a document that says, 'I confirm that this person is on the autistic spectrum', and then perhaps a fuller report for the actual person on the spectrum saying 'this is the evidence I have considered and why I reached the conclusion I came to', so that psychologist are not put in the role of having to produce legal evidence which isn't their skillset, or evidence which is going to be mangled by someone who doesn't really understand."*

"There is also an issue with using medical terminology like 'disorder'. Reports must make clear what is being diagnosed but not leave the person the report is about feeling that they are a broken version of an non-autistic person. We don't diagnose men as having a masculinity disorder which means they are defective compared to a female norm. It's the same with autism, it is perfectly valid to be autistic." | She feels that Clinicians aren't very good at writing reports for different audiences.

Report needs to talk to the person, and also different audiences. It needs to be in plain English with professional tone.

A straightforward document could state "We deem this person to be 'autistic'" due to the following evidence......

It seems that this participant particularly sought a diagnosis in relation to things at her workplace, yet realized thereafter that it is pervasive. |

What were the recommendations on your assessment for a way forward?	*"The psychologist, when she gave me her report, had recommended reading so I could go and find out more about autism, and she knew that I would be going back to the workplace with the disability adviser who had referred me and could follow this up."* *"With the psychologist's assessment I was simply being referred back to my workplace, yes I was autistic and so needed support. The psychologists' expertise wasn't in what support I would need in the particular job I had. She recommended some reading so I could understand autism, which was a start for me to understand my diagnosis and advocate for myself at work. The report may have made one or two comments about the workplace but I think that the report was just being handed back to HR at my workplace who would then have brought in experts on autism to have my workplace needs assessed. I've met some inexpert experts on autism in the workplace and the needs assessment process is hit and miss, but that can't be resolved by the diagnostic report writer."*	
On reflection		
What is your perception now? Do you feel any different now, on reflection?	*"It's been a long journey; it has surprised me how long it has been."*	

In hindsight, how could your diagnosis have been done better?	"The process with the psychologist was good but in terms of robust evidence it could have been stronger (more examples from my life about ways I behave and things I find hard) and in terms of a useful document at the end which I could have shown to people without shame it could have been better; in terms of signposting of services apart from the workplace it could have been better."	The people/individuals who seem to have gone private feel it's been a constructive experience. Yet they're given a report, but there is no follow-up. Does the actual report they are provided with suit their individual needs? The diagnostician and Clinician did not know how to write a report that's suitable for a work place. So what is the purpose of a report? What is the function?	
What was good about the process?			
What was bad about the process?			

What impact has your diagnosis had on the understanding of who you are?	"It has confirmed to me the truth about who I am. I'm autistic, this helps me understand myself, I'm not guessing I'm autistic, it is a fact, the truth about who I am. My own further reading on autism has helped me to understand who I am, so diagnosis was the starting point on that journey for me to understand whom I am and to try and un-learn all the stuff I had been told throughout my life, which was well intentioned nonsense and to try and put in place things that will work for me and to change the way I think about myself and that is a surprisingly difficult thing to do; I still try and allow myself to be myself and try and find things that work for me, and find ways of trying to hold relationships together that work for me, and not feel that I have to be what everyone else is; and that is still something I don't feel I am able to do at age 40, which is ridiculous; I just feel that most of my life has been wasted and I'm still on the journey of trying to put together things that most people work out as teenagers to be honest."	Self-reflection after diagnosis; she wishes she had been diagnosed as a teenager. Mourning after late diagnosis. This aspect of reflecting upon one's life and knowing how it could have been different. Basically, "You've had a wasted life, congratulations."
Is there anything else you would like to add?	"No"	

Christine: Matrix 2 (NHS diagnosis)

Questions	Responses	Researcher's Interpretation and notes
	Pre-Diagnosis	
Why did you seek a diagnosis?	*"My particular case is a rather messy one because I then went to my GP and said I needed mental health services, which were relevant to autistic people, and the local hospital where such services are delivered kicked up a fuss and said oh no, we only treat people we have diagnosed ourselves, which I thought was totally ridiculous because people could of course move into the neighborhood, and why is one diagnosis different from another? But I went along with this because they were the only service provider in my area, so I went for an NHS diagnosis at this local hospital."*	The NHS only see people for treatment that they themselves have diagnosed. For a well-known Clinical Psychologist, and for the NHS to discount it, maybe there needs to be a legal part of the document stating that under the law the NHS have to provide such services. Part of the vulnerability is that many families seem to believe that the NHS has their best interests at heart.
How long did it take you to seek a diagnosis?	*"I was on a waiting list for some months, but that's how the NHS works."*	Across the board with all the participants: the NHS takes far longer and does not have the expertise. The private sector is far more straightforward. But it's with the public sector that the problems and issues are there.
What knowledge of autism did you have prior to diagnosis?	N/A	

What were your expectations prior to attending?	*"I think that I was fairly ignorant prior to my assessment and if I had understood autism's messy history with the mental health profession and how diagnosis worked before I asked my GP for diagnosis I would not have allowed my GP to refer me to a mental health team or even used an NHS service at all, but because I didn't have this knowledge diagnosis was mishandled and I was blocked from accessing services."*	Refer to Adam Feinstein's book NHS may have broken the law and their own quality standards. GPs and LAs may try to ignore 'autism' as they know well for a fact that they are incompetent when it comes to 'autism'.
	Diagnosis	
Can you take me through your diagnosis as you experienced it then? **What were you thinking/ feeling at the time?**	*"I found the diagnosis process quite overwhelming, quite humiliating, stressful; my parents had to be involved, they found it to be very confusing; I felt mocked by the person doing the interview as if he thought my religious beliefs were very silly; I was interviewed at one point by someone who had English as a second language, who was supposed to be assessing my social skills."* *"The whole thing was ridiculous because I didn't know that it was a different type of assessment; I didn't realize that this was a mental health team who were only looking at autism as a possibility if they couldn't consider me to have some type of mental health condition; and being an adult woman of 32 of course they could easily assume that my symptoms were something else and they said I was not autistic."*	She felt very mocked and that the focus seemed to have been on her religious beliefs. A person who had English as a second language and was assessing her social skills interviewed her.

What was the environment like?	"*It wasn't set up to be a supportive environment for autistic people.*" "*The local hospital didn't have a clue*".	If the person goes through the NHS it's generally quite inappropriate environments, it's usually mental health based.
Was it suitable?	"*To get from the place where you could have a cup of tea to the room where I was actually seen was just a complete maze of corridors that badly needed a lick of paint; the whole place was a depressing, rabbit warren of a place; it clearly hadn't been designed with autistic people in mind at all. It was ghastly; the whole set-up made me feel really, really tense. It may have affected the assessment, but I think in their mind they didn't even recognize sensory overload as relevant when diagnosing autism. I think that the team assessing me didn't realize the building was going to produce some of the behaviour they were observing.*"	If the person goes through the NHS it's generally quite inappropriate environments, it's usually mental health based. Environment; private was great. NHS; no clue. This is a common theme. It seems that the NHS hasn't got the infrastructure. How this is important is that the physical environment will affect how a person functions in the assessment environment.
Did they make adjustments to the environment?	N/A	

| Did you feel that you were receiving a 'full profile' assessment? | *"The local hospital said that their test was better because it asked more questions and involved more people – like my parents, but actually I don't think they had the right skills; they were looking at everything from a mental health perspective and I don't think they understood learning difference, although they claimed to have better expertise in autism, they clearly didn't have a clue about how to handle or communicate with autistic people; I felt patronized, and I felt miss-handled by them. They didn't really know what they were doing, and their questions seemed irrelevant, and they said it was a full process but actually they weren't looking at autism from the point of view of an adult woman; they didn't look at sensory issues (they weren't a diagnosis criteria at the time but anyone with autism expertise would have seen that I was overwhelmed by my environment); they asked questions which were prejudicial to the process because they were looking at everything from a mental health perspective."*

"My parents were in the same room for part of the NHS diagnosis and part of the time they were interviewed separately. Goodness knows what went on in that room when I wasn't there. I can only guess that my parents either said that there was nothing wrong with me because they didn't spot the signs when I was a child or they didn't remember what happened 30 years ago or they didn't understand what the questions were getting at. I don't know what went on in that room." | The NHS, local hospital, there's a definite arrogance. The local hospital states that their test was better. As far as I'm aware they didn't know what tests she went through. They didn't understand learning difference and were looking at everything from a mental health perspective.

They didn't look at sensory issues.

They asked questions in a prejudiced manner, as they were looking at everything from a mental health perspective.

When they interviewed the parents, they didn't understand the questioning process.

The participant believes mother is 'autistic' as well.

If 'autism' had been explained in a positive light the family as whole could have forged a more positive identity.

In the context of family these things are so complex. Because if you have different neurotypes, inclusive of psychopathy etc., I think what needs to be investigated is how these neurotypes interact with each other. |

Parents' background is also important. Where a person comes from can dictate how they bring up their children; and when you add 'autism' in to that mix, and then bring in services and the wider community and how they treat people who are different. In professions as a whole there needs to be more dynamism

Should 'Autism' be taken out of the diagnostic manuals, as well as dyslexia and be considered 'thinking differences' and 'differences in learning'?

There may be a backlash for professionals and some organizations due to coming in to contact with other adults who weren't identified as children but may have formed more of a holistic view of their differences as a result.

"Autism' as a cultural difference: The male perspective of 'autism' may be in keeping with how 'autism' is constructed; however, the female perspective maybe more along the lines of a holistic perspective. Predominantly, the views have come from a male dominated profession, the majority of people identified have been male, but as more females becoming identified they may start to turn 'autism' on its head.

"The hospital were so inexpert they couldn't see that their evidence was faulty. I don't think they realized what I realize now, which is that my mother grew up in a home where she was parented ineffectively by someone who hadn't had their autism diagnosed. My mother's social role modeling was odd and she learnt to cope with a dysfunctional home by avoiding confrontation. I now think she is on the spectrum to a degree herself. So she would not spot or challenge an irrelevant line of questioning, I don't think she understood the questions."

"Autism is part of a constellation of neuro-diverse conditions. I was assessed separately for dyslexia and autism. It ought to be possible to have one assessment that picks up all kinds of issues like, dyspraxia, dyscalculia, attention deficit hyperactivity disorder and so on. Many people have traits of more than one form of neuro-diversity.

At the same time that diagnosis was to limited in its view (just autism and not neuro-diversity as a whole), it was also too broad, it included looking at irrelevant conditions. It is wholly inappropriate to see autism as a form of mental health condition and to diagnosis autism only if someone's behaviour cannot be explained as a mental health condition. An assessment of a neuro-diverse person's mental health needs, and their big needs, must come after their diagnosis of their thinking differences."

Rod Morris

What level/ type of professional conducted your diagnosis?	"The second assessment was carried out by a mental health team conducting a general mental health assessment in which they would only diagnose autism if my behaviour and difficulties could not be explained as a form of mental health condition."
	The assessment needs to be conducted on a humane base, e.g. what Asperger was referring to, than a systems base.
Was this suitable?	"They had the wrong view of autism, the wrong training and experience. They did the assessment as tick box exercise without understanding how autism presents in adults and in females. The subtleties of my social expression were assessed by a junior team member who did not have English as her first language. The team leader was a psychiatrist I am not even sure what training the other team members had. I was also given an IQ test by a junior team member and do not know why this was relevant or what her qualifications were to deliver this test or assess the results. I have had an IQ test every time I have had my needs as a dyslexic person assessed at work and I spent the whole test explaining that I'd done all the tasks before and asking whether that would affect the outcome. The team member was clearly too junior to know."

Post-Diagnosis

How did you feel directly after the diagnostic procedure?	"I felt literally punched in the stomach; I felt angry, confused, mishandled, cheated and humiliated and that the door to services was being slammed in my face for no better reason than the NHS does not want to spend money on people. It caused strain in my relationship with my parents, the friend who said to me that I could be on the spectrum couldn't believe the outcome and I was left wondering what on earth I was going to do."
	NHS experience very negative for her and family. Overwhelming and humiliating. She feels that her parents' involvement was a mistake. The NHS experience had a negative effect on relationship between her and parents. Parents felt guilty about their parenting when they were involved. It led to a lot of tensions between Christine and family. So actually the NHS could be breaking up families.

How/or/and/ when did it hit you?	"Three years ago when I left my job, I had space in my life to make some changes and that's when I went on a dairy and gluten free diet. The NHS hasn't understood how important that is for autistic people and I have been refused gluten free bread on prescription – and it's expensive, I have also had poor advice from a nutritionist who simply dismissed the diet out of ignorance. It took me a couple of years to adapt to getting the diet right and that's just one thing that has helped me. It took a long time for me to adapt to my diagnosis as a whole, I had to read up on it; I needed to know how to ask for support at work; I needed to meet other autistic people; I needed to change my diet and all this took several years."	Gluten free diet was taken up by her and she finds it useful. Yet in the NICE guidelines it is stated that such a diet should not be introduced.
Did the clinician/ diagnostician ask you to read and sign your diagnosis off?	"With the hospital report, I was not asked to sign it off, I was not asked for my opinion, I was being fobbed off with a diagnosis I didn't agree with; I tried to complain about how the diagnosis had been carried out as well as the conclusion. The hospital complaints process was useless; it simply involved asking the clinicians what had gone on; they clearly weren't going to say that they'd made a mistake. No, I wasn't asked to sign that off and I felt very patronized by that process and voiceless over and over again afterwards, because I was refused a second opinion due to autism being misclassified as a mental health issue, (at that time second opinions were only funded out of borough for physical conditions so I was offered a second opinion at the same hospital that came up with the first NHS opinion, which I refused) and then because the Primary Care Trust sat on my case an refused to come to a decision about referring my out of borough for a second opinion and this went on for three years until PCTs were abolished and because inaccurate information is stuck on my medical records to this day."	NHS professionals are misspelling their expertise, as she believed someone who was to diagnose 'autism' was seeing her. She tried to complain at the hospital but the procedure was ineffectual. She went back to GP and was told she couldn't go out of her borough. Her primary care trust lost her documents. This could well outline the picture of how the NHS can be incompetent.

Did you read it all?		
How did you feel when reading it?	*"The one from the NHS was just patronizing, and I am trying to get it removed from my medical records, but there isn't a process to have it removed from my medical records, so even though I know it's nonsense, I cant have it taken off my medical records and replaced by the psychologist's report because the psychologist's report is not an NHS document, so I feel really stuck. It seems to be a system designed to give people who can't communicate effectively a real runaround, and we as a nation waste a lot of money not giving people the support that they need to live their lives."* *"I knew what to do with a diagnosis of autism because I had already asked for disability support at work for dyslexia, but most people are diagnosed as autistic and there is no follow up support, no counselling, no information on autism, no information on where to meet other autistic people, no signposting to accurate information on benefits and how to read between the lines (that non-autistic skill) of the forms if you have a disability that isn't a medical condition, no information for family, friends, employers. There's just nothing and going back to your GP won't help because you'll have to educate them about what autism is. (Which you might already have had to do to be referred for diagnosis in the first place)."*	The assessment done by the NHS is the one on her profile, so the NHS is weeding out Autism, as it doesn't suit their service provision. The NHS did not ask for her feedback and/or for her to sign it off; they acted illegally and immorally on every account. Clinical Psychologist report; she asked to sign it off, it was not offered to her. She also had to say to the Clinician "No, don't send that to my employer". It could mean that she could lose her job; in turn research would then ay "all these people are unemployed because of 'autism'", and ask for more money. So it's unethical. She thought the diagnosis was going to be the same as dyslexia and the support was going to be there. People go in to a diagnosis blind.

Were you given the opportunity to preview your report and comment on it before it was finalized?	"This is a big problem, diagnosis is handed to people by medics, and they are the last people who should be telling someone that they are disabled. Disability is not something medics can fix, like flu, it's something disabled people live with in society and the health service doesn't really understand the social model of disability or disability empowerment at all."	People should be given specific contacts regarding disability rights. Training needed for medical professional in different models.
What did you think of the language and the perspective in the report?	"Not by the NHS"	
	N/A	
What were the recommendations on your assessment for a way forward?	"The NHS diagnosis concluded that as I was depressed. I couldn't also be autistic, so didn't offer follow on support on autism. Even in terms of my mental health needs it didn't refer me to anyone who could look at the different areas of my life, how I was coping with work? How was I coping socially? How was I coping with housing? How was I coping socially?"	The NHS were trying to construct an insurance policy, i.e. the report, for themselves and for the LA.

	"Diagnosis can only be conducted effectively by psychologists because it is they who understand autism, because it is they who have experts in learning difference. I will say again that autism cannot be diagnosed by mental health professionals or as part of a general mental health assessment – such assessment processes tend to miss rather than identify autism."	Christine believes that Clinical Psychologists should be doing 'autism' diagnoses. But maybe part of the reason is because her first diagnosis at the hands of a Clinical Psychologist was largely positive. Another participant had also outlined that he'd rather see a specialist in 'autism' than a "Jack of all trades". She doesn't think that a multi-disciplinary team is a good way to go about it. 'Autism' needs a separate profession?

On reflection

What is your perception now? Do you feel any different now, on reflection?	*"Looking back, if I had realized that the NHS assessment was a mental health assessment then I would have refused to attend, and neither I nor my parents would have been interviewed. In a mental health assessment someone is diagnosed autistic only if their symptoms cannot be explained as features of a mental health condition, which is like concluding that someone can only be dyslexic if they are not depressed. My parents thought they were answering questions on autism not my mental state in general. They have no understanding of autism or mental health and no ability to spot when a question has a hidden agenda. Also, I've never talked to my parents about things like being bullied at school, they didn't know about my mental wellbeing in childhood and youth or the incidents that point to autism that occurred outside the home. The stressful time of diagnosis was not the time to try and start a different relationship with my parents."*	She was under the impression that she was being assessed for 'autism', yet the mental health team was looking for mental health difficulties, suggesting that the NHS isn't informing their patients of what's actually happening by purposefully withholding information.

| In hindsight, how could your diagnosis have been done better? | *"For the NHS diagnosis, I don't think the diagnostic process for autism should go anywhere near mental health services or actually for that matter any kind of medic or the health service at all. In the same way that the Jobcentre is not run by medics, the state's diagnostic service needs to be based in the community. There needs to be a straightforward self-referral process (like walking into a diagnosis shop), the diagnosis needs to looks at neuro-diversity as a whole, and the people doing the diagnosis need to be professionals who have expertise in neuro-diversity. Diagnosis should be a simple process of looking at how someone thinks and copes now as an adult so your family circumstances won't block diagnosis – and lets face it autistic people are highly likely to have problems in their family relationships. Most of all diagnosis needs to be empowering and not shaming, this means not only ensuring that the person diagnosed is offered information on where to go for support, like local groups where you can meet other autistic people, but someone at the diagnostic service befriending the newly diagnosed person so that they have someone to go with them to their first group meeting."* | Are existing professions still based on outdated ideology? Given new scientific research and perspectives?

Is the medical profession acting unethically by prescribing a damning medical template on to a social construct? Such a diagnosis needs to be very neutral. Community assessment process linked in neurodiversity; refer to Luke's diagnostic model.

One consideration: If you have 'autistic' parents worrying about having an 'autistic' child then what does that say about how the parents view themselves?! Maybe the 'disease' is the aspect of normalizing which the medical model endorses. People may try to normalize whether they are diagnosed or not, it gets passed down the generations. It's almost like we've gone from blaming the parents, the issues are not caused by poor parenting, and has swung the pendulum the other way, e.g. one parent worrying about his/her child being taken away and being told that professionals don't view autism in that way anymore. Another participant mentioned fears about being viewed as having Munchausen's by proxy when seeking assessment. |

	"Finding the autistic community should not be daunting. It should be like walking into a pub and finding the locals are friendly and will chat and that actually they are your long lost family. Which is how I imagine gay people feel when they first come out and go to a gay bar and meet other gay people." *"So diagnosis should be a very empowering process and not medical or condemning in any way."*	How far does the psychosocial way that people deal with this stuff affect functioning and mental health? And how much is this then artificially put under 'autism'? Because if you are led to believe that you can't do something then that part of the brain will be affected in terms of functioning (fear about doing something).
What was good about the process?		
What was bad about the process?	*"The first assessment was me as an adult talking to a clinical psychologist who understood learning difference, the second one was an NHS mental health assessment involving my parents talking about my childhood, and I found it very patronizing, they just wanted to fob me off saying I was depressed. I had not recognized then that my depression was a lifelong issue, and that I was depressed because I was struggling to live with an undiagnosed disability. The diagnostic team confused symptoms with cause; it was a incompetent."*	Staff in the NHS are not open to new perspectives. Maybe the NHS is more about processing than actually seeing people as human beings, e.g. this aspect of what's been deemed as the culture in the NHS. She was saying that they just wanted to fob her off, saying that she was just a bit depressed. She recognizes that they were confusing symptoms with causes.
What impact has your diagnosis had on the understanding of who you are?	*"The mis-diagnosis that was the out come of the NHS assessment was confusing for my parents. I was said to be depressed, which isn't the whole story, I am also autistic. My parents felt guilty about letting me down as a child. They felt they had*	Mother as an ex primary school teacher was negative about the 'autistic' pupils. Christine needed a positive voice and found it difficult to handle this. Maybe it was also due to the mother denying the 'autism' in herself.

	caused the depression. But however, they had parented me I'd be autistic and there is nothing for them to feel guilty about. I deeply regret getting my parents involved at all: they felt guilty about the way they parented me, they felt confused by the process; they were confused by the fact that I had two reports with different conclusions, and that led to a lot of tensions in my relationships with my parents; and it's only now that my sister's three year old has been diagnosed as being on the spectrum that my parents understand that autism isn't something that is going to go away in our family; my mum wants to run away from it. Even though my mum is a retired primary school teacher and has had autistic children in her classes, she is quite negative about autism and I found that really difficult because I needed to find a positive voice for myself as an autistic person."
Is there anything you would like to add?	"Since my assessment I have spoken to others who have been seen at this hospital, the community mental health team have said to me that they have been surprised that some people they have referred to this hospital have been assessed as not being autistic, the hospital has a reputation for not thinking women can be autistic, and I have heard that they treat another form of neuro-diversity, ADHD with mental health drugs. I advise other people in my area not to go to this hospital for diagnosis or treatment which is tricky as they are the locally funded service."

"So, I had these two diagnoses; one which I very much believed because it was from a leading clinical psychologist and matched my experience of life and one from this local hospital which claimed to have some specialism in autism, but was really appalling. I tried to complain about the NHS diagnosis but the complaints procedure was ineffective; I went back to my GP and said that I want a second opinion, and because autism was classified as mental health, they said that they couldn't refer me out of borough and that the second opinion would have to be with the same people who did the first diagnosis at the hospital, (at that time you could only have second opinions out of borough for physical conditions), I didn't want a repeat of the first NHS diagnosis so said no thank you, and then my paperwork sat with the Primary Care Trust for about 3 years, they had to approve funding for an out of borough assessment and after 3 years Primary Care Trusts were abolished, and the Primary Care Trust had done nothing, no matter how many times my GP phoned them up."

"What I am now trying to do is get my medical records changed. DSM (Diagnostic and Statistical Manual of Mental Disorders) has changed its definition of autism and my diagnosis Asperger Syndrome no longer exists. So I need the clinical psychologist who did my workplace diagnosis to confirm that I am still on the spectrum, and I want her letter to replace this hospital report on my medical records."

No one should have to seek a new diagnosis as the two core components of both autism and Asperger's have been retained. The professionals should automatically adjust the diagnosis on their systems to reflect this change.

The DSM-5 and the changes have led to confusion for her as she is feeling as though she requires another assessment. Her LA and NHS have ignored the 'autism' diagnosis as they know they don't have the relevant service, they tossed it aside, so have focused more so on her mental health. So actually this NHS could have broken the law.

"In short, I have been completely messed around by a system I didn't understand and that my GP didn't understand, and found that the road to services was blocked rather than opened up to me as a disabled person. So here I am, a woman with a communication disability made to fight a nonsensical system, and I think one of the reasons why I wanted to do this research with you Rod was just to say how stupid my experience has been; and it was eight years ago but I don't think much has changed at the local hospital; it's still run by the same idiots".

People with communication difficulties being taken advantage of by a system that gives them the run-around without the right kind of support.

"I know that without my dyslexia diagnosis I would not have got any support I needed in the workplace, and that the same would be true for autism, no diagnosis no services."

They broke Equality Law by not making reasonable adjustments regarding her disability. Luke mentioned today, 18.11.2013 Monday, that LAs could be the subject of litigation. If the report she initially got from the Clinical Psychologist included elements of the law and taken this to her GP and the NHS team then she may have got further. In addition, GPs and these Clinicians need to talk to each other more. I'm sure that if other 'autistic' people read this thesis, and similar things come up, LAs should expect a series of litigation cases.

Isaac: Matrix (NHS diagnosis)

Current age: 65

Age when diagnosis was conducted: 55 (2003)

Current social and economic situation: *"I'm retired now. I had to give up work for medical reasons, not because of Asperger's. I was a postman."*

Official diagnoses by name: Asperger Syndrome

Questions	Responses	Analytical memos
Pre-Diagnosis		
Why did you seek a diagnosis?	*"We were having problems with the marriage and we went to Relate and one of the Relate councilors, who wrote books on Asperger's and she could see Asperger's in me. I had never heard about Asperger's up until that time. Even my GP had not heard of Asperger's and had to use the computer to look it up. That was the first time I had heard of Asperger's and that was in in 2002/2003. It did take me a while to get a diagnosis."*	Isaac sought a diagnosis due to difficulties with his marriage. It appears that his wife was pushing for a diagnosis. Isaac came across as having a dry sense of humor and appeared to have hidden intelligence in which his job as a postman would not have afforded him the opportunity to reach his full potential. There appears to be clear differences in neurology such as memory, which he did try and compensate for.

He first heard of Asperger's from a relationship counselor who he and his wife had been seeing. Even his GP had not heard of Asperger's and had to use a computer to look it up. It took a long time to get a diagnosis. |

How long did it take you to seek a diagnosis?	*"I had tremendous difficulty in obtaining a diagnosis because some of the places wanted my parents input, but my parents were deceased. I had it done at a hospital in Birmingham."* *"First place I went to was a place in Cambridge, but they couldn't do it without my parents being there, then I went to a well known charity and they gave me the name of the hospital in Birmingham where I saw a doctor which is where I had the diagnosis done. It took under a year (months)."* *"I went through my Doctors to get a diagnosis. I had to get a referral to the hospital and it was straight forward."*	He originally had difficulty in obtaining a diagnosis, because some of the places wanted his parents input, but they were dead. Is this a wider issue to diagnosis in older age as well as for people who have been fostered or adopted? One of the places that they investigated was over seen by one of the leading authorities in Autism, subsequently he ended up having to go to a charity who referred him to a hospital in Birmingham. He then went to his GP to get a referral it took under a year. How is it that a person that has worked and paid tax all his life and with his marriage at risk was it so difficult for him to obtain a diagnosis that has been formally recognized in all the diagnostic manuals for many years! GP's?
What knowledge of autism did you have prior to diagnosis?	*"None at all"*.	
What were your expectations prior to attending?	*"I just wanted an answer; had I got it or hadn't I got it, but according to this councilor at Relate she saw the behavioral patterns. I was nervous, as I didn't know what they were going to come up with. Most people with Asperger's have other problems as well, and I think I have Dyspraxia because I'm very clumsy and can get disorientated. That's just my thinking; I have not formally been diagnosed with Dyspraxia."*	Although the relate counselor saw the behavioral patterns he still had to go through a lengthy process. He was also nervous as he did not know what they were going to come up with. He did not know what to expect so he may have expected the worst.

Diagnosis		
Can you take me through your diagnosis as you experienced it then?	*"They wanted to know about my childhood more than anything, how I got on/treated at school, the family background."*	I suspect with him coming from a working class background that he may have had a certain view regarding individuals who were different or mentally ill and partook in ritualistic banter and ridicule as these types of issues were not understood at that time. I am sure it can be quite a shock to realize that you are the very person that you may be ridiculing others for.
What were you thinking/feeling at the time?	*"I had a good childhood, it was hard because my father hadn't a well-paid job but I was treated alright. I kept thinking what are they going to find; have I got more than this. It was in-depth, it lasted over 3 hours. The female doctor passed me onto someone else, he was asking most of the questions. There were 2 people involved in the process at the same time; a main consultant who asked me most of the questions and the other only asked me a few. It was NHS based."*	He seemed happy with the diagnostic process and said it was in depth and lasted over three hours. There were two people involved in the process. Is this suitable?
What was the environment like?	*"It was just an ordinary consulting room."*	
Was it suitable?	*"Yes, it was alright."*	
Did they make adjustments to the environment?	*"No adjustments made to environment, I was made to feel comfortable; the questions weren't probing and were quite easy to answer."*	They saw both him and his wife; he was made to feel comfortable but there were no adjustments made to the environment.
Did you feel that you were receiving a 'full profile' assessment?	*"It was in-depth, it went right back through my childhood, school and work; I have always worked and have never had a problem in finding a job. My wife was with me so some of the questions they asked us both together, others were with me on my own. At the end, the doctor and me and my wife were told that with the information we have you have Asperger Syndrome."*	

What level/ type of professional conducted your diagnosis?	"I believe it was a psychiatrist."	
Was this suitable?	"Yes, to me, the questions he asked were the right questions. I get thrown when people say Asperger Syndrome isn't a psychiatric problem, and then someone else says it is a psychiatric problem, so if it isn't a psychiatric problem why do they get a psychiatrist to do the diagnosis. It throws you a bit. I, myself don't see it as a psychiatric problem, if it was a psychiatric problem, you wouldn't have done what you'd have done would you, you'd have been having happy pills in a Psychiatric hospital. Some people say, you're not normal, and I say what is normal. I view Asperger's as a difference. To some people it is an advantage, to others it is a disadvantage."	This may be a view that he is still confused about. He does not see it as a psychiatric problem if it was he would be in a psychiatric unit taking medication. He questions the notion of normal and views Asperger's as a difference. He does not view it as a disadvantage although he knows that others do. He is aware that everyone has a different view on AS this leads to confusion. This raises questions regarding who should diagnose because if the individual does not see it as a psychiatric problem and one of the world experts refuses to diagnose on the basis of no parental input people may be put off seeking a diagnosis because of the stigma of psychiatry.
Post-diagnosis		
How did you feel directly after the diagnostic procedure?	"That was all right with me, because I knew there was a problem there; I couldn't do anything about it but it answered a lot of questions."	
How/or/and/ when did it hit you?	"At the time when it was confirmed. There were no pills so if you've got it you've got it. You've got to make the most of what you've got."	

Did the clinician/ diagnostician ask you to read and sign your diagnosis off?	*"That I can't remember. There was no follow-up, no letters, nothing."*	
Did you read it all?	*"I don't believe that I had access to my written diagnosis. They just told me that I've got this problem."*	Although he had no access to his written diagnosis they told him that he has got this problem is this problem they are describing called neurological traits or just patholagizing people who do not fit into current society?
How did you feel when reading it?	N/A	
Were you given the opportunity to preview your report and comment on it before it was finalized?	N/A	
What did you think of the language and the perspective in the report?	*"Everyone has a different view on it, haven't they; there is not one general view on it. There are loads of people who have different ideas on what it is and this is what throws you. I think it was the Relate counselor who said that Asperger's people just have a different outlook on life; we look at things differently to what somebody else does."*	

Question	Response	Analysis
What were the recommendations on your assessment for a way forward?	*"This is what upset the wife; it was just a case of just go away and live with it. There was no follow-up or suggestions. It upset her more than it upset me. It was just the case of if you'd got the diagnosis, there's nothing else we can do for you; that's your life now. Without follow-up it did have a negative affect on my marriage. I just get on with things; I'm what you would call a plodder, I just plod along and just carry on with things."*	There was no follow up and the issue of Asperger's seems to be more about his wife than him. He did state that without follow up it did have a negative effect on his marriage, certainly in this case it does highlight that when the social circumstances change then difficulties manifest it seems that those who diagnose for research purposes may only select those who fit their current pattern of research. It also seems in this case that the NHS feels no responsibility and is not knowledgeable of Autism and the human condition both with the process and the consequences of being given the label without any follow up.
On reflection		
What is your perception now? Do you feel any different now, on reflection?	*"No, I've just got on with life."*	
In hindsight, how could your diagnosis have been done better?		
What was good about the process?	*"It was very in-depth; there was nothing that upset me about the diagnosis; none of the questions upset me."*	
What was bad about the process?	*"I wish there was follow-up and advice for the two of us, me and the wife to help cope with this problem – strategies for both of us."*	

What impact has your diagnosis had on the understanding of who you are?	*"That's me, I can't change it, you can't change it; we just have to get on with life. I just plod along, I'm happy with my life. To me, there are more people who have actually got this than have actually been diagnosed, because you see people in the street and you thing he could have it because he is doing some of the things that you do, and you see other people doing it."*	Isaac seems to see Autism everywhere and believes that there are many more people who are Autistic than have been officially recognized. It could be that the more people, who are assessed, could address issues of stigma and introduce acceptance although this may not be something the medical profession wants as it would mean a loss of control and authority; hence changes in the DSM.
Is there anything else you would like to add?	*"I would like to see more done for Asperger people, but according to a friend of mine, in the DSM they are going to group it all together under Autism. I believe my sister had an Autistic problem (she died when she was 70) because in the 1950's she was sent to a boarding school for children with learning problems; two of her children have learning problems and they were sent to a special school. It has gone further because some of the grand children have got ADHD, so it's coming down through the line. This grandson, they were going to send him to a special school, but they have had second thoughts and are going to send him to a mainstream school. I am poor at math and it was my worst subject at school. I don't suffer with anxiety or depression but I have memory problems. On my father's side they are ordinary working class; my mothers side there's a couple of millionaires. I believe that every Asperger person is different; no ones the same, you can see odd things, but everyone's different. I have always worked apart*	The assessment went right back to his Schooldays and he recognizes the genetic components through him identifying other members of his family including grandchildren. If Autism is as serious as many conclude then why is diagnosis not conducted on a family level this also raises questions whether the medical profession is proper in this instant. Isaac believes that with a genetic link diagnosis should be done on a family basis.

Without him receiving a written diagnosis it is impossible to be sure that clinicians seemed to have missed additional diagnosis such as Dyspraxia, Dyscalculia memory issues. He does not believe that he has anxiety and depression which are thought to be the major comorbidities. |

from with medical problems, and I see many in Autism groups who have never worked. I have a friend I have known since I was nine, and another friend (dead now) who I had known since fifteen. I recognize the pushiness of society and competition compared to when I was younger when I never had that. Post diagnosis, I would like to see support for the people and the families, because there's nothing out there. If you are a parent with a child, there is support. The window cleaner came yesterday and his son had Asperger's; he is an 11 year old who has been in a Psychiatric Hospital, and he has ADHD as well now. They keep throwing bloody pills down kids. I believe this should all be done on a family basis, with the genetic link. You don't need loads of back up, but some. Someone to just listen to you or your partner with the problems that you face and see if they have any ideas."	He believes that post diagnosis he did not need loads of back up just someone to listen to. I feel that there is a place for others who have been through the process to formally offer paid low level support rather than every one with this diagnosis seen as the cared for and interventions that only neuro-typicals can provide. I feel that this process was not very good at all but it seems to be a consequence of having one profession assume over all control.

Jack: Matrix (Private diagnosis)

Current age: 70

Age when diagnosis was conducted: 65 (2008)

Current social and economic situation: *"Both good; It's something that I've always known was important to me and I have worked on both of them all my life; I have a strange habit of wanting to stay in touch with people that go back years. I play a lot of sport, which helps me to meet people. The social aspects of my life have always been important to me because when I was young I couldn't relate well to people; I wanted to but I didn't quite know how to engage, so throughout my life I was observant as to how people conducted themselves, and it is a learning process I am still doing."* Jack has had a successful career, has children etc.

Official diagnoses by name: Asperger Syndrome

Note: Ethically, the author of this thesis declares he has known this participant for many years, but this does not interfere with the content as the experiences presented here occurred long before first contact.

Questions	Responses	Analytical memos
Pre-Diagnosis		
Why did you seek a diagnosis?	*"My daughter, who was a speech and language therapist, worked with some people with Autism and said to me one day 'I think you and I, dad, may have it'. So, that was important for me to find out and at the time I was retired which gave me time to think about it and to negotiate a diagnosis and how to get one."*	Interesting: a speech and language therapist saying to her father that she and he may have 'autism'. Yet 'autism' is supposed to be a communication disorder. This highlights the generational factor of 'autism'. Where do you cut off this aspect of genetics of neurology and upbringing? Especially with behaviors etc. - where is the cut-off point? For example, when you get a dyslexic person who may exhibit dyslexia, say this accounts for 30%, and yet the rest of their difficulties may be more so due to the school environment whereby they are told they cannot do something.

How long did it take you to seek a diagnosis?	"Probably two or three years. The thought process I went through at the time, was reflecting on the aspects of my quality of life, and I was asking myself, do I want this because I couldn't see what good it will do me now, but then I looked at my quality of life and came to the conclusion that my quality of life I perceive as quite good, so there are no reasons why I shouldn't do it. But as it turned out it became an important question to me, so I decided to go after it. It took about two and a half years from the original concept that I might be, to mulling through it and eventually that I have to find out. It was a further six months before I received a diagnosis after I wanted to find out. I initially requested one from my GP, who said that 'I didn't know about Asperger's or Autism or anything like that, but I will back you'. Because it turns out they had to fund the diagnosis, which turned out to be quite expensive, I ended up having to pay privately for my diagnosis. The diagnosis cost me £600, which I thought was quite expensive just to have a couple of hours meeting. This was down in London." (Jack lives in the Midlands)	He was going through a reflective period at the time. He was looking at quality of life. What's interesting, is that he said that he was having a good quality of life so he didn't see a problem in seeking a diagnosis, which is he opposite of somebody seeking a diagnosis because they're having problems. GP: no knowledge of 'autism'. But said that he would back him.
What knowledge of autism did you have prior to diagnosis?	"None at all, apart from what I knew about myself. It was obvious that I did understand a lot because of all the self-analysis".	Went in to diagnosis without any prior information regarding 'autism'.

How did it come about?	"First of all I found out that there were very few people who were qualified to go through the process; secondly I found that there was no one particularly on my doorstep, and it eventually came to a choice of two, one was a national charity, and the other one was a guy in Sheffield. I wasn't too struck by what I had heard about the guy in Sheffield although somebody did recommend him and so I decided that I would go to the national charity. The lady who assessed me turned out to be a very well respected and well-known clinician in the field of Autism. She was very good at interacting and making both me and my wife comfortable for why we were there and what the process was about and that some things that she would ask me, she would need verification from my wife, because normally for a diagnosis they normally like people who were around for the whole of your life, well I couldn't provide that."	He said that there are very few people qualified to do the process. He did extensive research to choose the right person. Maybe professionals need to put on their website what perspective utilizing so that potential clients are aware of their qualification(s) and whether they believe in the neurodiversity theory; professionals should nail their beliefs to the mast. Professionals should be truthful about what they are offering. He and his wife felt comfortable with the Clinician.
What were your expectations prior to attending?	"What I was hoping for was a positive diagnosis one way or the other; I wanted confirmation, one way or the other and that is what I was looking for, and I was somewhat apprehensive. I didn't know what it would unveil but it was like waiting to attend your own court case, but I wanted an answer."	He said it was like attending your own court case.

Diagnosis		
Can you take me through your diagnosis as you experienced it then?		
What were you thinking/ feeling at the time?	*"I was considerably nervous; it was down in London and we had driven down there; we arrived early so therefore I had time to kill and my wife suggested that I have something to eat, but I didn't fancy anything, so we just walked. I was apprehensive, just straightforward apprehensive; I didn't know what to expect, I was nervous of what might come about, but I had this overall mission on getting a positive answer, yea or nea."*	He went private. He went to London, despite living in the Midlands; illustrates how far he had to go. He was extremely nervous beforehand and he didn't know what to expect; not knowing what to expect could affect the process. So maybe part of the diagnosis needs to incorporate things such as "Has the person had to travel?" He just wanted to be sure about whether he was 'autistic' or not. His driver, his mission on getting a positive answers either way.
What was the environment like?	*"We found it ok, but I had a Satnav and we could park outside her offices, so that was good. The secretary met us and we had to wait for the clinician to arrive. She then appeared and then we walked up this huge set of stairs and along a long corridor with high ceilings, then eventually into a large boardroom. My wife and me sat to one side, and she sat on the other side.*	Environmental aspects: secretary met them. Diagnosis was done in a boardroom?

Was it suitable?		
Did they make adjustments to the environment?	*She introduced herself, and she explained the process and I think she came across as very caring and understanding and she actually told me about her work with her colleague which made me feel as though she was qualified. She made me get to the point where I felt that whatever she said was true, so I had faith in her. She had a process that she was working to which she didn't disclose, but she didn't hide the fact that that she was doing it either, and she did say that there were times where she would need to ask my wife for verification of something, which was not that she doubted my word or anything. She was very good and she settled me down." Regarding background history and development and taking into account that his parents were no longer alive, Jack said that "She did ask those types of questions, and I was able to answer most of them. My initial experience of life was when I was about three years old and my very first trauma was just before I had to go to primary school and I had to wait for my mate to pass and watch him go to school and there was me not able to go to school because I wasn't ready for it and that is an experience that I carry with me, I can re-live that moment. I was able to not remember anything about whether I was bright or not, but the reactions of people and what they told me was that I was very bright and outward going, but absolutely and completely devoid of safety; if there was something to do I would throw myself into it, and I*	Clinician came over as being very caring and friendly. She was very good at speaking to them as a human being rather than taking the higher ground. Using the human approach in diagnosis. Part of developmental history came from his wife who had got to know his mother and father before they died. So it's a developmental history by proxy. His parents were dead so wife had to sit in, so there's no developmental history. THEME Limited developmental history. He was recalling the first trauma he had in his life.

	think the first trauma I had in life, I didn't know what it was until we discussed it and it turned out to be one of these little peddle cars that I could cycle up and down the side of our house, but then when I got proficient at it I opened up the gates and started to do fast turns on the pavement. We didn't have many cars around in those days, so it wasn't very dangerous to swing out onto the road either, but it was at that point that my parents confiscated the red car, and I don't think I took too kindly to that. I think there is a scar because of that, because people told me that it was so important and I felt as though I was treated wrongly."	He felt that he was receiving a full profile assessment even though the report was two pages long. This goes in to the area of him not knowing what to expect, and maybe the final report did not reelect the depth of the assessment.
Did you feel that you were receiving a 'full profile' assessment?	*"Yes, very much so. She covered an awful lot of things and I was able to give her an honest answer and as with this interview I probably gave more than I was asked for, so she got a good understanding of the truthful upbringing that I had and as it went on, my wife was able to start contributing, because she got to know my mother and my father before they died. We talked about things like clumsiness, how you felt in social situations, lots of things I don't remember, but I do remember thinking that applies to me, that applies to me in part, or no absolutely not. It was those sorts of answers to her questions that I was able to give, but she did cover a lot of ground. She also asked my wife similar questions about me also. It started to get quite interesting and amusing when I was telling her about when we go to see people, and in the car I will always ask my*	

		People looking for a diagnosis are looking for respected people; they want their diagnosis to be recognized, as there is an aspect of not being believed, so they seek out Clinicians who will be believed.
	wife what is it I should say and what is it I shouldn't say, and it's more important to know what I shouldn't say than what I should say. I will also talk after such meetings by asking that I didn't know what was going on, and she would explain it. My wife was able to put things into context for me and we got to know each other extremely well and therefore we know each other inside out, so I have always been open with her to the point of bluntness, and she has always understood and accepted me for who I am, and in the main, that's not difficult to live with, but now and again it can be."	
What level/ type of professional conducted your diagnosis?	Psychiatrist	
Was this suitable?	*"I don't think I could have got anyone better, as she was someone who had dealt with a lot of people on the spectrum over a considerable period of time, along with someone who I was assured was one of the guru's of the subject, and they were both working together for a long period of time. They didn't agree on everything, but they did agree on the basics and were respectful of each other, but she had her own views and professionalism, and it was a likeable situation and I felt at the end of the time, at the point that she was just about to pronounce that I could have faith in what she said.*	

It was interesting when she got to that point because she said that there are some people who need to have it proven in blood that you have the Triad of Impairments. She said to me that I don't believe that you have the triad and that she said that you don't need all the parts to actually be on the spectrum, and I think you are unquestionably on the spectrum." When asked about a fuller assessment such as assessment provided in the individual's real life setting as we would all do things in private that we wouldn't do in public, Jack believes that "the clinician wouldn't have learned anything because there are two me's; there's the me that I am and there's the me I portray, and I have become very successful in portraying something that I am not necessarily feeling. People often completely misunderstood me and it's all because they are reading into me things that I am finding difficulty with and they are reading the signs that they believe they are picking up and they are wrong. I think I do portray myself as someone who is far more confident than I really am. I think what the clinician was saying was that the stories that I told and the stories that I could share with her and that my wife could back up, she felt an absolute reflection of what she had seen in others, somewhat to a lesser degree, but reflected the same pattern of progress throughout my life and how you learn to cope with things and we told her a few amusing little stories which were very truthful	What she was saying that certain Clinicians state that they need to have the triad of impairments, and she didn't believe it, DSM-5 agrees with this as imagination has been taken out. "There are two mes"; this feeds in to the emerging female profile of being able to hide.

and open as to the way we were and how my wife had to treat me which was different to what one would expect. I think she understood that I was at a stage in my life where I didn't have much pressure because a) I'm still very happily married for a long time b) the type of job that I had done and the sort of things I have got out of it, the way I interacted and the way I could express myself, it was obvious that I wasn't having a traumatic time, but there were times in my life, which I shared with her, when that going gets tough that's when you need to dig very deep and that's when you find out what your weakness are; that's when you find out that you are not as strong as you think you are and you realize that anxiety and depression set in and all the nasty things that you wish you hadn't experienced, but I could start to see that the two were related, the condition and the actual effect. It wasn't surprising that I had mental health issues, yet nobody would pick them up, nobody would even understand, and that I think is effectively being misunderstood, and its always been very puzzling to me because you don't always know how people with mental health issues actually feel. I knew how I felt; it was different to the way I normally feel, but I had nothing to judge it against. Some people are born with talents and some people are born without talents, and some are born with abilities that are strong, and some people are born with inabilities that get in the way; I had very few inabilities, but the ones	Clinician recognized the social demands aspect of the situation (DSM-5). If you tie in the presentation aspects of mental health and who he really is, so mental health issues are just as hidden as 'autism'. So maybe we're looking at mental health time bomb? How does a person know if they are mentally ill?

I did have were very much of a social nature, and maybe the cause for my need to address the social aspects, because I knew it was a weakness and I didn't want to be weak, I wanted to be strong, so I wasn't shy in addressing the issues, and I used a lot of people in trying to develop my understanding that way, and I felt at the time of the diagnosis that this was all beginning to start to give me an answer as to why I had problems and what were the basic causes which I had never even had hinted at before. There were several occasions where she understood my coping strategies, and she was quite impressed, and found it rather unusual. I think she understood that despite the extra effort I had to put in, in any situation that I felt was worthwhile that I actually persevered with it, to the point where I was probably working double hard than anyone else, I was working with in order to just keep up." When informed about the change in the DSM-5 in Autism regarding "behaviors may only manifest when social demands exceed limited capacity" (APA, 2013) Jack absolutely agrees, stating "*I would very much say that, absolutely; when it gets to a certain point I just blow, and I have to retire and shut the world out. I knew how to protect myself; I wouldn't go into areas I was not capable of existing in; If I got to the point where I couldn't take part I would not continue to take part, either through switching off by thinking about other things while conversations were going on, or actually withdraw."*	Seeking a diagnosis to put his life and experiences in to context. He was looking to make sense of his life and a diagnosis gave him a different lens and perspective to view it. He agrees with DSM-5's social demands.

Post-diagnosis		
How did you feel directly after the diagnostic procedure?	*"Immediately and relieved. I felt that I had achieved something, which is extraordinary, but I now jumped a hurdle. Achievement in that I had confirmation that here was a light that said because of these reasons you are like you are. What do you do when you think differently to other people; why do you think differently; what's right for you, what's right for them, what's right for everyone else, is there an absolute right; you become a little philosopher, and this kind of gave me a tick and a star which said here is a tunnel to go down, which was brilliant, that was the immediate reaction."*	He felt immediately relieved, saw this as an achievement and a hurdle, "you become a little philosopher" - this feeds in to the female and male profiles. He's just turned it on its head. Ref: Tony Attwood.
How/or/and/when did it hit you?	*"Immediately"*	
Did the clinician/diagnostician ask you to read and sign your diagnosis off?	*"Yes, it was sent to me in the post; it was two sides of A4, it recalled the process that she engaged in, in order to come to her conclusion; she stated her conclusion, she signed it, and I signed it; she didn't sign it in front of me, she signed it to be sending it to me, then I signed it and sent it back. There were no amendments made as I felt that she alluded to the things that we discussed and agreed on, and all she was doing was reflecting the significant agreements. It was not so much of a clinical report in my recollection; it was much more a professional judgment of recognition of a condition, and my need to know where to look in order to understand."*	Document was agreed and signed off; gave it validity on both sides. It was not so much a clinical report but more so a professional judgment.
Did you read it all?	*"Yes I did; I read it several times and avidly."*	He read it several times.

How did you feel when reading it?	"A) I got what I wanted, which was a confirmed direction. B) Secondly, the words were not delivered in a way….. The way I read it was that I could put myself in her chair and see me through her eyes without any difficulty because she didn't use difficult language; there was no judgmental part to it whatsoever; it was a pure reflection of what we discussed and it was laid out in the sequence and the depth that we discussed it. Whether this is a good way of getting a diagnosis, I have absolutely no idea, and I was actually pleased by the humanity and the human approach of how she conducted the whole thing. I think I would have objected to a lot of medical terminology, so she didn't give me that."		This confirms why, as stated in the NICE guidelines, the social imagination aspect has been taken out: he used his social imagination to place himself in her shoes and imagined things from her point of view in relation to himself. This totally refutes the dominant theories.
Were you given the opportunity to preview your report and comment on it before it was finalized?	"Yes"		
What did you think of the language and the perspective in the report?	"She didn't use difficult language; there was no judgmental part to it whatsoever; it was a pure reflection of what we discussed and it was laid out in the sequence and the depth that we discussed it. Whether this is a good way of getting a diagnosis, I have absolutely no idea, and I was actually pleased by the humanity and the human approach of how she conducted the whole thing. I think I would have objected to a lot of medical terminology, so she didn't give me that."		Clinician's approach put him at ease. With a Clinician it's more about being the person they are rather than having all the knowledge under the sun.

Language is easy to understand. Most important: no judgment whatsoever. "I was actually pleased about the human terminology and approach she used", and he goes on to say that he would have refuted the medical language if she had. |

	Actual diagnosis was very good. Post-diagnosis things start to fall apart. You can have a really good Clinician and yet all this is undone post-diagnosis. Charities and regulation? Was eventually invited to a group where the setup wasn't reflective of the diversity of autistic spectrum. So the way they did things was very regimented and focused mainly on the aspect of providing a rigid environment. It was rigid from the point of view of the charity workers rather than the participants' view. They were treated like a bunch of zombies rather than having meaningful thoughts out of them. It was a place of fear. Double empathy problem. The charity worker did not exhibit the amount of empathy, understanding and reflection he had. The above ties in with regulations, qualifications and who can work in this theory. ABA for adults, that's what it was.
What were the recommendations on your assessment for a way forward?	*"There are societies around that you can approach in order to further your understanding of the condition, and this is what I was trying to get into, and then I actually went with my badge of honor as a new found recruit to this condition, and went to a well known charity and said 'what help can you give me?' They basically said 'piss off, there is nothing wrong with you mate, we can't help people like you because we have no time for people like you, we have time for people who are much more heavily affected'; they then expected me to run away, tail between my legs, and I said this was unacceptable and so I pushed and I probed, and they said 'look, I tell you what we can do, we can introduce you to a group that meets on a social basis, come along and see what you think of that'; so I did that and I was absolutely appalled by what I saw; I don't think it was good for the group who was there; I could see there was a lot of difference between the group who was there and me, because I had an awful lot of confidence that they didn't have and I had the ability to express myself and to look people in the eyes and to engage in a way that they appeared not to be able to; however, the amount of rules for the way that they were allowed to conduct themselves was so intense that it didn't allow them any time to express themselves. The rules that were imposed on them as being a member of this group; you couldn't speak for more than a minute; I know the reason why that is imposed, but that was a rule*

The role of the charity should be about facilitating the meeting(s) rather than trying to provide child-based therapy on adults.

and they didn't deviate from it, and everybody regarded it as a rule that was being broken if it was exceeded, so they treated them like a load of zombies rather than trying to extract any meaningful thoughts out of them, and to me they were looking for progress, they were looking for areas of how each of them could develop, they felt that the development they were looking for was because it was a social event, how well they socialized, and therefore how well they could stick to these rules and think of others rather than just themselves, and so on. I felt it was like a sword dangling above them, that if they did break it that this sword would slice them apart, and it was so strict and unfeeling that one or two of them actually broke away and couldn't take part any longer and so they were counseled by somebody else which then started to deteriorate because they weren't there around the table taking part and there was only one left doing that and he wasn't particularly skilled in what he was doing, I don't think. The amount of empathy he had, the amount of understanding and reflection on how it would affect him, had he had similar difficulties, was just not present. I was quite disgusted. He was an 'officer' with the charity; I don't think he was clinically qualified or a medical practitioner; I think he was employed by the charity to run these sort of groups. I don't think he was either qualified or knowledgeable, but he did work for the charity so no doubt he did understand the theory that they believe. That session around the table was only the second bit; the first bit, they met in a pub and they knew it was for a discussion and they formed their own social groups, which in the main was one large group which they all sat round and somehow took part depending on the level of their social ability and they also had the job of ordering food, which they did individually and they all paid for their meal and so on, prior to stage two which was this round table thing. The third aspect was you all go back and you all have your meal, depending on where you sit and who you are sat next to, you interact with them. That turned out to be an awful lot better, one girl and one guy in particular wanted to search for the meaning of their life, so we discussed that and that appeared to form a kind of bond between the three of us, and all three of us were expecting that perhaps next time we could take it a little further, but that time never came because they were only showing me and that this cannot be offered on an ongoing basis, and were unable to say that they could in future, again on the basis that they wouldn't be able to offer me anything after my constructive criticism and feedback which was either taken completely the wrong way by not understanding that it was constructive criticism, and nor could they defend or discuss it because they had nothing to say. The two people I was talking to: one was married and was trying to come to terms with his diagnosis and why his wife had to be so understanding etc. The other was trying to get a job and not feeling that she was succeeding."

Gave charity constructive criticism yet it was take negatively; illustrates double empathy problem and lack of Theory of Mind.

Rod: It seems that you were looking for commonality in other people, but others you came into contact with after diagnosis was not reflective of your experiences.

"Well, more than that, I felt that if they were running such a thing, then the beauty of being able to help each other should have been fostered, and it actually wasn't, it was frowned upon because I don't know, whether it is because of health and safety or whatever and you could get into the wrong hands; you could be because of your gullibility in being misled, and therefore the charity would be accountable for that, I don't know, but there was so much that they could have got out of taking the three of us that naturally got together and could be empowered; they could have done that, but they didn't. Totally controlling. The point that I wanted to make was that I couldn't find any positive help for somebody who they regarded as competent, and yet the difficulties that I have got, were as real as anybody else in that room, if not more so, because I could understand the implications and the difficulties and the impact; and all of those could actually be very soul destroying."

Rod – I would imagine that if you were put in a position of a mentor within that group, you might have the insight to be able to assist in a more positive way?

The beauty of trying to help each other was frowned upon. It wasn't therapeutic to anybody. This feeds in to the aspect that 'autistic' people ought to be mentoring each other and are in similar positions. People are attracted to people in similar positions in society so don't base judgments on pairing merely on the basis of a two or more people being 'autistic'.

Functioning levels aspects: the way he was treated did not recognize his difficulties, as he was able to hide his level of functioning.

Free people being treated as prisoners. Human rights legislation.

"Absolutely, and that was not considered. That was one thing they told me; the other thing I went to was a social evening where we played bowling, and again it was not a social evening at all, it was like a day release for mental patients where we were treated as such, although they were residing in the community and all legally classed as free citizens. It was disgusting. That was very scary; it was also very, very disappointing because what I was looking for, they weren't able to give me; they were possibly able to give me but they didn't have the time. I think that what should happen is that the people who are out there, so called societies to help everybody with the condition; if somebody goes along with a badge saying I am Autistic there should be room for help at whatever level and every level. It's about opportunity and my experiences are that there was none of that whatsoever, and that disappointed me horribly and I realized that on a national basis another charity was equally unfeeling; they had a wonderful resource on the computer which pointed you to various documentation, and they ran various campaigns, which were not actually providing the help that I think a national organization should. I think that most of the research is still based on children. The reason that I feel that I have managed my way through life is that I have a support structure in other people who accept me for who I am and without that support structure being in place on an ongoing basis, and at the end of a phone and/ or a knock at the door, or whatever way

I want to start a discussion or a chat of any form because something is not right and I want to understand it; I have that support structure in place; for many people who don't have that support structure in place, there is no structure in their social life and that is something that should be recognized and somehow that support structure should be explained, put in place, but enabled by the individual themselves to put it in place; so it is a set of skills that need to be passed over to people who haven't learned those skills or who find it difficult to understand why those skills are so important, because you need help in the community that is ever present; it's not good enough to run something once a month to meet a bunch of people under strict terms and conditions; what you need to do is have them in their own environment that they are comfortable with and a structure they feel safe with, and understanding people within that structure who understand their condition and their needs. Also acceptance by the community; I don't think that is difficult; there are many people now who have children who their children are being told that they have these difficulties and they are Autistic in nature, and therefore Autism is becoming something that is much more known about; but it is because of the nature of understanding of people at schools and such like, rather than the clinical fraternity who know sweet FA about Autism. I wholeheartedly, unquestionably believe that diagnosis should be conducted on a family basis, because this is what I mean by these networks,	He has a support structure from his family and the community, and yet he recognizes that this is not present in the community for others, and is needed. Individuals should have help to set up support structures in the community.

	and family is the strongest, closest, if it works, a group that should be enabled, and that means that you will find out when you have a diagnosis just how far apart they are, or are not. It is not just about Autism, but how do you care, and how do you provide the care and the understanding for somebody with a difficulty, which is not an illness; if it were an illness then everyone would say that I have a carer etc.; if it were just a difficulty and a social difficulty can actually be really annoying; if it were defined then it would already fit into existing service provision."	People with 'autism' can express emotion; he cried. Still finds identity crisis painful. Got help from Rod and by working with him. Through correct mentoring you have empowerment on both sides. So it's a form of therapy for both people. 'Autistic' people can develop a sense of a role within society. It can also provide a benchmark for which people can decide who's a friend and who is not a friend. So it can help in judgment. And this can also feed in to how 'autistic' people can develop a network.
On reflection		
What is your perception now? Do you feel any different now, on reflection?	*"Yes I do; very much so. I went through an identity crisis (participant crying), which I still find painful, and actually that is at that point that I needed help, and I got it from working with you; I wouldn't have got it any other way; I would have been as frustrated as hell trying to get the knowledge and understanding that I did by working with you; I don't think it would have been possible, and I would have ended up with a very poor understanding, and then I would have given up on it and then just dismissed it, where as I have found that being able to relate thought processes to being Autistic has been enlightening, and interesting and I have had the power and the knowledge to be able to put it in its rightful place and feeling the right way about it. There is a lot of philosophy going on and I don't think that other people will get that, and without*	

298

that I don't see how their lives would change, and I can see how if, say I was a little deeper into the Autistic Spectrum than I am, I think that I would become very isolated; there were times in my life where I just had to be isolated, but I think I would have withdrawn, and I chose as a coping strategy that the only way out of this was an affirmation of my previous decisions to have friends that I would trust and friends who would trust me; their availability at the end of a phone or whatever; people who have their different roles, so that social network that is missing from most Autistic people's lives; it is that in my opinion that has to be addressed, and you shouldn't be talking in terms of carers, you should be talking in terms as part of your social structure; you are part of this world, and you provided the Autism knowledge component to a wonderful extent; Maybe the role of charities, rather than provide social groups is to provide a network of similar people so they can be hooked up, but you need a group and a mentor in that group and you need them to sign up to an understanding of what a group is about, what it delivers and defined roles. I have seen many individuals, who when isolated they are not in a good place mentally, when they felt they had something to contribute that people valued, they became different people, and this is what groups and structures and groups would do and acceptance and bringing out those skills, and their role in giving as well as receiving."

He recommends that charity(ies) encourage(s) networking. When people feel they can contribute and help they feel valued and are able to give and receive.

| In hindsight, how could your diagnosis have been done better? | *"I would have liked a pathway of enlightenment, like we have discussed; as I say, I don't think people understand the re-living that I had to do, and I'm sure that I can't be on my own of going back on things in life, turning points in your life when you made a decision a certain way and then you analyze and think, well, that was a good decision, or that was a bad decision, why did you make those decisions, and now you can start pasting over what you did know at the time, the additional knowledge of what it is like to be on the spectrum, and then you become a little bit more enlightened. Until you have relived your life, you can't actually put that down. With regrets and me, I was fortunate because I think I have made an awful lot of right decisions, they haven't always been good for me in terms of not making my life easier, but they have been good because at the end of it I have felt improved as an individual and as such it has all been worth it. It may not have been worth it for the effort I had to put into it but I think that goes with the job as it were; it goes with the condition. I think my wife and me work very well together but I don't think you can receive help without wanting to give it; it's a two way process and as much as I receive help from her I think she receives help from me. She is obviously of a very nervous disposition naturally, but not many people would guess that; she is quiet but she always thinks things through and she always contributes and I think she has* | He would have liked "A pathway of enlightenment".

Giving and receiving is a two-way process; this is what he has learnt from his wife.

He's also written that his wife lacks confidence, and maybe it this aspect that has empowered him. |

	Him, like other participants, was aware and tried to analyze the problems in a systemizing way. Fitting in to Baron-Cohen's theory.
	become more assertive as we've lived together longer. She just lacks self-confidence, which is a trait in her family. It is interesting that her lack of confidence helps us to complement each other and empower each other; we are still happy with how the relationship is working. We have always analyzed things because I have always had to be analytical in order to obtain confirmation, which helps in social skills by ensuring an understanding of each other's thought processing. So, it is having the right type of support which is not something that is once every month, but hopefully and ideally is everyday and is continuous, twenty four hours a day, seven days a week. This won't be derived from service provision, but on the basis of family and/or community, with services initiating that. You need somewhere to have this discourse, and if you have a group of you, forget about the costing of money due to the travel and so on, but there are expenses involved and it does cost money to get from one side of town to the other if you do that where as if you introduce one neighbour to another, or being able to provide the skills so that you can do it for yourself which is the end result.
What was good about the process?	*Coming back to the process, good about the process is that it had a structure to it, a wide structure, probing structure and at any point I felt free to be able to go in there and probe it even further.*

What was bad about the process?	*Bad, is just this lack of what a diagnosis should be, it should be the start of a journey, a journey of understanding, and they have no one to hand you over to, they have got no ideas that they are giving you to take the next step; how do you get to understand it enough to be able to be able to understand what it means to you as an individual and so on; what's the point of a diagnosis if you don't have a path to do something about it. Looking in books, you can put your own interpretation on it and it ends up with no one saying it didn't mean that at all, what it really means is da di da de da and I can't learn unless I get that clarification, so it is a process, particularly in areas such as socializing, which is the fundamental issue in many ways to all of what we have been talking about, and I think that the difficulty is that empowerment, the ability to start the process off so that you've got the rest of your life to improve your skills in that, and I didn't get any of that. It's not to do with trying harder, it's about enlightenment; how do you get benefit out of a diagnosis, when you have no medicine to take; there has to be a way of pointing people down their pilgrims route that they then need to start addressing, and not only that, there is this need for other people to take that journey with you; it's a very lonely journey and it's an impossible journey. Another aspect is that diagnosis doesn't assess how your brain works and there is this aspect that when everyone is assigned the same label, it is assumed that everyone is the same*	Post-diagnosis: whether an individual needs time to process that? Say someone's at work, coming to terms and/or not coming to terms, can be more of an unconscious process. For example, if someone is still interacting socially at work and has bad experiences, then they go home and read a book, and it could just reinforce that what's happening to them is purely their fault. He didn't find books satisfying.

	where as we are all unique individuals and that doesn't come across to me from the professionals at all. I think that they are looked on as a Doctor who looks on a patient, and therefore it is a type of parent/child relationship, and actually you need to have it on an equal basis; somehow you need to create an environment where you can be equals in what your relationship is, and I think that is absolutely critical, and how do you go from a diagnosis to an understanding of what that means to you, how do you get your proper understanding, what does that mean to you and how can that affect your life."	You need an environment based on equality.
What impact has your diagnosis had on the understanding of who you are?	*"Tremendous: I feel better for knowing myself than I did before because there were parts of me that I didn't understand that I understand much better now because if there is something that I didn't understand, I re-thought through it, you know, why did I react like that? I now can understand it and I can manage it so much better now, and I can account for it so much better now. The thing that really hit me was when I just explained to just a few people, because I initially thought that I would have to go around and tell everyone I was Autistic, and I spoke to just a few people close to me and they were good enough to understand why I was talking to them and why I needed them for a couple of hours and we went for a walk and discussed it, and the wonderful consistent story that came back was that, yea we noticed that you were a bit withdrawn at times or a bit awkward, but that's you."*	Tremendous impact on self-understanding. Told a few people, close to him, and had a walk with them. His friends were very socially accepting as they knew him before he got a diagnosis, and post-diagnosis still accepted him, and that's something most families can't achieve. How is it that friends can be accepting and yet families can be rejecting? Rod's analyzing of other people's experiences has enabled him to understand his experiences better; this is a form of mentoring.

	Like Christine, he talks a lot about the process of what he would like to see. ASSESS IDEAS THIS PERSON HAS WITH OTHER PARTICIPANTS. How do you change it from a medical model to a social one?
Is there anything else you would like to add?	"How do you change the condition from a medical one to a community one? How do you change these charities and do gooders through a stage beyond understanding to one that we have just discussed that is a community, integrated type of resolution; realizing that there are many people out there who can contribute, could contribute if, and if treated right would contribute in a way that we just don't benefit from at the moment; and if you had that, the word benefit is an interesting one because at the moment they do get benefits and are actually written off and warehoused whereas what they should do is just understand a little bit of enlightenment to give people part of the game of socializing and that the give back they will give will enhance them as individuals and it's an ever increasing set of skills and it's not only a self-learning process, but it should be a natural self learning process, where as it is not a natural process to Autistic people because they are so wrapped up in the intricacies of trying to understand themselves that there is no time to understand others, and so they do need to be given a good education and what it really is that's going on and that will enlighten them and then they need the support structure around them to help them move

from one position to another. I can't see any health organization, any charity or anything going on in the community whatsoever to enlighten people with the condition and all those with them. How do you achieve that? Because it doesn't cost money."	Enlightenment of the 'autistic' community is needed. A community style revolution is required.
In relation to the deficit medical model of disability, Jack said *"There are two answers to that because there are two aspects 1) How did it effect me 2) Did I feel I was handicapped in any way, no, I didn't feel that and I have not had any of that sort of way of thinking up until the diagnosis, so I had no baggage; I had no pre-conception of what it meant. So that was my next thought, what does it all mean and lets start the journey. So, from that point of view, no I didn't feel handicapped in any way, but getting to know more about the condition has led me frustratingly to read very many books that haven't meant an awful lot to me, talked to an awful lot of people, most of which hasn't helped very much; tried to seek help from organizations where you'd expect it to be given, and not found; really getting quite angry that even though I was regarded as on the spectrum, there was no help, their was no guidance, there was no way of understanding that would be given to you, other than what you found out yourself, and that made me really annoyed. What are these organizations out their doing? They are raising other issues; they don't stick to their original cause and they wander way off."*	He didn't find books satisfying.

James: Matrix (Private diagnosis)

Current age: 59

Age when diagnosis was conducted: 57 (2011)

Current social and economic situation: *"I'm trained and work as a Social Worker. I'm comfortable being in the community and believe myself to be middle class, but not sure. I own my own house, am married with no children but I have two relationships with wife's children and am financially not too bad."*

Official diagnoses by name: *"Asperger Syndrome ('at the top of the scale', she said)"*

Questions	Responses	Analytical memos
Pre-Diagnosis		
Why did you seek a diagnosis?	*"It was quite a strange set of sequences. The first person to mention anything of the sort was my mother when I was 7 years old, I was a person who didn't fit in; strange; on the wrong end of everything; problems persisted even when working unless it was very precise and very ridged I couldn't do it. When I went to university to study social work, I met mothers of children who were Autistic, and prior to that I had worked with some service users who were Autistic and had Asperger's Syndrome, and subsequently became a subject I became engrossed with. Going to University expanded on that interest. I ended up transferring that knowledge to University and ended up doing a presentation on it and whilst working with service users I started noticing traits in myself, but was unsure but it*	Describing definite autistic traits, e.g. on the wrong end of things, a different cognitive style. Rigidality of thought. Not fitting in.

It seems strange that his mother had mentioned it was he was 7 and he actually worked with autistic people. It's like things had to get really bad, especially at work with his employer, that he sought a diagnosis. This links in with DSM5 regarding social demands exceeding limited capacity. When social demands exceed limited capacity this is the point where many adults may seek a diagnosis. |

Given the possibility as above, could it be that when an adult is recognized as autistic that this is the combination of differences and the current social situation? I'm alluding to this aspect that when an assessment is done may the autistic elements need to be separated from the social, i.e. the social pressures cannot be seen as medical. There are a lot of people out there who only believe the autistic person when you're under that kind of social pressure. There needs to be a paradigm shift through diagnostic assessments as communication tools so that the hidden nature of autism in line with social pressures are understood by individuals reading these assessments.

The social pressures were as such that he was desperate. GP said that there's an 18-month waiting list. Autism has been in the diagnostic manuals for a very long time, so why does it seem that there is a lack of professionals with relevant knowledge and expertise to diagnose?

"I'd lost who I was": he's been different all his life and through constantly being given advice by others on how to fit in he'd become in the middle of two worlds. The NT he aspired to and the autistic who he always has been. One could infer that he was seeking a diagnosis in the hope that he would find out who he was. "I was looking for an identity".

became more apparent the more research I did, so I had arguments in my head, am I inducing this or is it me, with everything going all over the place, I just couldn't put it together. I was having problems with concentration at University and ended up teaching most of the stuff to myself. I couldn't cope with University, getting around and getting there. I did more research and when things were getting difficult at work, so I talked to my GP about it, and she referred me for an assessment at the hospital, who contacted me and said the earliest appointment was in 18 months time, but I didn't know if I could last that long, so we decided to go private, with my wife paying."

"When we went for the assessment I was thinking we'll solve it, am I trying to solve anything, I'd lost who I was; that was one of the reasons I wanted the assessment was to find out who I was, so I can put it quite clearly, maybe this is just behavioral or it's just the way I think, I don't know. We went through the tests and I was looking for something, trying to explain why life had been so peculiar and so difficult all the

Question	Quote	Commentary
	way along. My wife was very supportive and she was with me throughout the assessment. I was looking for an identity, as I didn't think I ever had one. I needed to know whether someone professionally agreed with my thoughts."	How is it that a qualified social worker has to have his wife seek out someone to diagnose..? It's quite clear that even as a social worker, James was unaware of the referral process, in other words he wasn't aware whether he was going to be taken to the closes Psychiatric facility and/or what to expect from the process. This is something that the NICE guideline is looking to address. Note: Does the NICE guidelines give clear guidance and advice about what to expect from the process? It may be useful for alleviating parents' anxieties, but how about for the individual undergoing the process?
How long did it take you to seek a diagnosis?	"My wife organized it and researched over many months to seek the most professional, respected and qualified person instead of seeking anyone out who would just give a diagnosis. We discounted anyone who would give a diagnosis as long as you paid them. So, it was a couple of months. All my GP just said that if anyone cancelled then I could be seen quicker; by that time I was desperate so it only took a couple of months of raising the money and finding someone. Under the NHS I think I would have been diagnosed by a Clinical Psychologist; it wouldn't have been a multi-disciplinary team, it would have just been a straight forward assessment."	
What knowledge of autism did you have prior to diagnosis?	"I had a basic knowledge; enough to do a presentation on the Triad of Impairments. I didn't have an in-depth knowledge of exactly what goes on. I had an interest; I had suspicions but I wasn't self-diagnosing. I knew Autism existed and Asperger's Syndrome but I wasn't clear what the difference was. It was an interest but I was reading anything too in-depth about it."	Does having prior knowledge or not affect the assessment? If I had prior knowledge of autism before going for an assessment maybe I would have identified with such knowledge more so and therefore the behavior may have been more apparent. This is an interesting aspect regarding functionality.

| What were your expectations prior to attending? | "I thought it might have given me a reason of who I am, also I was apprehensive about where do I go if it isn't. I wanted an answer and for somebody to explain but I also wanted someone who could professionally do that, not just patting me on the head and saying you're on, because that's what happens to a lot of people I've seen since. My expectations were to have a resolution as to whether I was right or whether I was wrong, or another reason as to why I was having such difficulties in such simple areas. I've always had a concept as to why can't I just pick it up and do it like they do. I was just trying to put my life back on track so I could go in a straight line as apposed to going round in circles, which is something I was doing at the time. Regarding the diagnostic procedure, I knew it needed to take into account background. I work in an environment where a CP (Clinical Psychologist) has to do a depression assessment, you go in, you go out, you meet the criteria and it's all quite simple. I knew that the assessments for Asperger Syndrome were far more concise; there was a lot more traits to be taken into account. I was aware that it was to do with childhood; it was a lifelong assessment rather than just what is happening now. I was aware that any chronic issues happening around me now were not going to be connected to the assessment; everybody's opinion including my wife's would be taken into account. I feel it was a bit awkward not having my parents there for assessment, as they were dead. I knew it would involve tests and involve both verbal and observation components." | 1. His prior knowledge of assessment came from a professional perspective in line with simpler diagnoses that he was aware of, such as depression. He recognized that...

2. Parents were dead. As autism seems to require a developmental history, i.e. when the child is of an age before personality has fully formed but also before mental health problems develop (because it is crucial to differentiate between the autism aspects and possible mental health aspects).

How accurately can autism be diagnosed where there is a lack of developmental history?

Hypothesis: what you could have, for example, is somebody who seeks a diagnosis, have no developmental history because parents are dead, and this person may base their developmental history on what they've read regarding autism and actually obtain a diagnosis of autism despite not being so...?

Though why would anyone seek a diagnosis for autism if they weren't autistic? But you might have someone who is schizophrenic.

In every one of these cases it has been the person who has referred themself(ves). It has not been picked up and acted upon. If the issues were to do with depression, OCD or schizophrenia then maybe the individual would automatically be referred automatically for an assessment. |

Diagnosis		
Can you take me through your diagnosis as you experienced it then? What were you thinking/ feeling at the time?	*"The Clinician did not take into account early developmental history, as my parents were dead, but they did take into account later developmental history and the opinion of my wife. The Clinician asked about certain social situations and what the outcome was, did I have difficulties, were there any specific social issues that arose. She put the questions in a way that I could only give a direct answer to. There wasn't any loaded questions."* *"I was numb. I was apprehensive prior to going. I was quite worried and scared and questioning whether I have done the right thing; is this a good idea? Maybe we'd better forget it."* RM: "What was behind the fear?" *"I was trying to find a solution and it might not be there, so where do I go, what do I do after that. I was trying to put that out of my head. I talked about it with my wife; is prior knowledge a good thing or a bad thing; maybe you shouldn't seek a diagnosis if you have already got suspicions! That is what brought the anxiety up. When I got there, she was very specific in what was going to happen. I was told that 'no matter what happens in here, you are going to be the same person when you get out; you're not going to be a different person.' (These alleviated my anxieties and worries that I had prior)*	The developmental history would have come from him when talking with his wife, as she would not have known him at the age of 3, in terms of the diagnosis is this ethical? Could additional developmental history be sourced, e.g. school reports? When autism is so prominent, as is the case with this participant (monotone voice, clear black and white thinking, rigidity of thought) is the seeking of developmental history necessary? Possible theme: do the issues of like feeling anxious prior to attending diagnosis affect presentation and does that find itself in the diagnostic assessment? Aspects that are unnatural could find themselves in the description of that individual. Does the diagnostic environment provide for the correct assessment of the individual's natural state? 1. The aspect of functioning: how can this be measured in such cases? 2. Because other people, like employers, may be privy to the "report they may view as the behaviours of the report as being natural and continuous for that individual. How can one measure an accurate record?

Communication style was automatically formatted for the "autistic" personality type. [Questions were unambiguous and direct, closed questioning]

Regarding the criteria and repetitive behaviour, those that do not exhibit it are placed in a new category, not in 'autism', now for an adult like me, I wouldn't exhibit such repetitive behaviour. However, ask an adult whether they exhibit repetitive thinking and it is likely they'll say yes.

Behaviours may become more severe when social demands exceed limited capacity; this feeds in to new criteria.

Once it started, it was just a series of questions, which wasn't so bad; she gave me plenty of time to answer the questions so it took a long time. It got easer as the process went on. She was very straight with the questions; there was none of this 'what do you think'. There were time-limited tests, which were all very structured. She wouldn't say they were time limited until I was about half way through and if I was struggling where there was an expectation. She also interviewed my wife, both separately and together. She asked what my interests were and to what degree. She quoted the DSM and said that 'all her observation and evidence has to fit certain criteria; that it's not just based on her opinion, it's based on fitting the criteria and if you don't fit the criteria, you don't get the diagnosis.' She was a very frank person, which I view as good. I got less anxious as it went along. When it ended, she went to make her assessment and I was notified later on through the post.

What was the environment like?	*"It was quite a small environment; it was comfortable, there wasn't anything getting in the way. There wasn't anything influencing me from the outside and didn't cause any bother; it was a nice small room; the lighting was ok as it wasn't bright; it wasn't a clinical environment and it was quite a small place. It wasn't a huge building which was good. Parking was easy also."*
Was it suitable?	

311

Did they make adjustments to the environment?	"She did ask, 'is the environment ok?' and if there was anything that needed adjustment, to which I said there wasn't."	
Did you feel that you were receiving a 'full profile' assessment?	"I had a series of tests; I don't know how detailed an assessment is supposed to be; I knew it involved my life as a whole and the ability to do certain things. I didn't know how detailed those things were supposed to be; I was leaving it up to the professional as I didn't know enough to say 'you haven't done that bit', because obviously the younger you are the easer it is. At my age there wasn't any school reports to reflect back on. She went down the sensory profiling road and asked about that. Sensory issues causes me a lot of problems, such as the sensation of shaking hands and how that sensation affects me and not that I just don't not like shaking hands. She asked about other issues such as smells and similar issues and social interaction and asked if there were any issues with that and his wife backed this up from an observational, independent point of view, reflecting on particular instances that she observed and didn't know what was going on and that most of the interaction between me and my wife wasn't reciprocal at all. So, all these issues were covered; the sensory issues were covered which is something that I wasn't aware of at that particular time. As far as I was aware, from a Psychologist point of view, she covered everything at that particular moment in time. I believe that if I had	James didn't know how detailed the process is supposed to be, but he had a series of tests. Not knowing what to expect, will cause anxiety and therefore affect behavior and the answers given. Is this a true reflection of the individual and have these tests been built on a quicksand of deficit-based methodology in order to protect everyone else? He wasn't aware of the sensory issues both within a test aspect and also within and of himself. Suggests that most people don't communicate in how they experience the world. Is this the root cause of the difficulties? It is good that sensory issues were covered in the assessment. Note: compare with other participant. What test was used? Assessment consisted of sensory profiling issues with social interaction which were backed up by his wife and observational aspects of the interaction between him and his wife, which wasn't reciprocal. As there were no school reports or developmental history, assessment was conducted on the here and now. There were fewer resources to go on. Would this be the same for those who were

	been younger, there would have been more tests, although I don't know what the test for children are."	adopted? He believes that he received a full profile assessment. Bearing in mind that this was pre-DSM-5, before sensory issues were formally incorporated.
	"She went through my medical history, social interaction, childhood development, social interests and routine; she mentioned something called the AAA, communication, imagination, and motor co-ordination. She said that I was also displaying other traits."	She used the "AAA" (Adult Asperger Assessment) tool. Note: with the changes in diagnostic criteria and the recommendation of the tool in the NICE guidelines, does this mean that everybody has to be reassessed using that one recommended tool, but also in line with the new criteria? Additional assessments would be useful. Probably as other things, e.g. dyslexia, dyspraxia etc may have been missed.
What level/ type of professional conducted your diagnosis?	*"Under the GP, I think a Clinical Psychiatrist would have diagnosed me. It wouldn't have been a multi-disciplinary team as it was just an assessment. My occupational health doctor knew the clinician and this gave me more confidence as he said that she is an extremely competent person who he has known for quite a while. The person who diagnosed me was an MSC Health Psychologist, councilor for a charity, diploma in casework and supervision. That is her title. She does counseling in the subject as well specializing in Asperger Syndrome over a 10-year period, 1st class honors degree etc."*	James thinks that under his GP, a Clinical Psychiatrist would have diagnosed him rather than a multi-disciplinary team. The person who diagnosed him was an MSC Health Psychologist, councilor for a charity, diploma in casework and supervision. She does counseling in the subject as well as specializing in Asperger Syndrome over a 10-year period. Regarding appropriate person to identify Autism – It may not be about qualifications, but experience and who the person is!

Was this suitable?	*"I do believe that with the knowledge I have, that she was suitable. I don't know if a professional has to have a particular title before you can diagnose but she has many years of experience; she was well known and thought of by my occupational health doctor who thought highly of her. I assumed if she wasn't of a high standard or sufficiently positioned, she wouldn't have been able to give a diagnosis, or wouldn't have been allowed to. She seemed very detailed; I don't know if any of the other processes are any different. I didn't think at any time that it could have been any more in-depth, because I was an older adult and there were fewer resources to go on, but she seemed thorough. He doesn't know whether her title enables that."*	James believes that she was qualified to diagnose. Given that this woman is not a medical professional, will his diagnosis be recognized in law? Would it not be better if such a diagnostician have her assessments signed off by a psychiatrist, especially given that most psychiatrists would not have spent over 10-years studying the subject? Also, if he did see a psychiatrist, he/she could have ruled out other conditions. He does not know whether her title enables her to be thorough. Comes back to who makes a person qualified to identify autism!
Post-diagnosis		
How did you feel directly after the diagnostic procedure?		
How/or/and/ when did it hit you?	*"It is still hitting me. Immediately afterwards I thought the diagnosis was a solution or an identity, and I then thought what do you do with it! So what! That in itself doesn't solve any issues; that is when I asked myself, where does this leave me; who am I?. Can I work from this? I didn't know if anything was going to hit me out of the blue such as like that solves everything now. It explained a few reasons but it didn't give a pathway toward the future either.*	James is still coming to terms with his diagnosis two years on. What do you do with a diagnosis? And a hidden one. It costs a lot of money to get a diagnosis. For example, it can cost up to and beyond £1400

	"What do you do with it? Do you tell people? My wife told her sons and they said we don't know whether to say whether that's good or not. What do you do with a diagnosis, and a hidden one? A diagnosis made me feel better, but I wasn't sure how anyone else was going to react to it; its taken me 57 years to get to this stage; how long is it going to take everybody else. I didn't have any euphoria. I thought that this is a solution and then I suddenly realized that it isn't. It's like somebody giving you a new name; is that going to change your life! Well no, its not going to change your life, you're still going to be who you are; you can't cure it, cant do anything, just got to work with it, then I'm going to need support to work with it and I know that people say that you should work in your special interest areas, but that wasn't working at work; I didn't think it was going to solve anything at work; if I had lost a leg it would have been a lot easer. I thought I might have euphoria, but I didn't; it was a non-event."	for one. If an individual is led to believe that a diagnosis is going to make a difference, and this is not the case, is could be fraudulent? If someone was on the street was paid £5 to tell you some negative things about you, they'd be happy to do so. Get a Clinician at every corner, pay them and get a diagnosis! It has taken him 57 years to get here, how long will it take for everyone else? One of the common themes that is present throughout all interviews is that it seems individuals are led to believe, or they believed etc., that diagnosis would be recognized, that they'd be able to get positive help and support and life would be made easier. But after diagnosis their experiences didn't always live up to those expectations. Autism not recognized as a disability by society, despite being formally recognized in law. Is the law being broken? Is it legal to break the law?
Did the clinician/ diagnostician ask you to read and sign your diagnosis off?	*"Yes, she did. They signed it later after she did it. She sent it through the post with a request for it to be signed and returned. No amendments or changes were requested or made. My wife read through it as well and didn't see the need for any amendments."*	In his case, yes, the report was signed off. In other cases, it wasn't. Inconsistency exists. This is going to be one of the themes – inconsistency: 1. If everybody isn't permitted to sign it off, then how does anybody know that some of these reports are actually incorrect?

		2. When someone is asked to sign, often within a short period of time, it's on the basis that the individual has a decent knowledge of autism to do that. In addition, a person can go along with maybe decades of experience in autism, s/&he may be able to fake it.	
Did you read it all?	*"I did read it all."*		
How did you feel when reading it?	*"I found this a difficult question to answer as I didn't know what I was expecting to see in the assessment such as how technical it was supposed to be, but there were different quotes from the DSM criteria and how many I had to fill to reach the diagnosis, and what it would mean. It highlighted evidence; as far as she was concerned to say that I fitted the criteria. It didn't have an emotional effect as we just read it through without experiencing emotions."*	He didn't know what to expect at the assessment – did not know the format. Recommendation: a clear format, or several formats, of instructions and information for the participant. If all Clinicians used different pro-forma for different reasons and for different readers this would be useful.
Were you given the opportunity to preview your report and comment on it before it was finalized?	*"Yes"*		

Question	Quote	Commentary
What did you think of the language and the perspective in the report?	"It was all objective. It was understandable; she explained why she had reached her decision. She would pick out different criteria in the DSM and why I fitted it. I was happy with the language."	DSM is an American publication and he is a U.K. citizen.
What were the recommendations on your assessment for a way forward?	"She advised me to read more about the syndrome in an effort to increase the understanding of myself and the effect it has on my communication and interaction with others. I was advised to avoid becoming over stressed, which will cause more Asperger traits; I need to have a place that I can retreat to in order to enable me time to process and get things back into gear. I find it difficult to express emotions etc. She didn't offer any specific groups and there are not any groups where I live. She just advised me to do some more research. There were no specific recommendations other than carry out more research for self-knowledge. The onus was on me."	The Clinician has implied and asserted that this guy does not know anything about himself. It seems that Clinicians are more concerned about giving someone a label. It may be fine to a point, however, the diagnosis has to relate to the person as an individual. For example, if a person reads up Baron-Cohen's materials and thinks that it all applies to them they may think that the reason why they are isolated is because that's the way they are, however, that's not the reason. Society is not inclusive enough. Having a place to retreat to; is this like a quiet room they have for kids? Seems childlike. Is it fair for the individual to do all the research themselves? What was supposed to be the aim of this? Was it to imply that if he does a lot of research then he'll find out more about himself? And thus compensate for his difficulties? Does this imply a lack of Theory of Mind? Bearing in mind he's a trained social worker.

On reflection		
What is your perception now? Do you feel any different now, on reflection?	*"It has taken a long time for me to be who I am. I am still having problems conforming as I am not allowing me to be myself. In retrospect I see my diagnosis as the right thing to do. I feel different on reflection now, although I am still looking for who I am, fully, I do feel different because I have an outside view of myself now, where as I didn't have one before. Before, when things were going wrong, I didn't know why, but I now feel that I have a bit more control of how I react to others and how they react to me, and although I don't feel more confident, I feel more informed of what to do and how to do and that if an issue comes up, how I can cope with it. Whether or not you like it, you have to fit in; so I think it was worth it as it has resolved some doubts in my head and I was encouraged and boosted by the fact that the occupational health doctor new this person very well and had a lot of respect which gave me more confidence in her assessment. Some of the tests are quite intricate but are for people who are much younger. I am confused about what I have learned normally as an adult in life, and that I had coping mechanisms, which I hadn't realized were coping mechanisms in situations where I panicked and had to leave; and I didn't know what that was about; I thought it was about blaming me. I am not blaming myself as much as I used to. I am still hiding my differences, but I see that as good as it is for the benefit of other*	He feels like he can confirm better if he was actually left to be himself. That sentence alone suggests that he's having issues to do with identity. Are current assessments right for adults? As with this individual, he did actually say that his diagnostic test were for people much younger. Considering this person was diagnosed at the age of 57, wouldn't there need to be different and/or adjusted tests for adults? Is a diagnosis for the benefit of other people in the hope that it will eventually benefit the individual? Also, he's describing the aspect of unconscious coping strategies. How about if this aspect of lack of cognitive empathy is actually unconscious coping strategies that the individual is not aware? Maybe the lack of ToM are unconscious coping strategies? Maybe the brain compensates for all the 'interventions' people try and utilize with you. There is a lot written about the aspect of people covering up by pretending to be someone they're not, but how about this persona or character that doesn't exist? He's protecting something that he hasn't got, i.e. the persona he hasn't got.

	people. I have seen people speak and they say 'if you don't like it then get out', but that's the way I am; I don't tend to do that because I am still trying to fit in and projecting a character that I haven't got. I am still having difficulty coming to terms with that and having a hard time saying to people this is how I think due to the responses of them saying what are you going to do about it then. There are still a lot of problems and conflict at work as there is still an expectation that I can change and be able to do what everyone else does. I am frustrated by my workplace in that they don't understand Asperger's Syndrome and that it is my problem and that I can change and that is my responsibility. I have difficulty with situations where there are issues with mentalizing on both sides, with the Burdon being firmly placed on me, such as being told that I must fit in etc."	He's describing Damien Milton's theory of the double empathy problem.
In hindsight, how could your diagnosis have been done better?	*"If there were more family members it would have been more convincing for me, and if it had of been done sooner."*	Is he saying: maybe the diagnosis should be done on a family basis! Diagnosis can split a family. Would it be more ethical to state that: The person experiences these difficulties because of the lack of support. The medical diagnosis report alone justifies Local Authorities not doing anything.
What was good about the process?		

What was bad about the process?	*"I don't think there was anything bad about it. I don't know if I should be re-referred and that one assessment is enough. I have had a work problems assessment with occupational health and they have taken my diagnosis into account but until recently they haven't acted on it and no one has ever taken the diagnosis, such as the clinical depression component and put any recommendations into practice; they have just looked at it and then the process if finished. My diagnosis did not change anything regarding the workplace; everything went on as it did before; they just said 'so what'."*	Maybe within every diagnosis there should be quotes from laws, i.e. from the Equality Law, what the NHS should be doing etc. So it should actually be a legal document as anything else. There is this assumption on behalf of Clinicians that other professionals take these diagnoses seriously.
What impact has your diagnosis had on the understanding of who you are?	*"This is something I am still trying to work out. I am realizing that I am different and that my brain works differently and that there is nothing wrong with that and that I am more than an individual than I was as I was trying to be like everyone else. I still find it difficult to concentrate and to keep focus."*	He's coming across as though he is stuck between two worlds, e.g. he is different and that's okay, though he as to hide some aspects of himself in order to fit in with others. Maybe there is a gap between the diagnosis, i.e. that it's okay to be different, but the people around him have not. Thus causing a psychological dichotomy, which is bad when you have rigidity of thought.
Is there anything else you would like to add?	*"No"*	

Leanne: Matrix (NHS diagnosis)

Current age: 51

Age when diagnosis was conducted: 44 (2006)

Current social and economic situation: Has two jobs but are both part-time, both term-time, doesn't have a salary. *"I'm in a scary financial position, because my youngest son is 19 he is still in full time education for the next few weeks. In September the child benefit will stop and so will the child tax credits and family tax credits so I will be about £200 a week worse off, which is scary." "The last few weeks since my dad died, my boy has been brilliant and helped loads, he's answered the phone when I can't talk to anybody and he just tells everybody to go away; he has coped fantastically; I don't know what I'd have done without him and he doesn't get any recognition for that and he shouldn't have to have that responsibility but it's just the way it is."* Leanne has two sons and a daughter; *"both of my son's have been diagnosed but my daughter hasn't although this doesn't mean she is not on the spectrum."*

Official diagnoses by name: Asperger Syndrome

Questions	Responses	Analytical memos
Pre-Diagnosis		
Why did you seek a diagnosis?	*"I can't think of a short answer to these questions, so please be patient with me. My young son who was in a special school and, the short answer is that I was doing research because a couple of people independent of each other said the he had traits of Asperger Syndrome/Autism. One was a teacher at an infant's school that he had been permanently excluded from and I can't remember who the other person was; he ended up going because he was permanently excluded from three infant schools; that's pretty good going, so he ended up going to a special school, it was an EBD*	Leanne's first experience of Autism came from her conducting research regarding her son's difficulties. Simultaneously two people independent of each other said that he had traits of Autism. Despite major difficulties in getting her son diagnosed he was eventually correctly assessed this led her to recognize traits in herself. She self diagnosed and then sought formal diagnosis.

(educational and behavioral difficulties) school; he ended up being sent there because I had tried for a long while to get help because there was clearly something going wrong with the lad, he wasn't coping in school so we went through two CAMHS (Child and adolescent mental health services); where I live, we live on the boarder between two counties so if you get a doctor referral it could either be from one county or the other; it's just the way it works when you're on the county boundary, so we got sent to CAMHS in one county and then in another county and we saw various other people and it was all very difficult when you have a child on your own isn't it! I took him back to mainstream where they were holding back on it and I was saying can you look into it, and they were saying that 'he couldn't be autistic because he could talk', then when going all through that, 'it's not easy bringing up a child on your own, is it?' So, I did some research and I went on to a number of websites and I recognized the symptoms, so I self-diagnosed, went along to the doctors with loads of information and books because they wanted to put my son into a mainstream school and I really wanted to make sure he got the best provision, and because two people in his educational process had suggested that he had traits of Asperger Syndrome or Autism, so I wanted it pursued especially as my previous attempt had fallen short when I saw an educational psychologist who said he couldn't

Question	Quote	Analysis
	be autistic because he can 1: talk 2: he could understand words like patronizing. It was funny because about a year ago I was telling son about this and he said 'who's ed Psych? I thought there is no better example of somebody being on the non learning-disabled end of the autistic spectrum. It's just perfect, isn't it! I did some research, I self-diagnosed, I went to the doctor with all the research I got and he asked 'why do you think you have Asperger Syndrome?'"	Leanne paints quite a damming picture of professional knowledge of autism regarding her son stating that these professionals only considered autism if the person was non-verbal.
How long did it take you to seek a diagnosis?	*"6 months"*	
How did it come about?	*"I told him that I was researching on behalf of my son, then I recognized the symptoms/traits in myself, then I went to my GP and she referred me"*	As with Natalie who sought a diagnosis so that her children wouldn't feel alone in their Autism, Leanne was acting as a proxy for her son.
What were your expectations prior to attending?	*"This is where very personal, family history comes in. I was actually convinced that I did actually have Asperger's Syndrome, but I also have memories going back to my childhood of my mum saying 'why do you always have to have something wrong with you?' 'Why can't you just be normal?' 'Why can't you just be the same as everybody else?' 'Why can't you be more like your sister?' 'Why do you always have to have something wrong with you?' 'Why do you always have to be center of attention?' and so on, very negative things and I was just thinking, maybe I'm just making it up' maybe I just have to have something wrong with me. I was*	Part of Leanne's research prior to assessment was analyzing her family history. She has memories of her Mum being very psychologically abusive this is one component in her development where she lost her sense of self through experiencing the world in her own way and being told by everyone else that this was wrong (pretending to be normal) this aspect is often seen in families which is a natural form of ABA another psycho social interventions which cause untold damage and hardship to the individual. As a female she seemed to get on better with her Father more than her Mother. Is this consistent throughout female profiling of Autistic

	arguing with myself, but hold on a second, I wasn't looking for something to be wrong with me; I was looking for an answer for my son; I was being a proxy and it wasn't about me it was about my son; I wanted to know what is the right thing to do for him, I wanted the right way forward, I want to know what his issues are. So, that was where I was coming from. Apart from this, I can't remember having any expectations prior to diagnosis."	females and are the roles reversed for male Autistics? If so, this clearly highlights a need for the component of an assessment to be conducted on a family basis, especially if Baron Cohen is to be believed for example deficits in cognitive empathy, especially if these issues span the generations.
Diagnosis		
Can you take me through your diagnosis as you experienced it then?		
What were you thinking/ feeling at the time?	*"I think the overriding thing was how do I be autistic? When I realized I brought three books. I couldn't have picked three better books because they did what they said on the tin; yea, that's what it's like. So now I've got to learn how to be autistic; I spent so many years pretending to be normal, which didn't fucking work, but I don't know how to be autistic at all, so I was thinking crazy mad things." "I was thinking there was an interesting line in the skirting board; it was plastic skirting board and somebody made a really bad join and I was just looking at it all the time and she was wearing stripy trousers and ankle boots; I can't remember anything about what she looked like; I can just remember this wrong join in the skirting board in this little windowless office."*	During the assessment Leanne described Autistic traits such as attention to detail and fascination for certain things particularly with the skirting board and the clinicians stripy trousers and ankle boots.

What was the environment like?	"It was like they made a little office out of a bigger place, and they had not done the skirting board right and I was staring at it all the time thinking that was just wrong, and I can't answer any better than that."	
Was it suitable?	"From what I have read since, I think the environment was very low arousal."	Leanne didn't think the environment was suitable.
Did they make adjustments to the environment?	"No, I don't think they did."	They did not make adjustments.
Did you feel that you were receiving a 'full profile' assessment?	"Yes, at the time. Since then I have realized they didn't have a fucking clue how to do it."	Since reading further about Autism she realised that the environment was very low arousal and although at the time she assumed that she was receiving a full profile assessment she now realizes that the clinician did not know how to do it.
What level/ type of professional conducted your diagnosis?	"It was a person working in elderly mental health care and she must have downloaded this questionnaire off the Internet. She did the GADS (Gilliam Asperger's Disorder Scale) test, which is aimed at children. So I have a Pervasive Developmental Disorder, but I was 44. You know what, they didn't have a fucking clue; they just pulled somebody off elderly mental health care; I was only 44, you know; it's a joke."	Highlighting that she was a person working in elderly mental health care and using a questionnaire off the internet that was for children this raises issues regarding who is fit to diagnose and also what the individual doesn't suspect at the time.
Was this suitable?		

Post-diagnosis		
How did you feel directly after the diagnostic procedure?	"Being diagnosed was a bit of a relief, because I knew a little bit about Munchausen Syndrome; it was something that was mentioned some years prior to me being diagnosed. Can you remember Beverley Allitt; She had Munchausen Syndrome by proxy; it was still a very recent memory and Munchausen Syndrome by proxy is apparently when you hurt people to bring attention to yourself where as Munchausen Syndrome is where you hurt yourself to attract attention to yourself, so I was shitting myself that I had Munchausen Syndrome and with my son I didn't want to look for something to be wrong with myself; it was to do with helping my son to get him the right schooling, so I was relieved that there was nothing wrong with me. I thought when they told me that they were going to tell me that I had mental health problems or something terminal; it was awful and I was so pleased and relieved when it was Asperger Syndrome; but I also knew at the same time that if I had this Asperger Syndrome, then my family are going down like skittles; then they did; first it was my sons, then my niece, then my brother and family in Australia that I have never even met; it's amazing."	Leanne was led to believe that her child's difficulties were solely because of her. This seemed to have caused major difficulties with Leanne as she began to research Munchausen by proxy. This seems to be a classic case where a range of professionals took no responsibility for the situation, instead blamed the Mother leading her to believe (bearing in mind she was undiagnosed Autistic) that through her undiagnosed differences that she was abusing her child. This clearly highlights the double empathy problem with possible psychopathy on behalf of the professionals. Having spoken with Leanne it is quite clear that she is Autistic and how professionals didn't recognize that this couldn't just be put down to a lack of knowledge. After diagnosis she was very relieved that she didn't have mental health problems or Munchausen Syndrome by Proxy so was not deemed a child abuser. Another positive aspect is that more of her family members are being diagnosed. Diagnosis can really help families if done correctly but also with other family members investigated (and not just for Autism) so that any one family member is not singled out unfairly.
How/or/and/when did it hit you?	"Yes, because I was happy to have the label; I was really happy not to be mentally ill any more; I was really happy not to have to cope anymore; I was really happy not to have anything wrong with me anymore."	

Did the clinician/ diagnostician ask you to read and sign your diagnosis off?	*"I can't remember; I think she said the 'I am 95% sure you have Asperger Syndrome'; with the percentages she said that 'we always like to leave a little bit of room for doubt, just incase it's wrong' so they can say the we were 5% right. I don't need to say anymore, do I?"*	Although she feels vindicated it was bad practice for the clinician to use a ninety five percent ruling, which was probably designed to legally protect the professional rather than serve the patient. Either your autistic or your not!		
Did you read it all?	*"I read it all because it wasn't very long."*			
How did you feel when reading it?	*"The first word I remember thinking was 'vindicated'."*			
Were you given the opportunity to preview your report and comment on it before it was finalized?	*"I don't think it was applicable."*			
What did you think of the language and the perspective in the report?	*"The language was ok and fine. I didn't know what to expect; so, they told me I had Asperger Syndrome and I recognized that I had Asperger Syndrome; they told me that I probably had Asperger Syndrome with a 95% probability, so I was fine with that; I was a bit disappointed that I failed in getting 100%."*			

What were the recommendations on your assessment for a way forward?	"There was nothing in writing, but she said that she wasn't going to put me forward for any counseling because (to the best of my memory) 'you've got through all these things without any help; you should be fine'. At the time I didn't argue with it but in hindsight I would argue with it a lot; I think it should come as standard; if it had been a health issue; oh, congratulations Leanne, you have cancer; no, if it were a health issue, if it were any other sort of issue, you would be put forward. 'You've got through this far', right, you've had a broken leg all your life, you were born with a displaced hip; there's no point, is there. I wasn't even given a contact number; I think it's shit when you get diagnosed as an adult, and I was a mature adult of 44, I had got married, had three children, I own my own house, I've worked and had jobs etc. What makes people think that you don't need help! I can talk; I am really fucking good at pretending to be normal. When you go there should be a follow up which should be mandatory. You get a diagnosis follow up should be mandatory; it doesn't matter whether its physical, mental; what's the difference; why would there be any difference between cancer and neurological difference."	She believes that the language in the report was fine and although there was nothing in writing regarding recommendations the clinician didn't recommend referral to any services because she had got through these things without any help and should be fine. She wasn't even given a contact number. Is a diagnosis of Autism being used in order to prevent access to appropriate services which the person is legally entitled to, especially as Leanne is good at pretending to be normal thus being able to hide potential mental health problems in addition to Autism such as post traumatic stress disorder which Leanne may have perceived to be part of her Autism, certainly in this case diagnosis of Autism should have led to pathway for further assessment of other potential issues that may have been hidden. Leanne also thinks follow up after diagnosis should be mandatory.
On reflection		
What is your perception now? Do you feel any different now, on reflection?	"Yes I do feel different now on reflection because I've had a few years to get used to the idea that I'm autistic. My life has begun to make sense. Before I got my diagnosis I recognized that I had been hurt a lot, and I just want to say that if my hurt can help	On reflection Leanne does feel different now but I suspect the positive aspects have come from her interpretation of Autism rather than from external sources she now recognizes that her hurt can be used to help others. She sees her differences as a

	Participant quote	Researcher analysis	
	somebody else to hurt a little bit less, then my life has been a life worth living. Since my diagnosis, I have been put in a position where I can really help other people to be able to communicate with their children, to be able to understand themselves. One student who I work with recently said that I like working with you because you know what it's like, and that's a really good thing. By helping other people it gives us community. I've said this before, if people would just look at us as a culture, and we live in a multi-cultural society and people can embrace other cultures; it's a culture, and that's an easier thing to understand than a disability."	difference in culture rather than a disability (cross reference this with Christine's interview data) This aspect highlights an important role for Autistic people as mentors within the community and this should be offered in relation to post diagnostic support so that the person being mentored eventually becomes a mentor themselves thus making the process less open to chance and not such a lonely journey. (Cross reference with Jack's data)	
In hindsight, how could your diagnosis have been done better?	*"In all honesty I had already been masticated in the jaws of all these systems and processes before; it could have been done better; I wasn't expecting anything except to be sitting in an office talking to somebody; that was my expectation; I was 44: the first time I stepped into a psychiatrist office I was 9; you are brought up with it."*	She first stepped into the psychiatrist's office at the age of nine so she was well aware of how the system treat Autistic people she is pleased not to have mental health problems and not to have anything wrong with her. This highlights a further aspect regarding identity and sense of self as she may not have been mentally ill all along but rather she was led to believe that her natural state of being and functioning was an illness. There were similar issues surrounding gender dysphoria, where she now recognizes her need to be a boy is natural to her own being this fits in with Baron Cohen's theory of testosterone in the womb (check alongside Rachel the participant and Victoria's doctoral theses on gender identity)	
What was good about the process?			

What was bad about the process?		
What impact has your diagnosis had on the understanding of who you are?	"Its vindicated me; there is nothing wrong with me; it's helped me to recognize who I am; it's helped my children and other people I am close to; its given me a job, well kind of. Its allowed me to be who I should have been or who I was meant to be; I like who I am. I liked that fact that my dad was very positive about it."	
Is there anything else you would like to add?	"I was going to say something about gender; as a child I had three ambitions: 1. To read as well as they did on Jackanory 2. To be funny 3. And to be a boy I managed two out of three; I'm still working on being funny."	There were similar issues surrounding gender dysphoria, where she now recognizes her need to be a boy is natural to her own being this fits in with Baron Cohen's theory of testosterone in the womb (check alongside Rachel the participant and Victoria's doctoral theses on gender identity)

Natalie: Matrix (NHS diagnosis)

Current age: 39

Age when diagnosis was conducted: 38 (2012)

Current social and economic situation: *"Married with 5 children. Currently a qualified Science teacher and stay at home mum. Runs an autistic group."*

Official diagnoses by name: Asperger's syndrome (no additional diagnoses)

Questions	Responses	Analytical memos
Pre-Diagnosis		
Why did you seek a diagnosis?	*"One of my children (6 at the time) was having some problems at school and I researched his particular type of behavior and suspected that he fitted onto the autistic spectrum, specifically Asperger's Syndrome. I took him for a diagnosis with a really long list of attributes, he was seen by a speech and language therapist, pediatrician and an occupational therapist, he was diagnosed with ASD (Asperger type). I decided to research different things that would help him at school because the school were awful, and through that process I found more and more things that were actually relevant to me. So, I knew that I was the same, and I procrastinated for about a year whether I wanted to be diagnosed, and in the end I decided yes because I didn't want him to feel alone. I wanted to be able to tell him that mummy's the same; it's fine, I'm fine, you're fine and you can have a good life, because I found that the whole clinical side of it was very negative and I don't feel it needs to be negative."*	For Natalie her journey began with the diagnosis of her son (after he was having problems at school), this led her to seek her own diagnosis so her son wouldn't feel so alone with his diagnosis in the family. Through research into autism and her son led her to examine her own differences. • Should initial investigations be provided on a family basis as it seems a bit unfair to have a diagnosed child the focus, where as parents (who maybe in denial of their own differences) may project their undiagnosed differences onto their child. Was worried about the consequences of her own diagnosis and being investigated by Social Services and being labeled as an unfit mother. Luckily, in this case the professional put those fears to bed but fears such as this could have implications for other parents seeking a diagnosis.

		Was more of a clinical process rather than being reflective of a human approach. Natalie sees the clinical approach very negative. Is the NHS more about symptoms than dealing with human beings?
How long did it take you to seek a diagnosis?	*"A year"*	
What knowledge of autism did you have prior to diagnosis?	*"An awful lot of knowledge I've developed from research from various sources. I read all and anything I could about AS, including information specific to women."*	As Natalie researched autism before being assessed, and therefore saw it more as a process (as apposed to being diagnosed without any knowledge of autism) potentially leading to issues for any post-diagnostic support, if offered.
How did it come about?	*"I went to my GP after I had just had my youngest child for a post-natal chat, and I had the most stressful time getting there. Everything went wrong and I was running late, I hate being late, so I went in and she did the talk about how do you feel about having your baby, and I said that I'm a bit stressed. Then I just burst into tears and said oh, I think I may have AS, and she said 'it's alright dear, you're probably just a bit depressed', and fobbed me off. Three months later I went back in a more coherent form and saw another doctor, and just described what I was like as a child, and said that my son has been diagnosed, and I just want to know. I feel that I didn't need anything, but I would like to know so I could tell him that you're the same as mummy,*	GP with no knowledge.

The Identification of Autistic Adults' Perception of their Own Diagnostic Pathway

	and she sent me to a hospital, which has a specialist Asperger's unit. I saw a speech and language therapist first who made me do AQ10, which is a shortened AQ test, and asked me lots of questions to make sure I wasn't depressed or having psychiatric problems. I must have passed because I then went to a clinical psychologist a few months later, who put me through an official diagnosis, and told me at the end that I have passed the test and that I do indeed have AS. This was all based where I was living."	Initial assessment took place using a shortened form of AQ test (AQ10) with, a full diagnosis by psychologies thereafter. Initial test to make sure she wasn't depressed or having psychiatric problems! Psychologist: 'I have passed the test'.
What were your expectations prior to attending?	*"I expected it to be quite clinical and quite formal. With the speech and language therapist it was actually quite nice, she was friendly and I felt quite relaxed and she was quite chatty. With the clinical psychologist, she was far more formal, but she believed in the whole neurodiversity angle because she was very positive, which surprised me as I wasn't expecting that. It was pretty much what I expected, not one of the tests though because it was a children's test, which was a surprise. I had to read this children's book, and it felt slightly patronizing as I had to mimic brushing my teeth and things which made me feel a bit of a wally."* *"I suspect that the speech and language therapist is probably paid less than the clinical psychologist; she's probably the one who screens you to see if you're on the right track and I think it's the psychologist who does the real diagnostic work. I think it's a bit of a buffer to make sure you have gone to the right place. That was my perception of it."*	Good points: • Psychologist was very positive and believed in the neuro diversity perspective. • It was pretty much what she expected • Service was local Highlights inconsistency between professionals, highlighting potential issues regarding the use of multi-disciplinary teams. Seems dodgy to use child diagnostic elements, such as reading a children's book and emulating brushing teeth. Language therapist seemed to be the gatekeeper to formal assessment.

Diagnosis		Diagnosis of self:
Can you take me through your diagnosis as you experienced it then?	1. Diagnosis of self: *"That was a strange experience. I took the AQ test online and got 37 and I thought my husband would do worse, and he did it and performed fine, and that's a real shock. I thought there's something wrong with me, I'm defective and I felt quite depressed, then I did some more reading and research and then I realized that I am just different, and I was just quite cross about the clinical things I have read and the negative things I have read, and then discovered this whole other ethos, and then I just felt extremely positive. I wanted to bring my children up to be positive and also to reach out to other people and really dispel the whole myths of us having something the matter with us, so ultimately I feel very positive and very empowered, but also very frustrated. This positivity comes from me realizing that all my life I have been in these situations where people were really negative and I just didn't know how to deal with it. I felt that I was somehow useless and really blamed myself whereas I was just dealing the negative social behavior of other people who should have been well enough behaved not to have manifested it, so I suddenly realized that none of this is my fault. I have a different kind of brain, I'm smart, not defective and I just find the whole thing really interesting. I quite like learning for real that I am different rather than this horrible suspicion that I've had all my life, and wondering why the hell I don't fit in. So I approached it from that kind of angle."*	When first reading about autism Natalie felt defective and depressed, as the medical model is a direct reflection of the deficit social model. After further reading she discovered this whole other ethos, shrouded in difference rather than deficit. She suddenly realized that none of this was her fault. This call into question current approaches and methodology that currently forms a diagnosis. For example the affect this has on mental health and on other family members. This clearly highlights how the perception of the individual can directly effect their well being.

		Formal diagnosis	
What were you thinking/ feeling at the time?	2. Diagnosis by the psychologist: *"I was quite frightened because I had read some quite damning things about people with Asperger's as parents and I was quite worried that because I was being diagnosed that someone would tell social services and they would come snooping around my family with all these awful suspicions, so I was quite paranoid and a little bit worried. Before the diagnosis I cleared that up and asked if this diagnosis could be used against me, am going to be judged? Actually I'm not, they don't do that, and once she had reassured me that no, because I have never done anything wrong, that wouldn't happen, I went through the process and it was almost, well, I didn't really feel anything at all, I didn't really feel anything at all other than lets get to the end of it and you can just tell me and I'll have my piece of paper and that's that and I can move on."*	The formal diagnosis for Natalie was just a process of conformation in order for her to move on. The perception of stigma from others led to fears about the process and its outcome.	
What was the environment like?	*"I don't think they take on board that some people have sensory issues because they had buzzing strip lights. I can deal with it, it annoys me but there may be others with worse sensory issues than me and I felt that was a strange thing to have in a place where you were conducting these types of tests. I thought that would be a really obvious one not to have.*	Natalie's experience of the environment highlighted that sensory aspects were not investigated and no environmental adjustments were considered. For others this would have affected the assessment and highlight issues concerning the perception of behavior and functioning.	
Was it suitable?			

Did they make adjustments to the environment?	There were no questions such as *"is the lighting ok?"* *"How did you feel about the level of sound"*, *it was just straight into it as the psychologist wanted to get me out of the way as she had a lot of other work to do, so I felt like I was being a nuisance in some sort of way. I think these people have an air of importance about them and you're just another one who has turned up who is going through the same process. This was done through the NHS and I didn't have to pay for it. We are very lucky as we have this dedicated unit that does diagnosis."*	Natalie's experience is that of a process almost like a conveyer belt, where by she was treated by professional's as a non human, she highlighted arrogance of the professional's, Natalie was also treated like a child by being asked to look at children's books and to emulate brushing her teeth.
Did you feel that you were receiving a 'full profile' assessment?	*"No. I wrote them a letter of documentation before I went and mentioned that I clearly had some sensory issues and issues with noise which I self manage, I tend to try my best to just ignore, but deep down I find it quite painful at times although I have learned to live with it. I also have issues with touch and sensations as well. I had written to them about that and when I got my diagnosis through the post it said that no sensory issues have been reported. I guess I have lived 39 years and I've put up with it, I cut the labels out of clothes and people know not to touch me if I'm upset. They did no sensory test. I gave them the information on the day and they didn't bring it up at all. I have issues with taste as well so it's quite clear that I have a different sensory system, I guess that's just fine."*	The process was conducted through the NHS and Natalie didn't have to pay for it she felt that she wasn't receiving a full profile assessment for example no sensory test. Does this indicate across participant's experiences differences in how the two sectors conduct their assessments could the NHS be offering a poorer service to prevent correct and accurate diagnosis? • No sensory profiling was offered. • No additional diagnoses investigated • No developmental history from parent or caregiver. Should this have been conducted in the home?

What level/ type of professional conducted your diagnosis?	"I had a clinical psychologist.	
Was this suitable?	I don't know if she was suitable or not. She decided that I fitted the diagnosis. She said at the beginning of the meeting that she would have to go away and discuss it, and at the end of the meeting she just told me straight out and said that their was no ambiguity she was quite sure that I fitted the criteria, so I guess she was competent. She said that she would have to discuss it with her colleague, she said that "I probably won't be able to tell you today, I'll have to discuss it with my colleagues", and then at the end she just told me, so I guess if somebody is a bit ambigious, that maybe she has to have a conversation with the Speech and Language Therapist. I think sometimes people are invited back for further assessment, but I must be a screaming aspie! I just hanged loose and didn't behave myself or anything. She went and asked me about Star Trek, silly woman...	Natalie did not know if her psychologist was suitable, however due to the ambiguity of the psychologist Natalie was concerned about the professionalism and even though she was identified Autistic pretty quickly a professional did use very basic stereotypes highlighting a lack of knowledge which may leave others undiagnosed or misdiagnosed if these basic stereotypes aren't met.\n\nClinician didn't seem to have confidence in her ability to diagnose.
Post-diagnosis		
How did you feel directly after the diagnostic procedure?	"I was still a little bit worried about if it would have a negative impact on my family, knowing in my self and being secret, obviously I'm in complete control of who knows and who doesn't know, having it on your medical record as a disorder, I am still uncomfortable because I don't view it as a disorder,	Even after diagnosis Natalie was still worried about the negative impact on her family with having a mental disorder on her medical record. Natalie does not view this as a disorder but as a difference, which she believes GP's do not have very good knowledge of.

	and it does concern me the next time I have to visit the GP and when it comes up on the screen, does that mean that are not going to believe me when I'm not well, because GP's, I don't think have a very good knowledge of the condition."	Natalie had no doubt that she was Autistic and she saw the process as jumping though hoops. She had eliminated every issue including depression but needed guidance on how to deal with hostile people, even though this did not happen she did work out that she was different.
How/or/and/ when did it hit you?	*"The diagnosis? That was when I self diagnosed. I went through a range of emotions. There was no doubt in my mind. I completely fit the pattern. With the formal diagnosis I wasn't surprised at all as I was so sure I was right. It was almost like jumping through hoops to get it on paper. When I self diagnosed it answered a lot of questions. I did a lot of work on myself regarding depression and I thought I had eliminated every issue I had apart from being a bit rubbish when people are being hostile and I thought that there's the last little part I need to just sort out, and of course it didn't quite pan out how I expected, I haven't turned into this social guru who knows everything, but I have worked out that I am different."*	
Did the clinician/ diagnostician ask you to read and sign your diagnosis off?	*"Yes, she did, and I had another meeting where I had to go in and discuss it. She had a few things – I wasn't entirely sure that she understood some of my answers, but maybe that's part of the issue. I just signed it and said there you go. She just sat and watched me read it, she did try and hurry me up."*	Natalie did sign off her diagnosis and had a follow up meeting to discuss it.
Did you read it all?	Yes	

How did you feel when reading it?	*"I was horrified actually with some of the bits. She asked me to define friendship, especially with a friendship with one of my friends I had known since I was 5 years old and this is a person I love and respect, she is like my sister, and she said define friendship and I said 'well, its more than superficial interaction, isn't it'? She put it on my report, and I thought my god I sound like an android. I did say it, it was the first thing that popped into my head. The fact that it turned up on my letter; I hadn't thought that it would appear, and I thought that I sounded so uncaring.*	When Natalie was reading her diagnosis she was horrified. Professionals and researchers need to think long and hard how they view autism and how they communicate with people in order to, at least, attract affected people so as to gain a true picture of epidemiology of autism and research accuracy by encouraging proper participation.
Were you given the opportunity to preview your report and comment on it before it was finalized?	*I went back to the meeting and I said that 'no, I love my friends', she said 'that's not what you said', and I said 'no it isn't'! That's interesting isn't it! What would you say to a stranger? Would you gush emotion? I generally wouldn't!"*	The psychologist misinterpreted some of the things that were said indicating that there was a two-way theory of mind issue and clear power dynamics with the psychologist having false expectations on socializing in general there are clear issues of interpretation with power but not necessarily competence with the psychologist.
What did you think of the language and the perspective in the report?	*"It was alright. It was very formally written of course. I felt that it had a clinical slant on it, but I guess it is a diagnosis, and that's right. I would like to see more as – we've established that have a different neurological type, and that's really exciting, but it was very much that it was Asperger's Syndrome and I had the following difficulties in childhood blah blah. It felt a bit like we care but not now. It made me feel a little bit uncomfortable but I don't think the GP's even read them; I think they just read the first page."*	The report was very formal and clinical where as Natalie would have liked to have seen it in the mode of a different neurological type. She felt that they cared but just not now.

What were the recommendations on your assessment for a way forward?	"They said that I could go to their social skills training group. I'd like to do that just to see how it's done because I might be able to pick out elements to use with my children, and they asked if I had any interest in joining a women's group, which I did, but they haven't actually sent me the information. It's been about a year now and I haven't chased it up either. They are NHS based groups. They have them at the hospital where all the psychiatric patients go, so I was quite perturbed, like going to a place for diagnostics where they have all the people who are sectioned in there, so it made me feel uncomfortable to be going into that type of environment. You don't see any of it; the place is so quiet, it's dead, I didn't see anybody on my way round, and it's just the department of learning disabilities tucked around the back, but I was concerned and I said to my husband 'oh my god, having it here, I don't want to go in there because I don't have any psychiatric problems', but I guess for them it was a logical place to put it."	Natalie was offered a social skills training group as a way forward, however without recognizing the neurological and psychological differences behind such difficulties it could be dangerous to make this recommendation, these groups are also NHS based where psychiatric patients go making her feel uncomfortable this is obviously inappropriate, it may be logical to the NHS but it shows clear divide between NHS assumption and patient need.

Worried about having to attend a psychiatric hospital for assessment. Should this have been conducted in the home? |
| On reflection | | |
| What is your perception now? Do you feel any different now, on reflection? | "Having gone through this whole process of discovery? I think I'm very fortunate to have this service near by, because I've heard of people who struggle with diagnosis. I think it's quite backward in its approach, I think the whole clinical approach to it is a bit irritating. After diagnosis it would be very nice for them to give you a talk about what it really means rather than just to give you this label and assuming that you know because if someone goes along and they haven't done a lot of background | Natalie sees this as a process of discovery with a clinical approach quite backward having a local service is good but she feels that is she hadn't done a lot of background work previously it could have lead to the individual having a damaging perception of themselves. Natalie feels that the process is a little bit insulting and if she went through the process when she was younger it would have been even worse. Natalie recognizes that there isn't really anything for adults. |

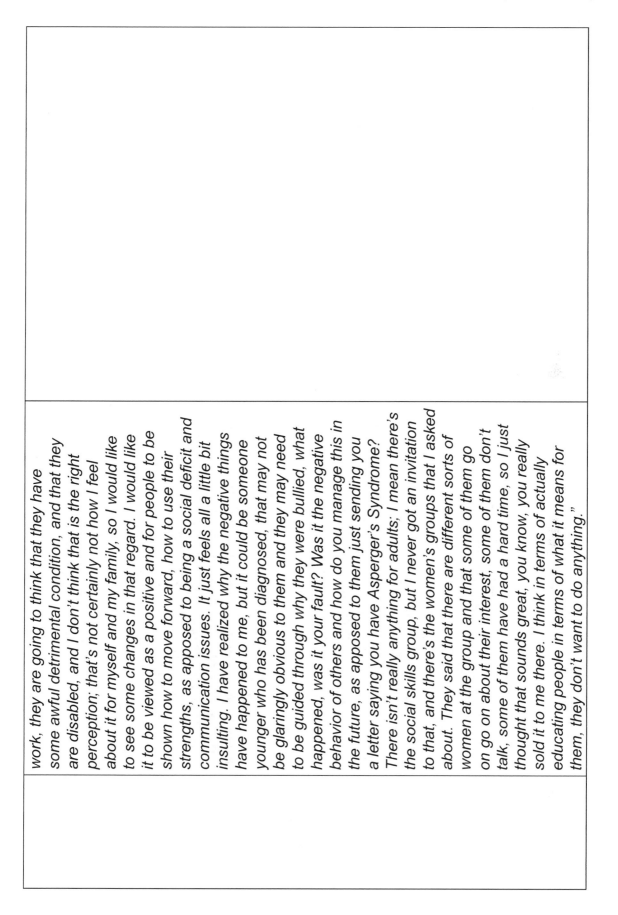

work, they are going to think that they have some awful detrimental condition, and that they are disabled, and I don't think that is the right perception; that's not certainly not how I feel about it for myself and my family, so I would like to see some changes in that regard. I would like it to be viewed as a positive and for people to be shown how to move forward, how to use their strengths, as apposed to being a social deficit and communication issues. It just feels all a little bit insulting. I have realized why the negative things have happened to me, but it could be someone younger who has been diagnosed, that may not be glaringly obvious to them and they may need to be guided through why they were bullied, what happened, was it your fault? Was it the negative behavior of others and how do you manage this in the future, as apposed to them just sending you a letter saying you have Asperger's Syndrome? There isn't really anything for adults; I mean there's the social skills group, but I never got an invitation to that, and there's the women's groups that I asked about. They said that there are different sorts of women at the group and that some of them go on go on about their interest, some of them don't talk, some of them have had a hard time, so I just thought that sounds great, you know, you really sold it to me there. I think in terms of actually educating people in terms of what it means for them, they don't want to do anything."

In hindsight, how could your diagnosis have been done better?		
What was good about the process?	"I think for me, the speed at which I was seen and diagnosed was very good. I probably would have been seen even sooner but I insisted that I had my appointment in the school holidays so that my husband was off work. So the speed was good, I think it's nice to have a dedicated place to go to. I think the process needs to be pretty much what it is as they are looking for things that are very hard to see so I think giving questionnaires and tests that show up your differences are probably the only tools they have."	She recognizes that the speed of her diagnostic pathway was very good and that there is a designated place to go. She recognizes that the tools are inadequate but that that is all there is.
What was bad about the process?	"I think post-diagnosis, there needs to be more for people."	Common thread - there needs to be more for people post diagnosis.
What impact has your diagnosis had on the understanding of who you are?	"It's filled in the final piece of the puzzle for me as to why I'm different. I suppose that I always know I was different, and it's very peculiar actually, I remember in my teens when I was depressed I thought I must be nuts, and that's not a very nice way to feel about yourself, so it's nice to know that I'm not nuts. I guess for a long time I have decided that I don't really get on with very many people and I never knew why, and now I know why, and I think it is very useful, I have certainly enjoyed the community where I have just started this group where I want to help and enable others if I possibly can and I think it's been positive."	For Natalie the process has provided the missing piece to confirm that she is not nuts but that she is different and that authors need to be very careful on how they construct autism and the cause and effect this will have on the reader.
Is there anything else you would like to add?	"No"	

Rachel: Matrix (Private diagnosis)

Current age: 39

Gender: Transgender (male to female, currently in transition)

Age when diagnosis was conducted: *"When I went to see the Doctor for depression I think he initially figured out I had Asperger's, I was 28 (2002) at the time but it wasn't until I was 30 (2004) that I saw him again specifically for getting an Asperger's diagnosis from him."*

Current social and economic situation: *"I'm married and we have a mortgage and I'm an IT consultant and run a limited company and I do freelance web design work as well"*

Official diagnoses by name: *"I think it's Mild Asperger Syndrome. I've not got depression at the moment but did have in 2002. I think the main reasons for that were a mixture of relationship problems with a previous relationship and it was around the first anniversary that my father had died and things were getting stressful at work as well, so with all that going on together it caused depression at that time."*

Questions	Responses	Analytical memos
Pre-Diagnosis		
Why did you seek a diagnosis?	*"Around 2003 to 2004, when I was in the early stages of the relationship with a lady who I went on to marry, she suspected that I might have Asperger's, having noticed some traits within me that she recognized from the son of a work colleague who also had Asperger's, and then she suggested that I should get a diagnosis of it just so there is a record of it."*	As with other participants, Rachel first came into contact with Autism from someone else. It is vital that when an individual first comes into contact with this knowledge, it needs to be presented in the right way as the first impressions of autism may sow the seed as to how the individual proceeds to develop a further understanding of themselves and autism. The aspect of seeking a diagnosis so there is a record of it could be referring to protection regarding employment etc, like insurance if things go wrong in ones life.

How long did it take you to seek a diagnosis?	*"It was fairly quickly to arrange an appointment; it was only a few weeks as this was done privately, because I had seen him for the depression and that was paid for by health insurance I had with the company I was working for at the time; I think I probably paid myself for the Asperger's diagnosis. I have a feeling that rather than go through my GP, I went directly to him, as I had already seen him for the depression, although I did get a GP referral for the depression at the time."*	Rachel found diagnosis easier because she knew the professional (they have met before when he was treating her for depression) Trust and familiarity is key to accurate diagnosis. Again, highlights differences between private diagnosis and NHS. Why is it that private insurance companies don't cover autism and is this the same with National Insurance and the NHS?
What knowledge of autism did you have prior to diagnosis?	*"Yes, I had quite a decent understanding of Autism before then as well; mainly through books and the internet."*	I suspect that prior to diagnosis, she had identified herself and had somewhat come to terms with it.
What were your expectations prior to attending?	*"I expected that I would most likely have a diagnosis of Asperger's before actually attending."*	She had expectations and prior knowledge. This is something professionals need to take into account, that the individual may have more knowledge, thus leading to a type of test of knowledge and trust.
Diagnosis		
Can you take me through your diagnosis as you experienced it then?		

What were you thinking/ feeling at the time?	*"I wasn't particularly apprehensive, so I think it was just going on to see the Doctor and expecting him to say I have Asperger's, but not worrying too much about it. By knowing the Doctor before this prevented a lot of anxiety, because that last time I saw him I was in a lot worse state by a long way. I was in a very bad state of depression, so seeing him again when my mental health was ok; it really wasn't much of a problem. If it had been a stranger I think I would have been more apprehensive, but because it was somebody I've met before, I didn't have that much fear."*	Again, trust in the professional is key to an accurate assessment, and will reflect nature and severity of presentation and information the individual feels they can impart, especially given the aspect of stigma. A case could be made for the family doctor to return – a professional who knows the family as well as the individual through house calls? This could be a solution to address the apparent disconnect between professionals and the service user! This could also be an alternative to multi-disciplinary teams!
What was the environment like?	*"It was basically a room at the clinic which is a private hospital in Somerset, so I think it was the same place I had been to before to see him previously. It was a private hospital; the parking was ok; it was in a suburban part and not in the center. In terms of sensory stuff, the kinds of things that trigger my sensory stuff is like a supermarket on a busy day is the type of environment that effects me the most because you've got the bright lights, people getting in your way, lots of noise, all the products of clashing colours on display at the same time."*	Familiarity with the environment will help to assist autism more effectively as anxiety components will be in the background, thus enabling a more accurate diagnosis. Although Rachel states that she does not suffer anxiety (which highlights that mental health problems are not an inevitable part of autism) it is wise for the process of assessment of autism to take place in a way that the components of possible anxiety and depression not be identified as autism, but should be coded separately and addressed with approaches where autism is present.
Was it suitable?	*"Yes"*	
Did they make adjustments to the environment?	*"They didn't ask or make any adjustments."*	

Did you feel that you were receiving a 'full profile' assessment?	*"No, I think it was because I had figured out about my Asperger two years ago; it was just to rubber-stamp the fact that I had Asperger's. The time I saw him for depression was a more in-depth discussion and he noted that on my records at the time; the second time (for Asperger's) it was a quicker meeting. I was not aware of his inclination of Asperger's when I went to see him for depression. When I went to see him for the Asperger's diagnosis he said at the time the main focus was getting the depression treated and sorted, so he didn't want to cloud the issue with mentioning Asperger's. It was me who approached him for the Asperger diagnosis."*	It would seem that the process of assessment has in this case occurred over many years for Rachel. The issue here is that the doctor did not seem to appreciate the potential underlying causes for Rachel's depression. It would seem that the doctor may have suspected autism, but may have felt that by going down this path, it may have induced anxiety and therefore further depression, although identifications if done right can alleviate both. Alternatively, the doctor may not have had the correct knowledge of autism, so it fell to Rachel to first convince the professional and then to educate him.
What level/ type of professional conducted your diagnosis?	*"It was a consultant Psychiatrist. Very much the right professional with the right qualifications."*	
Was this suitable?	*"Yes"*	
Post-diagnosis		
How did you feel directly after the diagnostic procedure?	*"Good, I think – Just getting a name to it and just confirming that I had Asperger's after all; it also put my partner's mind at rest at the same time as well."*	Rachel was at the point that she had already confirmed her own diagnosis and was seeking a formal confirmation. Assessment of autism may not always be about diagnosis or identification but just confirming the conclusions that have already been reached. (possible theme to contrast with other participants)

Question	Quote	Analysis
How/or/and/ when did it hit you?	"It didn't seem to be that much of a big deal to be honest. I guess it was something that I have lived with for some time before."	Rachel may have already have been through the process of self-identification and post-identification realization.
Did the clinician/ diagnostician ask you to read and sign your diagnosis off?	"No, he just sent the letter off through the post. It was a letter saying that he had reached the conclusion that I had 'mild Asperger Syndrome'. He might have mentioned a couple of reasons. It was one sheet of A4."	If this is standard practice for this professional, then this is inappropriate, but it would also suggest that professionals may be producing reports reflective of what they believe their patient is seeking, or what would help or protect their patient (for example saying no cognitive impairment where this might effect the persons standing in the workplace).
Did you read it all?	"Yes"	
How did you feel when reading it?	"It was ok, there wasn't a problem at all because it was what I expected. I felt good that I have got this on paper."	She felt good at being recognized. This maybe a type of vindication (another theme) of having beliefs and experienced formally recognized.
Were you given the opportunity to preview your report and comment on it before it was finalized?	"I didn't ask to, so I guess I didn't in that case."	Should it be down to the patient to ask, or should this be automatically part of the process? Bearing in mind that these participants are free citizens under the law and should reach an agreement with each other.
What did you think of the language and the perspective in the report?	"It just seemed fair enough; there wasn't any issues with it; the Language was fairly formal, but that's what I would have expected in a letter from a Psychiatrist."	

347

Question	Response	Reflection
What were the recommendations on your assessment for a way forward?	*"There were no recommendations either verbal or written. I think that it was because it was a fairly mild case that he thought there was no action to be taken."*	With this notion of severity, how do we compare and cross-reference this in different individuals? The notion of using the term mild is a flawed paradigm as it provides the individual with a false anchor and sense of self especially if/when social circumstances change.
On reflection		
What is your perception now? Do you feel any different now, on reflection?	*"I think it's put things in to context a bit more about how, for example I try and avoid particular situations' now, like avoiding supermarkets during busy periods, because I know that's one of the triggers that freaks me out. Traffic jams as well and I've Never felt like I've fitted in to social situations involving alcohol, pubs and clubs either, so I suppose that kind of makes sense as well. Career wise it makes sense that I have gone down the path of working in IT. That seems like a popular career choice for people with Asperger's. The only times where I have told them at work is when I've made the tea."*	Rachel has taken responsibility and strategized around her differences. She has the freedom and the ability do this, although I suspect that if social circumstances were not as favorable, and then the situation will be very different. Rachel has fallen into the trap of stereotyping when mentioning Asperger's and IT. Could those diagnosed individuals be just as bad about stereotypes and inevitable stigma as everyone else?
In hindsight, how could your diagnosis have been done better?		
What was good about the process?	*"The good was that it was a quick process and that he had already done the work about two years previously to the diagnosis. There wasn't any hassle in getting the diagnosis."*	Again, Rachel's diagnosis was more about formal confirmation, with the process occurring over many years. Maybe this is the future of diagnosis?

What was bad about the process?	"What would have been better is some follow-up in terms of advice and support afterwards, but I guess because I did it off my own back via a private consultation instead of something more structured, this may have been the case. I could have gone back to my GP and asked for more information, but I didn't at that time."	An obvious theme, which is common, not just with participants, but with most diagnosed individuals. It may have been that if Rachel had provided her GP with the diagnosis, the NHS may not have accepted it and required she sit their own assessment. Additionally, with patients not providing GP's with their diagnosis, what will this do for research and record keeping? Also, if Rachel were to seek medical assistance for another condition which may be made worse without knowledge about the person's autism?
What impact has your diagnosis had on the understanding of who you are?	"It's made quite a significant impact. It's made things a lot easier in terms of my marriage because my wife knows now that I have Asperger's specifically and we are both more accommodating of each other because she is disabled too and she has some mental heath issues including bi-polar and stuff, so we support each other. We know what makes each other tick and what situations to avoid. She knows never to send me to the supermarket in the middle of the day."	Highlights that through proper understanding and a correct diagnosis, people can be supportive of each other, and not just through formal systems support. Part of post-diagnostic support should be to assist in helping everyone become more understanding and supportive of each other while facilitating ideas around strategies.
Is there anything else you would like to add?	"I have good days and bad days. I find that if there are too many things going on at the same time, I find that difficult as well as prioritizing time." Rod: Diagnosis can bring up issues of the past, which can be a good thing or a bad thing. With poor experiences it can make the person re-evaluate those past experiences and that could be a good thing or it could be a bad thing.	Rachel seems to see these things in layers. Autism is in the background for her. It's helped her to come to terms with things. She's got a partner, after having gone through depression she's going through gender transformation - layers of identity? She highlights issues with executive functioning.

The following has been retained in order to highlight how communication/discussion with someone who has been through the process can assist and provide a role in the post-diagnostic process.

"That was the case with me because in secondary school I was a major target for bullies as I was bullied quite a lot, but at the same time I was bright academically, so I guess I threw a lot of effort into my schoolwork, which helped me."

Rod: Good you had an escape route.

"I was frustrated and board at primary school but found my interest in secondary School which is where I excelled. I left School with GCSE's and A-levels and went on to study chemistry at Oxford, and graduated with a 2.1 and then went on to work in IT not long after graduating. I did see an educational psychologist when I was about 7 because of behavioral issues and they said that I was in the top two percent of the population intellectually and I was put in contact with a national association for gifted children, which ran Saturday morning courses. I don't think I did as well as I expected at University due to difficulties adjusting to the different method of teaching compared to school. The whole gender thing, having transition has made it easer for me to cope with the Asperger's, ironically. I know somebody else who maybe interested in speaking with you. They also think they have Asperger's or something similar and they are in transition as well. The main differences (I believe) between Asperger's and Autism are that most people with Asperger's are good at communicating verbally and contextually,

whereas a lot of people with Autism wouldn't be. I was lucky in the third year of secondary school onwards because a lot of the bullying occurred in the lunch hour and in morning break, but from the third year onwards, I used to go to an electronics club that was held in the physics lab in the lunch hour. Although we had electronics taught in the physics classed, the extra lessons made me more advanced in those lessons. The main worries at the moment are mainly financial and needing to find another IT contract fairly soon. Other than that, I think the main pressures have been my wife's ongoing health issues, who was in hospital for most of April with kidney failure and she was in intensive care, she was that bad. She was disabled from birth with a spinal condition and has to use an electric wheelchair and a hoist, so her health isn't that good compared to most people. The other thing is that my Mother is in a care home with dementia and we are trying to sell her house to pay for care home fees. What gets me is that there is ex amount of people unemployed that don't have any illness or disability; they are not finding jobs, so if you've got an illness or disability, the employers are going to go with those without disabilities first, even though they are not meant to half the time. I don't see Asperger's in my case as any sort of major deficit; I just see it as thinking a bit differently, which ironically has benefited my career. Everybody should be treated with dignity."

Rod Morris

Rod: We just socialize differently!

"Yes, I like to socialize with specialist groups. A lot of our friends are either involved in the LGBT or through my Asperger's group, or through the church. At school I found some subjects harder than others, but I just thrown more energy into those I guess. I like Science and chemistry and music. Being given a computer helped me with algebra. People with Asperger's have a much clearer idea of what is really going on behind the scenes and underneath the surface than a lot of NT's fed all the bullshit."

Russell: Matrix (Private diagnosis with NHS elements)

Current age: 58

Age when diagnosis was conducted: 51 (2006) *"I was told unofficially by a psychiatrist with specialism in autism about 10 years ago (48 years old), then 3 years later I had an official diagnosis. (51 years old) I went back as I needed an official diagnosis."*

Current social and economic situation: *"I work full time for BT and I have worked since I was 16, I do work too hard for some of my peers and they don't like how much work I do; at home I am very lazy and I can't be bothered to do anything; I employ a cleaner to do everything; I'm divorced; I was married for 18 years; got divorced, again at age 48; I currently have a girlfriend whom I have been seeing for 8 years, but we don't live together; financially I am ok with no worries; I don't have any friends and I don't go out; If you took away all the professional people I know and my girlfriend, I wouldn't have anybody. I see a councilor and have regular massages. I find it hard to socialize in the normal way; there has to be something keeping us together, like work or school, in the school days. I have no children as I couldn't have any with my wife; I never found out why; we did have IVF for a few years."*

Official diagnoses by name: *"Asperger's Syndrome, Dyslexia, Dyscalculia, potential long-term memory problems which I am trying to get assessed but its like banging my head against a brick wall, Depression, Stress and Anxiety, very poor sleep."* (These were all diagnosed separately but around about the same time – between the ages of 48 and 50)

Questions	Responses	Analytical memos
Pre-Diagnosis		
Why did you seek a diagnosis?	*"I became initially aware that this was a problem through a TV program, which covered a family where the husband had Asperger's; not long after that my wife left me, so all the old problems reared their head such in socializing and trying to find another partner, during that divorce I went to Relate, and for many weeks, it teared me apart; they look into everything, even what colored socks*	Russell's diagnoses are numerous including core neurological aspects and secondary mental health problems. Apart from the professional people he and his girlfriend know he wouldn't have anyone so socially he does not have a support structure to enable this. It seems that he receives some inter personal skills from his girlfriend and a counselor, he became initially aware of Asperger's from a TV

	you're wearing, and it was with a view of getting me back together and not the marriage because it was excepted that the marriage had broken down. One of the things we looked at was my intelligence and my abilities; it was then decided to investigate these things including whether I had got Asperger's, whether I'm Dyslexic and what my IQ was, which was high, where as I always thought I was below average, and I have now ended up in MENSA, which is unbelievable and has given me another interest."	program but it wasn't until social demands exceeded his capacity to function which was in the form of his wife leaving him. Russell also found out later in life that he had a very high IQ, all of these late diagnosis must have led to a feeling of injustice through reflection of what his life could have been if these aspects had been identified sooner.
How long did it take you to seek a diagnosis?	*"The first one I saw, once he had interviewed me, he asked me why I wanted a diagnosis, and I said that I wasn't bothered about an official diagnosis or having a bit of paper; I just wanted to know what is happening; it has come to me realizing that something is wrong with me; something is stopping me from socializing in the normal way, particularly with women, finding partners and girlfriends. After the divorce I felt that I was back to square one, back to when I was in my teens and no better off, so I wanted to know what it was, and if it wasn't Asperger's then I'll carry on looking. He said that I had Asperger symptoms, so no need to look any further, but warned me that a diagnosis might damage my career, but I said that I wasn't bothered about an official diagnosis, and it was left at that."*	He went through two processes the first one was informal without a formal diagnosis. The first psychiatrist recognized Asperger's but put Russell off formal diagnosis through unwisely warning him that an official diagnosis may damage his career despite disability legislation being in place, this says more about the psychiatrist perception of the work place and of coarse a diagnosis is just a recognition of autism so the person does not automatically become Autistic when they are diagnosed. The psychiatrist could therefore also have said that a formal diagnosis could provide him the legal protection if issues arose in relation to Autism. Russell went for a second diagnosis as his work place were trying to force people into call centers and he knew that because of his differences he new that he would not be able to do that.

	The reason I went back and saw a different Psychiatrist was that, even though I was working for the same company, I lost my post at work and had to find a new one, and they were trying to force people into call centers, and I knew that there was no way I could work in a call center; so I went to get an official diagnosis to help me with this, so that they would have to treat me as disabled and make reasonable adjustments for me."	
What knowledge of autism did you have prior to diagnosis?	*"Not a lot. I always thought of Autism as that of little kids in a world of their own, who don't communicate with people. This was my view of Autism before I knew about Asperger's. Although I watched the program, I didn't conduct any research thereafter. It was only after the divorce that I was having real problems again that I started looking into it. I am still friends with my ex wife and she came with me to the assessment."*	Aside form the employment aspects Russell's secondary focus was with women.
How did it come about?	*"I initially went to my GP. He wouldn't refer me to anyone who specializes in Autism to start with; he just wanted me to go to my local mental health unit and be interviewed there. Fortunately, they then agreed to send me to a Psychiatrist who specialized in Autism. The second time I went, I paid for it privately, as I thought the NHS wouldn't be too happy if I went back wanting to go through it all again with the NHS paying."*	The first diagnosis was done by the NHS which beggars the question is the NHS putting people off receiving a diagnosis because they haven't got the capacity or service provision regarding this group, which is why many are refereed to mental health his second diagnosis was private and he said that the environment was much better.

| What were your expectations prior to attending? | *"With the first one, when I just wanted to know what was wrong, my expectations were that it was Asperger's and that I was hoping that I was right. I wasn't looking forward to putting in all the work, time and energy trying to find out what it was if it wasn't Asperger's. I was very unsure of myself back then and I didn't know that I was intelligent; I knew that I was different; I felt different; I felt that I couldn't get on with people like other people do, so I was searching for answers, and that with an answer I could do something about it and improve my life. I was nervous going to it. My wife supported me and she accompanied me to the assessment, even though she had announced that she wanted to leave."*

"With the second one, I was still unsure because I believed that I didn't have the symptoms that badly, some of the people I have told since don't believe I have Asperger's as they can't see that I have a problem. So, I was nervous the second time round but this surrounded the question as to whether I was bad enough to have a diagnosis, and I didn't know how this diagnosis thing worked, how bad you have to be to have a diagnosis. I was also worried about my job situation; without a diagnosis they would force me into an unsuitable post, which would make my mental health worse and leave me having to leave the job, and we don't like change." | Recognition of intelligence leads to better confidence and empowerment – Identity.

Others have told Russell that he doesn't have Asperger's and subsequently believes that his symptoms are not that bad. How does one identify levels of symptoms and functioning is this appropriate? Russell shows through his difficulties presented here core aspects of the new Autism diagnosis of social communication difficulties and rigid behavior I suspect that maybe the repetitive behavior aspect is one exhibited more in private or when under stress and anxiety. |

Diagnosis		
Can you take me through your diagnosis as you experienced it then?		During diagnosis he felt the questions were to blunt and out the blue and difficult to answer. Given the aspect of social demands and face to face questioning it could be problematic for a psychiatrist to write down what the individual said as I could be inaccurate as well as give others a false impression of the individual particularly if the diagnosis is going to communicate to a range of different people the questions Russell was asked were mainly to do with his sexual life and this does not seem appropriate even if Russell's mind at the time was focused on interpersonal relationships.
What were you thinking/ feeling at the time?	*"Regarding the official diagnosis, I was nervous going through the interview; I was quite upset, nye on crying; some of the questions I felt were (even for someone with Asperger's) too blunt and out of the blue, very personal questions that were just dropped on me out of the blue which I found very difficult to answer honestly to a stranger about. They were questions to do with my sexual life. My ex wife came a second time but the Psychiatrist didn't see her a second time as he obviously thought he didn't need her input as he had seen enough of me. It was difficult and I was very worried about the outcome, and if I didn't get a diagnosis, what else could I do. Psychiatrists do look back into childhood; unfortunately my parents are both dead and my youngest sibling was 8 years older than me, and they left home when they started work, so they weren't true brothers and sisters that I had, they were more like extra parents to me. I am very sure that one of my brothers has got it and both my ex wife and my girlfriend said oh yes, he's got it. They can see it and I can see it, and he's aware of it; I think that my brother is ignoring it for now."*	As with other participants Russell didn't have parents or other family members to describe his developmental history although Russell does recognize that one of his brothers has Asperger's. With the new diagnostic criteria of Autism in DSM 5 weighing so heavily on developmental history, could the diagnosis of Asperger's which requires no developmental delay and thus no developmental history served as an alternative to autism, and with Asperger's disappearing, could many find themselves in the new category of Social and Communication Disorder.

What was the environment like?	"The NHS one was very clinical, hospital type environment, the second one where the official diagnosis happened was at a private clinic so it was quite homely."	Again regarding the environment the NHS doesn't come out of this very well at all with a very clinical hospital type of environment and the second private diagnosis was more relaxing and homely. It would appear that the NHS does not have the practical resources to assess Autism as it is geared for mental health problems alone. This could not only affect the information contained in the diagnosis but also the research on how Autism is presented.
Was it suitable?	"The only problem there was that it was late in the evening so my ex wife was left waiting in a waiting room for the duration of the diagnostic process in a very cold environment with the heating turned off."	
Did they make adjustments to the environment?	"They didn't ask me if any adjustments were needed to the environment. I have some sensory issues, but there was nothing that bothered me at the time of the interview."	Potential sensory issues not investigated into account.
Did you feel that you were receiving a 'full profile' assessment?	"I think there could have been a fuller assessment of me and my life but maybe they only probed as much as they felt necessary because, certainly on the second assessment when I was officially diagnosed, I was quite upset, so they might have thought not to push it any further. They didn't discuss my other diagnoses such as Dyslexia, but they focused on what was bothering me, which was the interaction with other people component. This was within the social aspect, personal relationships, work and being asked to look at jobs in call centers as this is to do with people and being in a room full of my peers and dealing with the public. So, it was interaction with people, which was my big problem at the time."	Russell does not believe that he received a full assessment as the sensory aspects were not investigated they didn't discuss his other diagnosis and they focused on the social aspects that were bothering him at the time rather than an assessment of his life path.

What level/ type of professional conducted your diagnosis?	"I think they were quite high up specialists in the field. On both occasions, one person was assessing me. I think they were appropriately qualified as one was a professor, so they weren't any old local authority Psychiatrist's. They were not local professionals, but they were both psychiatrists, one of which was in Leicester."	He states that the specialists were high up in their field with one being a psychiatrist with one being a professor, they were not local to the region so they may not have got an idea of his social circumstances in the physical environments he was expected to function in. Russell states that he was quite upset in assessment and indicated that they pushed him to far. Is the level of professional that important? Could it be that a highly qualified professional who may have the clinical expertise but not the interpersonal ones to gain an appropriate assessment whilst leaving the Autistic relatively unscathed by the process. An aspect that Russell mentioned and which other participants have also highlighted is the aspect of not reading about Autism before diagnosis as he could subconsciously present symptoms that he has read about. If individuals seeking an assessment can put as much care and thought into their diagnosis why is it that professionals can't seem to do the same!
Was this suitable?		
Post-diagnosis		
How did you feel directly after the diagnostic procedure?	"I felt happy that I had discovered what it was and eager to find out more about it then because I hadn't looked into it much before diagnosis because I recognized that when one knows about the subject, even subconsciously, you could be presenting the symptoms that you have read about. So, I purposely didn't read up on it, but after diagnosis I found out quite a lot about it and joined support groups and things like that. I was happy and felt that perhaps that I could do something about it."	

How/or/and/when did it hit you?	"It was pretty instant but I felt relief and happier, and once I started reading up on it and going to support groups I almost felt a bit guilty because I saw people in the support groups who were a lot worse off than me, who couldn't get work, who couldn't have anywhere near a normal life. I felt some displacement where I didn't know which camp to put myself in, but I still go to a support group now after all these years, and there are those in the group who have classic Autism and Asperger's Syndrome as well other diagnoses; but I enjoy going because it's structured."	
Did the clinician/diagnostician ask you to read and sign your diagnosis off?	"No, I can't remember that happening at all; I just got sent his report, which was copied to my GP. I think that the report consisted of about 8 pages."	Russell was not asked to sign his diagnosis off which was also sent to his GP although in comparison to other participants his report consisted of eight pages the fact that he was not provided with the opportunity and a right to reply to aspects of his assessment make it troublesome especially when clinicians don't get to see the long term results of their handy work.
Did you read it all?	"I did read it".	
How did you feel when reading it?	"I was a bit annoyed that the clinician got something wrong; it was stated that I had raised a family, which was incorrect. It wasn't a big mistake and of no great consequence, so I never did anything about it."	When Russell read his report he was a bit annoyed that the clinician got something wrong, it was stated that he had raised a family, which was incorrect. Although this was of no great consequence to Russell this highlights by not having the written information confirmed with the individual could lead to dire consequences.

Were you given the opportunity to preview your report and comment on it before it was finalized?	No (read previous comments)	
What did you think of the language and the perspective in the report?	*"I thought it was ok; I didn't have any strong feelings about it."*	
What were the recommendations on your assessment for a way forward?	*"To research more about Asperger's and to contact support groups. There was no mention of contacting any particular organization. I was advised to learn more about it."*	Regarding recommendations and in line with many other participants they were totally inadequate and pointed the individual to research more about Autism and contact more support groups. If a clinician was truly knowledgeable about Autism then that person should have a range of book titles that he or she could recommend, very specific titles which are dependent on the individual who has just been assessed. Even if a clinician disagrees with a title these should still be recommended to an individual in relation to their needs..
On reflection		
What is your perception now? Do you feel any different now, on reflection?	*"I feel a lot different now. I think that because of my diagnosis and my need to improve, as I felt that I must improve to have a happier life, so I was driven to make the most of what I have got and also to try and learn all these skills that other people learn automatically. People have commented, with one*	As with other participants the onus was on Russell to change and improve in order to lead a happier life. This methodology does seem more psycho social than relating to neurology or though through this Russell says he has become more confident and happier.

Like most participants he felt happier and relieved having been officially identified.

person saying recently that I appear to be a lot more confident. I have learned that it's an ongoing thing that I just have to push myself to do things, because if I don't do them, then I will always be poorly skilled at those things; unless I do them, I won't improve. I do protect myself from some things but the things I want to achieve have a cost associated with them, and that cost is that I have to put in the effort to keep on doing things and to learn from my mistakes in order to gain social skills; and unless I do that, I will just be lonely, depressed and unhappy; so I have to do things which are very uncomfortable perhaps initially, not perhaps in terms of going into a call center, but by joining organizations and groups and going to places on my own to mingle with a bunch of strangers and to try and socialize, and to also learn the skills which I feel is totally different for example to differentiate between sexual relationships and personal relationships, which is a hard thing to do. I drove to Germany this year, I was prepared to go on my own, but I had someone to go with me, to a personal development workshop, and it's not the first one I have been to that this organization has run, but it was the first one in Germany I have been to. I do try to talk to people more."

| In hindsight, how could your diagnosis have been done better? | *Post-diagnosis, there isn't a lot out there; the initial group I went to is an independent group which has been set up and run by a mother whose husband and son have been diagnosed with Asperger's; that was great to start with, but it has become too popular, too big and too noisy, so I don't go any more as I don't enjoy it; when it was a really small group I enjoyed it. The second group I went to was one funded by the NHS and run by a Psychologist and that was really structured and like a formal meeting and the Psychologist facilitates the meeting; where as the other group was more of a social group, this was more structured where he made sure everyone had a chance to speak and he would control the ones who couldn't stop speaking and we did practical things such as designing leaflets for hospitals and they had speakers in who would educate us; such as a speaker on psychotic drugs and a speaker on benefits, which was of no interest to me. A lot of the others are on benefits and can't work. We had speakers from organizations who help disabled people into employment. That was quite a good group and it's the only one I still go to. It is no longer funded by the NHS and the group has to now find its own funding; so it's more like a business now, which is not as good because too much of time in the meeting is taken up as a business meeting, focused on who is doing what and where we are going to get funding from, so it's less enjoyable now. The* | As with other participants Russell found initial difficulty with Autism groups as he saw people who were worse off than him where it seemed that he was questioning his identity. He enjoys going to groups because they are structured.

Russell gets a lot out of his groups but found he had to leave one as it got to big and to noisy he has been through several groups which all involved aspects relating to the people running them, either losing sight of what Autism is or not taking into account individual needs or differences for example Autism and Autistic traits become the focus of the group rather than individual differences. Many of these groups do seem to be about luck where I think different groups need to be about different people rather than the same label. |

		The bad things about the diagnosis was that it took them a bit of time which was down to not having a referral route. It would have been better if it were local and just like other participants he needed advance notice of the questions as he is not good at thinking on his feet thus affecting the answers in assessment.
	third group I used to go to was run by a charity and every month they would just go out for a meal at various local pubs and restaurants and this was really nice as there would only be half a dozen of us and it was nice and quiet and by having a meal there was something for us to do, if we were just sat there supposingly socializing without a meal, I think a lot of us will just be staring into nothingness, but a meal gives you something to do. I went to this for about a year, but I stopped going because of health conditions related to diet. Those are the three groups I went to."	
What was good about the process?		
What was bad about the process?	*"The bad things were; it took quite a bit of time and I had to go via another health worker before I got to a specialist; I had to travel and it would have been better if there were more local facilities; it would have been really nice if I had some notice of what the questions would have been, as I am not very good at thinking on my feet and some of the questions can be a shock when they are read out to you and you are expected to answer. It could be that it is designed that way to highlight difficulties in answering the questions, if they are that clever.*	

What impact has your diagnosis had on the understanding of who you are?	*"I feel a lot better about myself and a lot more worthy and not as rejected by other people; I feel loved by some people now; I feel a lot closer to people; my girlfriend's family is great. The more people get to know me, the more they can see it in me; when I first told my girlfriend, her reaction was to dismiss the diagnosis and say there is nothing wrong with me, but now she sees it and I have done and have said things which are inappropriate and she sees that I miss-reads things and take things literally."*	The first impression of his diagnosis from his girlfriend was to reject it, and now she accepts it as do other people tis has made him more confident he feels loved and a lot closer to people especially his girlfriend's family.
Is there anything else you would like to add?	*"I wish that I was diagnosed earlier and that my intelligence didn't covered up my learning difficulties and my learning difficulties didn't cover up my intelligence (until I was 48). I think that children as early as possible should have their IQ tested, and then if their academic skills don't match up to their IQ then they should be investigated to see why they are not succeeding. It's not just the Dyslexia, Dyscalculia and the memory problems that are my learning difficulties, I think a lot of it is down to the Asperger's in that I have very narrow interests; anything outside that I don't want to know. I don't know whether I have a bit of ADHD, but I can't really read that well; I couldn't read a novel although I can physically read; my mind would be elsewhere. I also have trouble with hearing a little bit although there is nothing wrong with my hearing, it's just that if the environment is noisy, if there is more than one conversation going on at once, then I can't concentrate on what someone else is saying, so that obviously affects learning at school and the fact that by not socializing at school affects*	In relation to his intelligence and his disabilities he describes the twice exceptional problem in that his intelligence Allowed him to cover up his learning difficulties and his learning difficulties covered up his intelligence subsequently he believes that every child should have their IQ tested and if they are academic and their skills don't match up to their IQ then they should be investigated to see why they are not succeeding maybe IQ tests should be mandatory on Autism assessments?

learning as well. I am pretty keen in saying that things should change for children; that children should be looked at better and assessed better and if they don't achieve in relation to their IQ level then they should be investigated and helped. I couldn't believe it when I had my IQ tested and I was in tears, I was crying. They told me that I was in the top one percent, and I left school with just a few CSE's. The English CSE, they wouldn't even let me take the exam I was that poor; they wouldn't even let me attempt it. I am a bit annoyed that I could have got a lot of help in the early days, which would have made my life a lot different. My IQ was tested after going through the diagnosis of Asperger's, but they were all within the same few years.

There was the Asperger's, the Dyslexia/Dyscalculia diagnosis, and the long-term memory problems came out, and my marriage broke up, I lost my post at work, I found out that I was very intelligent; all this happened within the space of two to three years. I am not sure whether it would have been helpful to have all these elements tested at the same time because I believe that it is better to see a specialist rather than to see someone who is a jack-of-all-trades; so I am unsure which would be better. I do believe that the professional who diagnosed my Asperger's should consider the co-morbid elements to give some idea of what else might be a problem and point the individual towards other professionals in whatever field is appropriate; but with me, they didn't seem to look at other problems."

Regarding comorbid diagnosis Russell was not sure whether it had been helpful to have all these things tested at the same time he believes it should be a specialist rather than a Jack-of-all-trades. Where would this lead multi disciplinarily teams and Luke's idea about having one person to assess Autism. Russell seems to believe that by setting up multiple path ways to different professionals for different diagnosis as a flaw with Russell's pathway is that the professionals didn't seem to look at other problems or other diagnosis that he had been given.

Printed in the United States
By Bookmasters